THE URBAN MISSION

Essays on the Building of a Comprehensive Model For Evangelical Urban Ministry

Edited by
Craig W. Ellison
Alliance Theological Seminary
And Nyack College

UNIVERSITY
PRESS OF
AMERICA

In tribute to the late David Gillespie,
God's enthusiastic and compassionate servant.

The essay "Racism and the Evangelical" originally appeared, in slightly different form, as two articles in *Christianity Today*, and is used here by permission. "The Psychodynamics of Racism" (October 9, 1970), © 1970 by Christianity Today, Inc. "The Psychopathology of Racism" (January 15, 1971), © 1971 by Christianity Today, Inc.

The essay "Black-White Understanding: Communication and Participation," © 1973 by Graham Barnes. Reprinted by permission.

The quotation on page 1 by Ralph Covell is from "Urban Crisis: Test of Our Missionary Concern," *World Vision Magazine* October 1969.

The urban crisis is "God's provision to the church to test our integrity, to force us to be honest, and to keep us from congratulating ourselves for a ministry abroad that we are loathe to practice at home."
— *Ralph Covell*

CONTENTS

PREFACE

I have been progressively impressed that the challenge of the essays that follow — as of the Bible itself — is the call for a Christianity not bound by cultural mores, a Christianity that dares to risk, a Christianity that gives evidence of the fruits of the Spirit.

The focus of this book is on the central city, because it has been fled or avoided by most American evangelicals. There are many reasons for this, as these essays point out. Some are legitimate; many more are the products of selfishness, insecurity, and secularism.

The urban fad is over but reality remains. Millions of American central city dwellers are ignored, despised, or feared. The evangelical faces a gigantic challenge, and an opportunity to share Christ with these persons. Christians of every race must begin to communicate and cooperate with each other. They must begin to see the city as a place over which Christ is weeping, because of the millions who are strangers to his claims. They must begin thinking and acting in ways that incarnate the love of Christ. This will call for self-examination and growth, both psychologically and spiritually. It will not call for paternalistic missionary forays into the city by day only to escape from its dangers and challenges after dark. When we address ourselves to the task as Christian communities, those who are thus freed to minister, and who know that God is calling them to the urban mission, must be constantly supported in their efforts.

My personal concern over the central city began when I was first exposed to life in the inner city of Detroit as a graduate student. Over a period of several years I saw and experienced the ups and downs of trying to relate Christ to inner-city residents. I learned about the patience and vision needed to persist, to love, to teach responsibility. I have seen and experienced the difficulties of cross-racial and cross-cultural communication and cooperation. I also learned the reality of the fleeing church. It was painful to watch churches move out to expensive new facilities in the suburbs, from where they sent hundreds of thousands of dollars for overseas "missions" while being apparently unconcerned about the millions of persons just twenty miles from their location. Equally painful was the absence of communication and cooperation between those Christians remaining in the city.

During my years in Detroit I became involved in the Central City Conference of Evangelicals, an interracial and interdenominational group of believers, most of whom were involved in central city ministry of one form or another. The purpose of this conference was to facilitate communication, provide fellowship and opportunity for mutual prayer, to develop common vision for the city, and to find ways to assist each other so that resources and efforts were not needlessly duplicated. During the close of this time in Detroit I became aware of similar groups in other parts of the country. The need for a representative setting forth of the challenge of urban ministry became clear to me.

About the same time a teaching position opened at Westmont College in Santa Barbara, California. Here I have been involved in another facet of urban awareness through involvement with an Urban Internship Program and in minority affairs. Even in the small city, the considerations here discussed in reference to the large city are pertinent.

I have been challenged and encouraged by my contacts and correspondence with the contributors to this volume. Their thinking has affected mine, and their efforts and commitment have been an inspiration. I also appreciate the interest shown in this collection by a number of other people centrally involved in urban concerns who were unable to find the time to contribute an essay. The caliber and dedication of people from coast to coast who are seriously taking to heart God's call to urban ministry should inspire all Christians. I am convinced that we are at the headwaters of a great new flowing of God's Spirit in our urban centers, through the sensitive, interdependent ministry of those from different races, denominations, and social and economic classes. Events that have transpired during the process of publishing *The Urban Mission* seem to bear this out. The November 1973 Chicago Evangelical

Declaration of Social Concern, signed by some of America's most outstanding Christian leaders, including a number of contributors to this book, would seem to signal the beginning of a new concern on the part of Christians for exactly those people and needs represented by our urban centers. My prayer is that God's mission to the city will overshadow self-interest and mistrust. These essays point to many concerns and suggest many procedures for implementing a more effective city ministry. But many of the answers and directions will have to be worked out in the crucible of experience and exchange.

The Psychology Department and administration of Westmont College have been most helpful in providing financial assistance in the volume of correspondence and duplication that went into the development and completion of this book, and I thank them. A special word of appreciation is extended to Mrs. Donna Kennedy, Mrs. Shirley Gay and Miss Sharon Thornburgh for secretarial assistance. Also, thanks to Marlin VanElderen, Editor-in-chief of Eerdmans, who has patiently and with quiet confidence supported the development of this book. Finally, my deep appreciation to my wife Sharon, who has been a sensitive critic, and whose own sense of God's call to commitment has significantly affected my perspectives.

Craig W. Ellison

PART ONE: INTRODUCTION

1: CITIES, NEEDS, AND CHRISTIANS
by Craig W. Ellison

The city is a place of paradox. Historically the center of economic and trade functions, it is also a place where great poverty co-exists with great wealth. The crucible of much of man's culture, it seems also to be the focal point of social deterioration. Its life-styles and anonymity attract millions, only to motivate many to leave subsequently in search of community.[1] It is a place that fascinates and a place that is feared. It is a place where the most overt forms of evil flourish, and yet continuing acts of human courage, kindness, and sacrifice are commonplace.

CRAIG W. ELLISON is assistant professor of psychology at Westmont College, Santa Barbara, California. He is a graduate of The King's College, Briarcliff Manor, New York; and holds the Ph.D. from Wayne State University, Detroit. While in Detroit he was active in the Metropolitan Action Center; in the Central Alliance Church, located in the inner city; and as originator and director of the Central City Conference of Evangelicals. At Westmont he has been involved in the Minority Affairs Committee and the Urban Program Committee. He has published articles in the **Journal of the American Scientific Affiliation, Inside, The Other Side,** *and* **Christianity Today,** *among others. He is Executive Director of the Western Association of Christians for Psychological Studies.*

In 1970 the Census Bureau reported that 73.5% of the American population lived in metropolitan areas. A simultaneous influx and outflow of persons characterizes the contemporary urban scene. Since 1945 blacks have moved in increasing numbers from the South to Northern central cities, so that today more than two-thirds of the black Americans living outside of the South live in the twelve largest metropolitan centers. Between 1950 and 1966, 98% of the growth in black population occurred in cities. At the same time, the flow of middle- and upper-class whites from the city to the less-crowded suburbs has been joined by the movement of lower-middle- and lower-class whites (as well as middle-class blacks) and Jews. The suburb is no longer uncrowded and has begun to mirror some of the problems of the central cities — pollution, delinquency and crime, drug usage, sophisticated alcoholism, etc.

It is with the central city that this book is most concerned. Most cities have a "Gold Coast" or "Lafayette Park" area, where the well-to-do can be found; and these well-to-do need the gospel as much as any sinner. But that is not the focus of this book. Millions of people without the personal presence of Christ live in the central city. Many of them society has labeled undesirable: they are poor, of a different skin color and a different life-style from the middle class, not well educated. Many of them are elderly, many more children. The central city is a place of change, but much of it is brought on by external forces insensitive to the needs of the city-dweller. It is a place of diverse value systems, various needs, and, frequently, depression.

In such a place Christ needs to be demonstrated and proclaimed.

These essays challenge the general evangelical community, which has feared and ignored the city, to listen to the voice of God and to the voices of millions who need to see Christ incarnated in the lives of caring, loving, risking Christians. They also provide encouragement and new perspectives for those already ministering in the city.

The Urban Situation

Many Americans caught a glimpse of the living conditions of the urban blacks during the late 1960s, when the frustration and despair of being forced by closed housing policies to live in deteriorating urban areas resulted in civil disorders that could not be ignored. But the disorders ended, the chaos was largely forgotten, and most of the oppressive living conditions that generated that reaction continue for both black and white city-dwellers.

Michael J. Flax has compiled massive statistics that help indicate the quality of life in eighteen large American metropolitan areas.[2] I will mention here the data for only five of Flax's fourteen categories: unemployment, poverty, health, mental health, and public order. Many additional indicators would be needed to assess definitively the quality of urban life, but these provide a sound basis for statistical comparison.

Unemployment. The average unemployment rate in the central city areas

Flax surveyed in 1969 was 3.8%; in suburban areas it was 2.9%. In other words unemployment was 1.34 times higher in the central city. Typically, unemployment percentages for central cities bear the brunt of national recessions when the total unemployment rate goes higher. At the time I lived in Detroit, for example, unemployment for the general metropolitan area reached approximately 6%, while that in the central city was near 25%.

Most of the unemployed in the central city work force are young black males. The psychological effect of not having a job in a society that measures worth largely by the size of the paycheck is devastating. Furthermore, unemployment brings boredom, a lack of means to improve one's living condition, and an inability to afford basic essentials like proper food. There may develop what some sociologists call a culture of poverty.

Poverty. According to 1969 statistics 17.5% of central city residents were below the poverty income level of $3,000 per year; only half that percentage were below the line in the suburbs. Try to imagine how you would live on $3,000 per year. The stark reality is that many Americans do not make enough money to eat properly. Even hamburger at today's prices is a luxury at that income level, and potato chips and soda pop become staple fillers to keep children from crying and the minds of adults off their stomachs.

A 1967 study by the Massachusetts Department of Public Works indicated that in a representative section of Boston's inner city, two-thirds of the nonwhite households and nearly two-fifths of the white households had a weekly income less than $100. Despite this, only six percent of white and twenty-two percent of nonwhite householders received any public assistance.

The physical ramifications of living in poverty are aggravated by the life-style it brings on—frequent frustration, depression, and aimlessness on the part of those without material means to lift themselves out of the situation.

Health. The average central city-dweller cannot afford health services when he is sick or injured, much less preventive health care or proper diet. The advent of government programs like medicare and medicaid have not assisted much, and recent changes in the rules have made it more difficult for persons without transportation, like the urban elderly, to get needed public health assistance.

The effects of the horrendous inflationary rise during the past year (1973) have yet to be analyzed and documented, but the stress must be horrible for those on poverty-level incomes. When the average cost increases for food have amounted to approximately 20%, and the cost of basic staples such as beans and potatoes, flour and sugar, has jumped 200-300%, the perspective is dismal. Although there are many persons overseas who desperately need food, and whom we should help as we're able, the stark reality is that right in the central cities of America there are thousands who are barely surviving, or doing so for the time being on nutritionally inferior diets which can't help but affect their motivation, cognitive functioning, emotions, behaviors and spiritual states.

Flax's specific indicator of health was the infant mortality rate. Using 1967 data he found an average of 25.3 deaths per thousand live births in the cities, compared to 19.1 for suburban areas. It is well known that the United States does not rank well among industrial nations in this area, and the central city obviously bears the brunt of that.

Heavy pollution created by automobiles that travel on freeways built for the convenience of suburban commuters and by large industry, few of whose executives live in the vicinity of these urban areas, also contributes to poor health.

Mental Health. The culture of poverty produces depression in many inner-city residents. Frequently it results in the break-up of families, either because of the inability to feed everyone and the possibility of federally supported fatherlessness, or because of the tension of living in constant uncertainty. Family structures like that spawn a variety of emotional problems among adults and children. The physical environment of the inner city, with its typical grayness and lack of space for play or meditation, and the press of people may contribute to mental health problems.[3]

Flax's study indicated that suicide rates in 1967 in the central city areas studied were 1.43 times higher than the rate for the suburbs. The 1968 data for metropolitan areas indicated that the rate was increasing.

Public Order. A major concern of recent political campaigns has been "law and order." Following on the heels of urban-centered racial unrest, the appeal undoubtedly confounded racial attitudes with some objective facts and led in many cases to an almost hysterical fear of the city. Indeed, the number of violent crimes seems to increase somewhat as the size of the city increases, as does the number of property crimes, according to FBI statistics. However, most violent crimes are not the product of premeditated street ambushes, but are crimes of passion involving friends or family members.

Flax found that the number of reported robberies per 100,000 people was 600 in the central city compared to 59 in the suburbs. Not infrequently city-dwellers, though they own little, may be victimized by several burglaries in a period of time.

Recent research has indicated that a major factor differentiating delinquents from non-delinquents is the quality and cohesiveness of marital and family relationships.[4] Bad housing and inferior education seem to be less relevant causes. Sheldon and Eleanor Glueck indicate that in families which are not properly "integrated" or proper and consistent discipline by a father is absent, the percentage of boys turning to delinquency and crime soars. In the inner city a multitude of forces combine to help create family instability.

Challenge and Opportunity for Evangelicals

We could go on to discuss other pressing urban problems—alcoholism, drug-abuse, anonymity and loneliness, transportation difficulties, educational inferiority, inadequate housing. Countless books and articles have been written about these problems. Our purpose is not to duplicate these statistics but to emphasize that the vast and interconnected web of needs and problems that characterize America's central cities forms the daily experience of people—human beings for whom, the Christian confesses, Christ died.

Not only are millions of city-dwellers forced to live in the misery of the conditions already described, but they face the very real possibility of spiritual death. Not all Christians are called to full-time ministry in the city, but surely more are called than are currently serving there. Do we love our property more than these persons? Have those Christians still in the city taken seriously the call to disciple and to share Christ, or are we also drifting in evangelical pockets of semi-comfort? Is our vision broad enough? Does it reach flexibly to people's needs and demonstrate Christ's love in a way that can help bring them to Christ? Do we recognize that God created us as whole persons?

Each of us must ask himself questions like these. What does God want us to do about the city?

Urban ministry is usually not comfortable or convenient. It requires the best of God's people. It demands a deep, sustained, personal walk with Christ, and a willingness to take risks and to live with uncertainty, to confront evil and its destructive influences in the lives of people and to incarnate the good news.

Risk and Uncertainty. The traditional evangelistic methods of suburban churches and evangelical organizations may perhaps be effective with those who are middle-class in outlook. The diversity of race, life-style, social and economic status, ethnic heritage, and values makes their application difficult in the inner city. There is no guarantee, for example, that a racially mixed congregation can be ministered to in such a way that each individual member is built up and supported spiritually and psychologically. (It appears, however, that cultural and educational backgrounds are more important factors than race here.) People will probably not be sufficiently exposed to the gospel through proclamation in the 11 o'clock worship service, so that new methods of outreach have to be developed.

Effective urban ministry must be experimental and flexible. It calls for people who can tolerate uncertainty and vulnerability. It calls for people whose faith is more real than their fears. It calls for people who are willing to move out of comfortable and habitual ways of doing things. Most of the evangelical community would do well to reread Paul's words in II Corinthians 6:3-10 and take them seriously. Perhaps we could be delivered from our conformity to society's standards: our jealous guarding of our own property, our fear of the city and those who are different. Without such deliverance, without God's help, we will be ill-equipped to minister to the city.

Confronting Evil. There are those, like Jacques Ellul, who suggest that the very essence and structure of the city is evil.[5] I have difficulty with this view, though I believe many of its structures sustain and even further evil. The presence and effects of evil are readily visible in the city. Frequently its form is overt and dramatic, resulting in the kind of fear that keeps many Christians from considering urban ministry, though evil is by no means unique to the city, or to the minority groups and lower income persons who live there.

The fact of evil in the city should surprise no one, least of all the evangelical Christian. People live there, and God indicated long ago that "none is righteous, no, not one" (Rom. 3:10). But the pervasiveness of evil in more dramatic forms may shock the urban evangelical reared in a nonurban environment. There is sexual evil in the prevalence of prostitution, pornographic theaters and bookstores, homosexual and go-go bars. There is the destructive abuse of drugs and alcohol, the effects of poverty against the backdrop of the greed of slumlords who charge exorbitant rental fees. There is the wickedness of policemen who encourage and participate in graft to supplement their own low incomes.[6] There is the violence of attacks against other persons—armed robbery, rape, murder — and property—arson, burglary, vandalism.

How does the Christian respond in each of these areas? Should he respond with judgment and complete separation or should he find ways to relate Christ? Should he encourage reform of evil systems and structures or should he "preach Christ" to those affected by them and benefiting from them? Is it a part of a Christian's urban ministry to become involved in community efforts designed to counteract some of these evils? It would seem that if we are to be salt (Matt. 5:13), we must apply ourselves in areas of the urban setting that are being victimized by evil, as well as involving ourselves in church services and personal evangelism.

Christians who are involved this way, trying to "bear witness to the light" in areas where men's deeds are evil, will find ample opportunity to proclaim Christ in power. Victims of evil, as well as those perpetrating it, will listen to those who come bearing a perspective of deliverance from oppression (Rom. 6:21-23; Gal. 5). Christ himself moved among those who were oppressed and identified with the poor, bringing good news to them while sharply criticizing the structures and persons who either perpetrated the evil or who thought themselves above sin.

The urban evangelical must call for repentance by those involved in more gross forms of evil as well as by the multitudes who simply have not allowed God to take over their lives.

Incarnating the Good News. Probably more than any other segments of American society, city-dwellers need to see Christ incarnated by his followers.

For those oriented more toward behavior than words (as many from lower socio-economic backgrounds are), it is essential that Christ be demonstrated. For those experiencing crushing needs, words alone are usually meaningless. (If you doubt this, think of what a touch—in contrast to words—has meant at a time when a loved one has been lost.)

Christ himself took the first huge step of making God's love concrete. He took spiritual experience out of the abstract realms of philosophy and religious form and made it real (Phil. 2:5-8). He did not just speak. He acted sacrificially. He demonstrated God's love by healing those who are sick, raising loved ones from the dead, forgiving sins, and absorbing the impact of sin on the cross.

We who are called Christians must be willing to incarnate Christ. The urban Christian must identify with the various city-dwellers. He must be willing to rub shoulders, to be "all things to all people that some may come to know Christ." This is not convenient Christianity; this is the call to a challenging and vital mission..

Some Assumptions

There are a number of underlying assumptions that provide a thread of unity throughout the diversity of the essays that follow.

Salvation by Faith. "All have sinned and come short of the glory of God," Paul tells us (Rom. 3:23). Each person must recognize this personally and be redeemed individually, through belief in the atoning work of Christ's death and resurrection. A proper relationship with God cannot be established by works; it is by faith that we become God's children (Eph. 2:8, 9).

Saved for Good Works. Although we are saved by faith and walk by faith, our walk is to be one of good works (Eph. 2:10). These do not save us, but they are the proof of our salvation. This theme is pervasive in the Bible. We should be remembered for our "work of faith and labor of love and steadfastness of hope in our Lord Jesus Christ" (I Thess. 1:3). Our faith should be "active along with [our] works, and . . . completed by works" (James 2:22). We are saved not into retirement but to "do good to all men, especially those of the household of faith" (Gal. 6:10). We are to let our "light so shine before men, that they may see [our] good works, and give glory to [our] Father who is in heaven" (Matt. 5:16).

Special emphasis is placed on acting beneficially toward those who are poor (Ps. 41:1-3; Prov. 19:17; 21:13; 22:22-23; 29:7, 14; James 2:1-8) and acting to correct injustice (Isa. 59:14-16; Micah 6:8).

Our Purpose Is To Please God. Evangelism, worship, making disciples—all these are definitely important dimensions of the life of the individual Christian and the church. But our basic purpose is to learn how to please God (I Thess. 4:1). With that motivation underlying our behavior, various kinds of actions will be pleasing to God. There is no single form of activity or vocation for every Christian. This allows a great deal of flexibility in our approaches. It also allows us to accept the individualized work of God's Spirit through us. We should not feel guilty if we help someone without immediately proclaiming the gospel. On the other hand, when the Spirit indicates, verbally proclaiming Christ is highly pleasing to God. This suggests our next assumption.

Prayer Must Precede. To be sensitive to the Spirit and the needs of those we run into, we must accompany our ministry with prayer at every point. This is not just a security device. It is an absolute essential for the kind of discernment needed to ferret out the needs that we are to address ourselves to. Many of those in the central city have complex needs. The Christian will not want to waste his time meeting superficial needs, but neither will he want to prejudge certain classes of apparent needs (nonspiritual) as superficial. As many foreign missionaries have found, people are frequently brought to Christ because someone has shown them Christ love in dealing with a physical or emotional need.

Love Must Be for the Whole Person. To see only people's spirit as valuable is to fragment them as badly as to ignore their spiritual needs. God made us integrated beings. The Christian must address himself to the whole person — physical, social, psychological, and spiritual.[7]

Love that does not address itself to the concrete needs of the person, spiritual and nonspiritual, is self-deception (I John 3:17-18). Unfortunately, many Christians prefer to interpret the passages of Scripture that talk about our responsibility for the whole person figuratively. In so doing, they twist Scripture to serve their own desires, and fail to see others as God would have us see them.

Certainly we are to loose the spiritual bonds and bring spiritual restoration, but such passages as Isaiah 58:6-12 will not allow us to avoid our basic responsibilities to the whole person if our *own* relationship with God is to be healthy. The Christian should be sobered when he reads in Matthew 25:31-46 that unless we have engaged in this kind of compassionate service, glorifying God, we may find ourselves cast out from his presence.

David Moberg has thoroughly investigated the roots of the current dichotomy between evangelism and social concern, and rightly exposes it as nonscriptural.[8] Man has been pulled apart by both the backers of the social gospel, who ignore the spiritual needs of men, and those evangelicals who minister exclusively to the spirit, and ignore his social needs. For effective urban ministry, it is time that man was put back together and treated correctly.

Paternalism Will Destroy. The very term "mission" is both advantageous and disadvantageous. At its best, it suggests selfless and sacrificial incarnating of God's love to those without Christ. It brings to mind those servants of God throughout history who have ministered to those without Christ and in sensitivity to God's Spirit have brought many into a salvation relationship with

Christ. It brings to mind those who have loved others, treating them with sensitivity, as equals.

At its worst, however, the term mission suggests imposing one's own culturally based attitudes and habits on someone from another culture in such a way as to suggest they are scripturally based norms. It suggests the subtle—or not-so-subtle—attitude that those being ministered to are inferior. It implies that the ministering agent really knows best. It is the failure to become servants, "looking to the interests of others" and "in humility counting others better than yourselves" (Phil. 2:3, 4). It is a failure to identify either with Christ (Phil. 2:5-7) or with the persons being ministered to.

An urban mission effort of this latter type would work against the cause of Christ in many lives. There is a great deal of caution today on the part of black evangelicals, for example, about the involvement of white evangelicals in urban ministry, at least those that relate to black people. I believe that there is a place for multiracial urban ministry and for interracial congregations, but the guidelines and the relationships will have to be carefully guarded.

We may not realize how paternalism destroys the opportunity to build sharing relationships until we stop and think of times when others have been condescending toward us. Even if it has been with the best of intentions, it has hurt. Everyone likes to be treated as a worthwhile person, not as a project to be helped or someone to be put up with because the Christian is supposed to love everybody.

The City as Place of Mission. To be a missionary is to be one sent by God with a specific purpose. Urban areas are greatly in need of evangelical Christians who are sent by God, not by feelings of guilt or visions of adventure. Paul's missionary mandate in Acts 1 began with the witness closest to home and progressively spread to the uttermost parts of the earth. Many Christians today see the city as a troublesome, threatening, massive area to be avoided, and, reversing Paul's priorities, prefer overseas missions.

Overseas missions are surely part of God's call, and many courageous people have responded to it. But what about those who remain behind in comfort and in apparent disregard of the needs next door? Is not our neighbor the one in need (Luke 10:29-37)? How can we continue to ignore those in need who live right near us, and be self-satisfied in our disregard? How can we as evangelicals fail to believe that God wants his people sent into urban centers where the greatest concentrations of population are. God wants all people to be reconciled to himself: how dare we avoid so many people? Even Paul's missionary journeys were predominantly to the urban centers of his day.

Those evangelicals already in the city, who have comfortably settled into their own religious communities, need to reassess their view of the city as well. Do they see those around them with compelling spiritual and personal needs? Are they willing to become involved with those who differ from them and are somehow regarded as inferior? Are they willing to become flexible, to abandon tradition in order to reach people with the message? Are they serious enough about God's call to abandon denominationalism, which needlessly prevents fruitful cooperation? to put aside provincialism? to give up their own empire-building? to ask how people can be effectively reached for Christ? The mission must become the common point of cooperation. It must become more important than denominational or congregational sovereignty, nonscriptural tradition, or factors of race.

The city is a place of mission, of ministry with vision, creativity, persistence, tolerance, acceptance of others, prayer, and lay and ministerial involvement. It is a place needing the *best* in missions, now.

The Structure of This Book

This collection proceeds from a historical and theological setting to specific programs and a comprehensive model for evangelical urban ministry. It includes the abstract and the concrete. It is written to provide an understanding of the scriptural and historical bases for urban involvement, of some of the factors that keep evangelicals from vital involvement in the central city, and of some of the elements that must be included in effective ministry. In addition, one major section focuses on the need for specific evangelical educational programs to produce leaders who are sensitive to and involved in the city. Each section begins with an introduction describing the thrust of the articles in that section. Unlike books of readings, this is a collection (with one exception) of original articles designed specifically for this book by the editor. It represents the individual viewpoints of each author within the framework provided for consideration of the specific topic assigned. The book may be read by taking an isolated chapter at a time, but each section, with its individual chapters, has also been designed around a specific purpose and one section builds on the other. For example, after the section considering factors that have hindered urban involvement among evangelicals, the essay "Making People Aware" suggests some of the ways to increase evangelical awareness and introduce urban ministry as a priority for evangelicals. Section IV then goes on to describe several educational programs that are helping do this among the young evangelicals who will be tomorrow's pastoral and lay leaders. Some options for training evangelical minority leadership are also considered.

Notes to Chapter 1

1 Will Herberg, "City and Suburb in Symbiosis: The Urban Problem in New Perspective," *The Intercollegiate Review,* Spring 1973, pp. 161-163.

2 Michael J. Flax, *A Study in Comparative Urban Indicators: Conditions in 18 Large Metropolitan Areas* (Washington, D.C.: The Urban Institute, 1972).

3 Cf. Georg Simmel, "The Metropolis and Mental Life," in *Man Alone: Alienation in Modern Society* (New York: Dell, 1962), pp. 151-165; John B. Calhoun, "Population Density and Social Pathology," *Scientific American,* February 1962, pp. 139-148; also, R.C. Schmitt, "Density, Health and Social Disorganization," *American Institute of Planners Journal,* Vol. 32 (1966), 38-40; H.H. Winsborough, "The Social Consequences of High Population Density," *Law and Contemporary Problems,* Vol. 30 (1965), 120-126; and J.A. Desor, "Toward a Psychological Theory of Crowding," *Journal of Personality and Social Psychology,* 1972, 21(1), 79-83.

4 Sheldon and Eleanor Glueck, *Delinquents and Non-Delinquents* (Cambridge: Harvard U.P., 1968).

5 Jacques Ellul, *The Meaning of the City* (Grand Rapids: Eerdmans, 1970).

6 Cf. Peter Maas, "Serpico–The Story of an Honest Cop," *The Reader's Digest,* May 1973, pp. 280-327.

7 See Charles Y. Furness, *The Christian and Social Action* (Old Tappan, New Jersey, 1972) for a Scripturally based treatment of Christian social action in relation to a variety of issues such as: racism, poverty, civil disorders, demonstrations, and violence.

8 David O. Moberg, *The Great Reversal: Evangelism Versus Social Concern* (Philadelphia: Lippincott, 1972).

PART TWO:
A CONTEXT FOR COMPASSION —
HISTORICAL AND BIBLICAL PERSPECTIVES

INTRODUCTION

The appeal of this book is best understood viewed in the dual context of historical evangelical involvement and scriptural expectations. In this section, William Nigel Kerr demonstrates the precedent for whole-person urban ministry set by outstanding saints of the eighteenth and nineteenth centuries. Evangelicals in England and Europe consistently led society of their day in economic and social reform, practical concern for the poor and rejected, and demands for justice. Ross Nelson then explicates the consistent scriptural command to be our brother's keeper. The Christian is to be a vehicle of God's love, to show compassion and concern for those around him. With the tremendous concentration of human life in urban centers, suffering and need are inescapable. The Christian community must face this reality if it is to be true to the commands of Scripture.

The late L. Nelson Bell pointed out that "compassion looks deep into the heart, suffers with and understands the need of the other person, and communicates that understanding. Compassion ignores the unlovely as it sees God's image. . . ."[1] The compassionate Christian is a responsive person touched by suffering and offended by injustice. He takes active steps to restore wholeness—spiritually, psychologically, socially, and physically.

Effective compassion for the city-dweller is not sentimental. It is not just an idealistically inspired feeling. The realities of city life can easily transform an emotionally based compassion into bitterness and self-pity. The Christian cannot enter urban ministry expecting to be appreciated for his demonstrations of concern, for many of those for whom he sacrifices the most energy or resources will show little overt gratitude. His compassion must have no strings attached; he must do, not for the approval of those done for, but knowing that God approves.

Often the most needy city-dwellers have experienced little genuine love. They have been manipulated and have learned to manipulate; they have learned to cover up feeling because they have been hurt so often. The urban evangelical must accept this and love unselfishly. Compassion that is not paternalistic do-gooding is aware of the suspicion of its recipients and willing to risk rejection. It will eventually get through.[2]

Second, Christian compassion seeks practical outlets. Whether it is helping persons without transportation get to the store or hospital, assisting in obtaining decent housing, getting buses to pull to the curb for the elderly, calling for an end to racially motivated job discrimination, finding a job for a father of a family of four, or seeking restrictions on industrial or auto pollution that poisons the air of the inner city, whatever the expression, God will honor it if it is done to glorify him (Col. 3:23). Here Christian laymen and professionals have a major, as yet unfulfilled, responsibility in the city. If people in the city are going to listen to the message of Christ, they must see practical demonstrations of that message in the lives of Christians (Jas. 2:15-17). It is easier for Christians to say, "Let the government do it," or to condemn those in need as deserving their state, than it is to put faith into practice. Yet Scripture seems to indicate that those who claim to have faith and do not evidence it in practical compassion may not even be genuine Christians (cf. I John 3:17f.; 4:7f.).

Genuine Christian compassion is an expression of who one is. As Dr. Nelson points out in his essay, the expectations that Scripture sets can be met only by one who is a transformed being. The stresses and strains of urban reality, the incessant demands, will quickly wear out a compassion that does not spring from who one is. Compassion cannot be pretended. Though it is our duty, it cannot be properly sustained out of a sense of duty. The urban evangelical must walk daily and closely with his God, if he is to have the power to be a vehicle of God's grace.

Fourth, the compassion of the urban evangelical must be tuned to the area of need felt by the one being ministered to. We must avoid the temptation to think we know best how to meet a person's need. God may give us wisdom to discern superficial and underlying needs, but we must learn to listen carefully and not impulsively impose our preconceptions. If the person has an apparent spiritual need, we must be prepared to meet that need, wisely, through the counsel of the Scriptures and prayer. If he is primarily hungry, we have a responsibility to address ourselves to that need. We need not feel guilty about this, for we are following the example set by Christ.

Abraham Maslow has pointed out that each person has a hierarchy of needs.[3] At the bottom, or foundation, are physiological needs. Building upon this are his needs for safety, for belonging, for being loved, and for self-actualization. If a person's lower level needs are not being met he cannot experience fulfilment on the higher levels. If a person has the need for belonging and we present him with food, or with a Sunday School quarterly, he will not be reached. If he is in need of self-fulfilment and transcendence of his situation, we may have an optimal opportunity to show compassion by sharing the gospel message. If he is hungry, and we preach about spiritual salvation, the message he will probably get (even if we offer food afterwards) is that our compassion has hooks in it.

Finally, the kind of compassion that the Christian is called to demonstrate in the city must be expressed both in personal involvement and in structural reform. Both Nelson and Kerr give numerous examples of how Christians through the ages have been willing to be involved with others. The impersonal city, with its anonymity and loneliness, makes personal compassion a powerful avenue of Christian witness and incarnational expression. But structural reform, as an expression of compassion, must not be overlooked. The Christian must be involved in introducing compassion into corporate, institutional structures. Where injustice is being perpetrated by law, he must seek reform of the law. He may be called on to exercise personal compassion in helping a person to get a job; he is also called on to exercise compassion of a structural nature if job hiring practices are keeping a whole host of city-dwellers out of jobs.

We must not defend inaction in this area on the basis of a naive understanding of the passage that tells us that rulers are not a terror to good conduct, but to bad (Rom. 13:1-3), so we should not resist authority. We are to exhaust every channel to bring about such reform, because we know that it is right and good. If we are still refused, we must realize that perhaps the rulers do not want what is right, and must be willing to suffer with those who are the objects of structural injustice for the cause of Christ.

How can such compassion become a fuller part of evangelical experience? Three factors seem essential: exposure, sensitivity to God's concerns, and the ability to put oneself in another's place.

The Christian community will not become sensitized to the urban challenge unless they are exposed to the scope of the city's need. Most evangelical Christians are exposed to a very confined part of life, which does not include the reality of life in the core cities. The extent of urban need gets far less emphasis than overseas missions; some leading evangelical periodicals never address themselves to urban ministry; there is little communication between pastors, youth, and congregations in the inner city and outlying areas; exposure to the inner city consists of riding above it on expressways on the way to a ball game. Programs such as those mentioned in Section IV seem absolutely critical if the evangelical community is to meet the urban challenge.

Believers need to become more sensitized to God's will as expressed in the Scripture, a challenge penetratingly portrayed by Nelson. As this happens, more evangelicals will become burdened by the urban situation. A danger in some of the pietistic movements that characterize evangelical Christianity is that they become self-focused. True piety begins with my relationship to God as an individual and then moves to the incarnation of Christ's love in my relationship to others. Nelson points out that the two are inextricably intertwined throughout Scripture. Many Christians live selfishly most of the time. We need, with God's forgiveness, to become immersed in his concerns. Genuine compassion will flow when we become his imitators (Eph. 5:1f.).

Finally, we have to learn how to put ourselves in the place of others, to see how things look from other people's point of view (Phil. 2:4). As we do this we will begin to experience, with feeling, the plight of millions who are suffering, crushed, and blighted by urban living.

One frequently hears of a dichotomy between evangelism and social concern. For the evangelical Christian, however, both are expressions of godly compassion. Naturally both may express something less — evangelism may be an attempt to escape personal involvement and to gain status, social concern an attempt to circumvent spiritual regeneration or build God's kingdom without God.

The scriptural way—and the historic evangelical way—is for evangelism and social concern to go hand in hand. Neither is a substitute or escape from the other.

Notes to Part 2: Introduction

1 L. Nelson Bell, "Acting Like Christians," *Christianity Today,* Vol. XVII, No. 30, July 6, 1973.

2 For the evangelical beginning work in an urban setting, studies like that of Charles F. Kemp, *Pastoral Care with the Poor* (Nashville: Abingdon, 1972), can provide a helpful point of orientation.

3 Abraham Maslow, *Toward a Psychology of Being* (Princeton, N.J.: Van Nostrand, 1968).

2: HISTORICAL EVANGELICAL INVOLVEMENT IN THE CITY

by William Nigel Kerr

The evangelical of the eighteenth and nineteenth centuries was very much a creature of his time, reflecting its strengths and weaknesses in both his personal and institutional efforts. He shared the Enlightenment's heightened awareness of the physical world and man's creative role in it. The evangelical, however, brought to bear his biblical heritage and refused to secularize the truths regarding man's rights as God's creature in God's creation. Nor would he bow to the view that man could be perfected by education and the improvement of his environment. He called out with others for the freedom and rights of man,

WILLIAM NIGEL KERR is dean and professor of church history and world missions at Gordon-Conwell Theological Seminary, South Hamilton, Massachusetts. He is a graduate of Wayne State University; and holds the Ph.D. from New College, University of Edinburgh, Scotland. His special field of academic interest is the history of modern evangelicalism, and he has researched eighteenth- and nineteenth-century social concern at several foreign libraries. A member of ECUMB, the Evangelical Theological Society, and the Latin America Mission, he has contributed to **Scottish Journal of Theology,** **Christianity Today,** *and* **Baker's Theological Dictionary,** *among others, and is co-editor of* **The Encyclopedia of Modern Christian Missions.**

but interpreted this in the light of God's sovereign authority. God, not man, was the measure and measurer of things, and so the evangelical insisted on the significance of revealed truth as found in Jesus Christ and in the Bible as God's written word.

The evangelical was not unaware of the predicament of the poor brought on by the Enclosure Acts, the Industrial Revolution, and the mushrooming of urban centers. Frequently he was a victim of these and ministered in the midst of most pressing circumstances. Moved with compassion for the laboring man, the poor, and the homeless, he reached out with the means at his disposal to alleviate the distress by reforms that would correct social problems. Because the evangelical responded reflexively and immediately reached out to meet the crying needs of the poor he is often accused of treating the symptoms and not the disease. However, he found it difficult not to be involved at this level while also evaluating and seeking to remedy causes when possible. The caricature of early evangelicals sitting in total isolation in small chapels preaching fire and brimstone to each other carries little weight. Overton and Relton, after looking somewhat negatively at Anglican Evangelicals, admit:

> With all these drawbacks, they seasoned the life of the time with salt, and this illumined a dark age with gleams of heavenly light. They were used—as the instruments of Him Whom they had learned to love, and Whom they taught many thousands to love also.[1]

The role of the English religious liberal, often considered the major source of reform, has been reassessed by R. N. Stromberg, who concludes that they "were scarcely reformers." As for the deists, "it is hard to find evidence of that 'tremendous interest of most deists in the public good', quite commonly alleged." While dismissing "the cult of benevolence," Stromberg remarks that "the notable late [eighteenth] century movement of social conscience was created by religious philanthropists, among them Wilberforce, Granville Sharp, Clarkson, Howard, and Miss More."[2] All of these people were evangelicals.

Ministry to the Whole Man

On Princes Street in Edinburgh stands a statue of the Rev. Thomas Guthrie with the Bible in one hand and his arm lovingly around a lad from the city slums. How typical of the early evangelical, who was concerned with the total man though he did not question that the greatest service one could perform for another was bringing him into fellowship with God.[3] Among a large number of those early evangelicals, there was no sense of a dichotomy between the responsibility to witness and the call to act responsibly as an agent for good in society. Evangelical leadership gave to and participated alike in city missions, world mission, and philanthropic societies, while at the same time using every influence for social and economic reform through parliamentary channels.

Their involvement was unself-conscious, for they were Christian citizens who would "do good to all men." "So unwearied in well doing were certain groups of Bible Christians," notes David Owen, "that in the public mind the word 'philanthropist' became all but synonymous with 'evangelical' and 'philanthropy' was applied to the good works that appealed most to evangelical tastes."[4]

When we search for the source of this evangelical interest in the whole man, we find it, at least in part, in the pulpits of their churches and on the shelves of their libraries. Henry Venn, the father of John Venn, pastor to the people of the Clapham Sect and a frequent visitor to Clapham, wrote a most influential book, *The Complete Duty of Man.* It is typical of the input of late eighteenth- and nineteenth-century evangelical devotional material in England and in the United States. In the section on "The Temper of a Christian Toward His Fellow Creature," Venn calls for justice and mercy in the most practical terms. Quoting extensively from Scripture he demands understanding and generosity toward the poor and the underprivileged. "Their pains and diseases of body, their troubles and distresses of mind, their necessitous circumstances, their unjust suffering from others will receive liberal relief from your bounty."[5] On the Christian's motivation for extensive and sacrificial service, Venn says,

> If you ask, What is there peculiar to the real Christian, by which a disposition so extensively merciful is excited and maintained? I answer, the reverence he pays to the command of God, and the full persuasion he enjoys of the truth of His promises, but still more, the sense he has of his own redemption by Christ and agency of the Holy Ghost in his heart. . . .
>
> By His agency, through means of the motives offered in the written word, he is delivered from the unfeeling selfishness or the partial good-will natural to the human heart. For the fruit of the Spirit which distinguishes and infinitely enables every true believer in Jesus, is expressly affirmed to be love, and to be in all goodness. . . .
>
> No duty is more frequently urged than this: Be ye therefore merciful, as your Heavenly Father is merciful. . . .[6]

There are many Christians, Venn says elsewhere, who

> content themselves with the form without the power, liking mightily to sing psalms and hymns, hear sermons, say prayers and receive the sacrament; all which are means and good means of grace, fit and proper to be used; still they are but means, and of no effect unless they lead to the end and purpose of them, namely, good works toward God and toward man. These are the vitals, the essence, the sum and substance, of the Christian, the one and only true religion.[7]

Meeting Social Needs

Evangelical faith, within both the established church and nonconformity, provided certain elements not commonly found in society. First, it supplied an integrity for the individual. It aided him in conceiving of himself as a person through the perspective of the gospel. Because of Christ he knew that he had a heavenly Father, that his sins were forgiven, and that he was one with others in the church of Christ. This faith met one of man's deepest needs—to belong. In so doing it assisted him in meeting the uncertainties of the new industrial society. Second, it provided a new concern for the urban masses. This concern had a far deeper meaning for the Christian, who had a Christlike compassion for the rootless crowds, than for the Enlightenment. Out of this concern came programs, institutions, and campaigns that ministered to the needs of city society by providing help for the starving, the sick, the unwanted child, the ignorant, the imprisoned, the prostitute, and the unprotected laborer.[8] Hannah More and William Wilberforce are mocked by Sydney Smith, W. D. Morris, and the Hammonds for seeing the vices of the poor and not the rich.[9] This hardly fits the facts, as Wilberforce's *Practical View* and More's *Estimate of the Religion of the Fashionable World,* both written for the upper classes, clearly show. Standish Meacham's chapter on social life at Clapham gives a number of incidents of the desire of the "Clapham Sect" to influence its peers in matters of religion and service.[10] Third, evangelicalism called out against the existence of a society where the rich and influential, even the Christian rich and influential, simply closed their eyes to the cry of the poor and refused to bear the burden. Morris writes that "if it was the policy of the church of England to 'indulge the rich and keep down the poor', this was not true of the Evangelicals."[11]

Of Chalmers' ministry to the city of Glasgow it was said, "He had warmed it."[12] This incarnationally centered humanization of society was one of evangelicalism's greatest contributions. A vivid example of this is seen in the approximately five hundred Methodist ministers who around 1800 adopted voluntary poverty, not for personal ascetic reasons, "but because the needs of the poor around them ought to keep them poor by the call on their charity."[13]

William Wilberforce joined Thomas Bernard and the Bishop of Durham to set up the "Society for Bettering the Conditions of, and Increasing the Comforts of the Poor" in 1796. "Let us therefore make the inquiry," they said, "into all that concerns the *poor,* and the promotion of their happiness, a Science—let us investigate practically, and at one system."[14] The report of the Society in 1800 said that they would transcend the "petty and unstable objectives of affording caprious or monitary relief; but in the well founded hope of conferring permanent benefit."[15] The Clapham people gave their personal services to the relief of people in their own parish, assuring all of assistance in medicine, employment, and education. Hannah More, though not cognizant of the scope of the poverty problem, was willing to sacrifice as shown in a letter to Wilberforce:

I have greatly lessened my house expenses, which enables me to maintain my schools and enlarge my charity. My school alone, with clothing, rents, etc., cost me £250 a year. . . . As I have sold my carriage and horses, I want no coachman; as I have no garden, I want no gardener.[16]

Henry Thornton before his marriage, it is reported, gave 6/7 of his income to charity,[17] and in a single year donated £6000.[18]

Germany — "Die Innere Mission"

Several of the finest examples of earlier evangelical concern in urban areas come from Germany. F.J. Hurst notes that "German Protestantism has given birth to some of the greatest charities of the present age, whether we take into account the number of beneficiaries or the faith and self-sacrifice of the founders and their successors."[19] Notable among those was John Falk, who turned from a promising literary career to help the starving population of Weimar during the Napoleonic Wars. Operating in the streets Falk reached out in Christian love to the orphans and the children, often desperately wicked. His "Reformatory" had no locked doors, believing instead that "love overcometh." "We forge," Falk said, "all our chains in the heart." He established also a plan to end begging in Weimar and set up a training school for boys. A true evangelical, his grave bears his own words: "Underneath this Linden tree, lies John Falk, a sinner he, saved by Christ's blood and mercy."

Pastor Fliedner at Kaiserwerth found his parish in destitution when the local factories went bankrupt in 1826. He set up a relief program which expanded rapidly to minister to the poor in neighboring regions also. His special work, however, became the assistance of the sick among the poor. He ministered to them in the largest house in Kaiserwerth, which was purchased in 1836, beginning his Deaconess Institute. After a period of opposition the idea spread to Holland, Switzerland, and France, and later to Alexandria, Bucharest, Constantinople, Smyrna and other locations. The nurses and instructors took their training at Kaiserwerth. Florence Nightingale profited from training there and wrote a book on the institution.

Johann Hinrich Wichern (1808-1881), a Lutheran pietist, founded at Hamburg, Germany, an institution for boys called *Rauhe Haus*. Organized as a reformatory, it helped abandoned boys to prepare for a useful life under Christian influence. Wichern's method was one of trust, love, and a community of mutual support. His aim was a Christlike character and personal economic independence. A faith-work, depending largely upon pietistic people to support it, it grew to be a national institution with over 250 branches in Germany alone.

Along with the work of Falk and Fliedner, *Rauhe Haus* formed the base for the emergence of "Die Innere Mission." This movement dates from 1848, when in the face of revolution a church diet was convened at Wittenberg. Here, at the site of Luther's work, Wichern made a moving appeal for spiritual renewal and cooperative concern in social needs. The first report delineated as its purpose "that the Christian Church with all its resources, and through all its agencies, may fill and quicken the whole life of the people in all ranks of society, inspire all social arrangements and institutions, with all the might of a love, energizing heart and life—and through all its living members labor to save the neglected and the poor." The work was more than humanitarian: it made "temporal and material aid a means of spiritual redemption" and aimed "at realizing in sacrificial service the priesthood of the believer."[20]

England: The Plight of the Poor

No social problem in 1800 was as important in the public eye as poverty. While it was generally felt in England that there was no way to eliminate poverty, it was seen as the duty of the more fortunate to supply at least the marginal subsistence needed by the unfortunate. In 1795 Eden's *State of the Poor* had laid out theories of poverty but arrived at no conclusions, though it did draw serious attention to the severity of poverty in Britain. Some ten years later Colquhoun, the chief magistrate of London, in his *Treatise on Indigence* spoke of "innocent indigence" and called for relief of those who had experienced bad fortune.

Chief among those in nineteenth-century England who sought a solution to poverty and its related problems stands Lord Shaftesbury. The full story of his work and his influence is told in a three-volume work by Edwin Hodder. Disraeli said that "The name of Lord Shaftesbury will descend to posterity as the one who has, in his generation, worked more than any other individual to elevate the condition, and to raise the carriage, of his countrymen."[21] His crusade included better treatment of the mentally ill, improved housing, better health, sanitation and recreation facilities, better schools, labor legislation, improvement of mining conditions, and opposition to the opium and the liquor traffic.[22] His concern as a Christian to serve his society derived largely from the ministry of an "obscure disciple," his nurse Maria Milles, who taught him to know and love Jesus as Lord and to seek to apply the truths of the Bible to contemporary problems.

A great part of Shaftesbury's effort was directed at housing conditions in London. He reported to Parliament that of 1465 families in St. George's Hanover Square, London, 929 lived in one room each, and his personal investigation had found situations where two, three, four, and even five families lived in a single room. Nor were these the worst quarters in London, for conditions in the lodging houses were even more disgraceful. A report of 1845 showed that in one situation a space fit for three hospital patients (33' by 20' by 7') often held from 50 to 100 men a night. The poor paid three pence a night to sleep in vermin-infested rooms often without beds or ventilation. Where beds were offered, frequently eight people would occupy a single bed. Shaftesbury was behind "The Society for Improving the Conditions of Laboring Classes," which showed what could be done to alleviate these conditions. The Model Lodging-houses established as a result of his pleading demonstrated their value in the cholera plague of 1848-49. Although nearly fifteen thousand Londoners, largely among the working classes, died of the cholera, the inhabitants of the Model Lodging-houses were singularly spared from the disease.

The Model Lodging-dwellers had clean and bright conditions by contemporary standards and paid no more for accommodations than was charged by the filthy hovels. These new quarters operated on a six percent profit basis, while slum landlords were drawing thirty to forty percent from their investment. Shaftesbury was no advocate of socialism, but he deplored those who used private resources to exploit the slum poor. He also fought the "window tax" which drew a levy on each window in the house and could amount to as much as seventy pounds on a single Model Lodging-house. This strange tax placed a financial premium on the very conditions that fostered filth, crime, and disease. Charles Dickens saw as "the best act ever passed by an English legislature" Shaftesbury's bill entitled, "Registration and Inspection of Common Lodging-houses." This bill enforced an elimination of the hideous conditions that were the lot of thousands of London's unfortunate poor by opening them to public officials who had power to deal with what they found. When new streets were put through the thriving city of London in 1853, many tenements were torn down. It was Shaftesbury who took up the call for care and decent housing for the poor left in the streets.

The social conditions in the English cities produced prisons of the worst sort. These medieval structures were scenes of hideous oppression which struck evangelicals as out of keeping with basic human decency. The Quakers had long had a concern here and their voice was heard. Among evangelicals the work of John Howard (d. 1790) stands out. Howard's work had an impact not only in England but, because of his frequent journeys, on the continent as well.[23] The picture of petite and cultured Elizabeth Fry (d. 1845) walking alone into the horrors of Newgate prison to begin a work of Christian grace challenged the nation and the world to act in the improvement of prison conditions and ministry to the prisoners.[24] The need for prison reform, for alteration in debtors' laws, for the assistance of released prisoners, and for a reduction in the number of capital offenses was made known by evangelicals who vigorously campaigned in the reform effort.

Scotland: Challenges to Poverty

Chalmers, while ministering at Glasgow for four years, set up a scheme for helping the poor of his parish.[25] His works *On Charity* and *On Poverty* were widely read and received the more notice because of his ability as a scholar. His pamphlet "The Influence of Bible Societies Upon the Temporal Necessities of the Poor" was already in circulation. Chalmers began by conducting a survey of the 11,000 members of his parish and noted the conditions of each. He discovered that two-thirds were alienated from the church and that a large percentage existed on relief and were depressed psychologically. Chalmers divided the newly established St. John's parish into 25 units and personalized the assistance offered. The sums for distribution were kept low and the avenues for help increased. Important in the scheme was the care shown in recruiting workers and the training which they were given. Though not having the advantages of the kind of studies later available to General Booth, the scheme was quite successful and copied widely. Perhaps its most important contribution was the stimulation it provided for the production of much needed concentrated studies on poverty. Chalmers' assistance left men and women their respect. "Help is to have a moral and educational end, and not a demoralizing one."[26]

Thomas Guthrie was minister in Edinburgh at Old Greyfriars after 1837 and a man deeply concerned for the poor. He established parish savings banks, libraries, and schools, and campaigned for the Scottish Education Act of 1872. He noted in *The City: Its Sins and Sorrows:*

> So Long as Religion Stands by silent and unprotesting against the temptations with which men, greedy of gain, and Governments, greedy of revenue, surround the wretched victim of this basest vice . . . it appears to me utter mockery for her to go with the Word of God in her hand, teaching them to say "Lead us not into Temptation."

Guthrie was deeply impressed by the labor of John Pounds, a cobbler of Portsmouth who, like a good shepherd, "had taken pity on the ragged children, whom ministers and magistrates, ladies and gentlemen, were leaving to run wild." Guthrie noted that Pound, "looking for no fame, no recompense from man, he, single-handed, while earning his daily bread by the sweat of his face, had, ere he died, rescued from ruin and saved to society no fewer than 500 children."[27]

The Disappearing Church

The city mission movement owed much to evangelical David Nasmith (d. 1839), founder of the Glasgow City Mission as well as missions in Dublin and London.[28] Early in the century societies were formed in New York, Brooklyn, and Boston. Best known among the city missions were McAuley's Water Street Mission in New York and the Pacific Garden Mission in Chicago, established by Col. G. R. Clarke.[29] Samuel Hadley, a convert of the McAuley mission, founded more than sixty city rescue missions in the United States. To the work of the hundreds of independent evangelical missions in European and American cities is added the well-known effort of the Salvation Army, founded in 1864 (1880 in the United States). General Booth's *In Darkest England* and *The Way Out* were a clarion call for the church to serve in the cities. Out of an 1871 visit to Paris by Rev. Robert W. McAll came the establishment of a hundred city missions in France, a third of them in Paris and environs.[30]

The ecumenical character of these efforts among evangelicals, points out Timothy Smith, "was rapidly awakening a new sense of responsibility for those whom a soulless industrial system had thrown upon the refuse heap of the city's slums."[31] Evangelical endeavors such as that led by Anglican clergyman Stephen H. Tyng of New York acted as a catalyst encouraging a variety of efforts which aided the city poor. Edward Norris Kirk, an evangelist in Boston about 1842, saw that "the rise of urban poverty in America posed a new challenge to religion." Kirk insisted that "when men love their neighbors as themselves, the causes of poverty will be sought out, and the remedy applied as far as possible."[32] This evangelical compassion for the underprivileged spread so that The Independent in 1855 deplored "Sabbath feasts of taste and music" as the church turned away from the destitute masses.[33] The same periodical in June 1855 "regretted the spasmodic nature of most poor relief, especially its failure to deal with the economic factors in urban destitution." The evangelically motivated banded together in cross-denominational efforts to meet the practical necessities of the poor with bread, housing, jobs, and personal salvation.

In 1886 S. L. Loomis delivered a series of addresses which were published as Modern Cities and Their Religious Problems. A reading of Loomis shows that the dreams of the evangelicals of 1800 had not been realized. The mandate was still the "advancement of the Redeemer's Kingdom among the neglected masses of the great towns." By Loomis's time the mass abandonment of the city came and an attempt was being made to stem that tide:

> When a down-town church finds its old supporters moving away to the suburbs, instead of picking up its hymn books and hastening after them, instead of selling its old building for a warehouse or a skating rink and abandoning the neighborhood with its increasing multitude of dying men—why should it not recognize the changed condition of affairs to equip itself for day the new kind of work and reaping the new harvests. . . .

While the endeavor of the evangelical churches in missions and settlement houses did much to alleviate the problems of some, the problems of the man in the inner city were not at all solved. However great and glorious the story, "distress was met more often with relief than reform."[34] Reforms were called for, and in many instances effective, but it was often too little and too late to alter the situation.

The Evangelical Contributions

Evangelical involvement in eighteenth- and nineteenth-century social reform was largely carried out apart from ecclesiastical structures, at least until the end of the period. The originating forces were not the churches but concerned individuals who provided direction and vision for the emerging programs of assistance. Often the established churches and denominations opposed and undermined moves to involve the larger Christian community. In a sense, then, there was a secularizing of Christian philanthropy, as faith acted in love away from the brass altar in the "stained glass prison." Here is a re-institutionalizing of Christian work, a moving of it outside of the courts of formal religion. The gospel moves from the temple into the byways, and men are confronted with the healing and helping power of Jesus Christ.

What can we say about this crusade of evangelicals to better their nations and to "bind up the brokenhearted"?

1. The evangelical, when he became aware of social problems, presented his talents, time, and his resources to alleviate conditions.

2. Perhaps more important was the way in which he dedicated himself as God's servant to the task.

3. This made possible the establishment of relationship with those who were in need, thus supplying the personal factor that alone can humanize and Christianize such efforts. This was quite in contrast to both the isolationism of the humanistic drawing room discussion of "men's rights" and the philanthropic "do-goodism" of the later nineteenth-century church.

4. Evangelicals tended unconsciously to keep a balance between philanthropy, personal faith, evangelism, and world mission. They refused to shut anyone out in favor of the others.

5. The public conscience was alerted, sensitized and enlightened by the two-pronged effort of printed page and personal example. Both the conscience of the Christian to act meaningfully and the consciousness of the masses of people to Christian behavior were affected.

6. Through evangelical labor there was the righting of a multitude of wrongs, and society benefited greatly from this crusade to effect an application of divinely revealed principles to the everyday world in which men lived, thus honoring the Creator God.

7. The nineteenth-century evangelical had rediscovered what it meant to be salt-like in society. As *The Epistle to Diognetus* put it:

> What the soul is in the body, that Christians are in the world. The soul is dispersed through all the members of the body, and Christians are scattered through all the cities of the world.[35]

Evangelical Perception of Today's World

It must be noted that evangelicals have never really lost their desire to act in the world. In the spirit of worldwide expansion that characterized the nineteenth century, they threw themselves into the task of mission with an exemplary zeal. Today's world church and the temporal blessing that accompanied those missionary efforts are witness to their effectiveness.

Unfortunately, at the turn of the twentieth century a bitter battle with a radical and often destructive liberalism took place. Struggling for his institutional existence, the evangelical was in no position to act as forcefully in his rightful heritage of Christian social concern. Furthermore, a major psychological barrier was built up by false dichotomies that were pressed on evangelicalism by those who felt that the human establishment of an earthly kingdom of God was the task of the church. Frequently personal religion was totally sacrificed to the "social gospel." Consequently, evangelicals began to read their Bibles through narrower lenses and hesitated to implement a biblical social ethic as had their great forebears from the Reformation through the nineteenth century. Fortunately, with a new interest in serious biblical studies much of this is being recovered.

In the first half of this century an attitude of otherworldliness in religion seems to have swept across evangelicalism. This Spirit did not, however, seem to curtail the effort of many evangelicals to become materialistically affluent. A false concept of God and his world in many segments of the church almost totally wiped out a sense of social responsibility. The writings of Herman Bavinck, Abraham Kuyper and other Reformed theologians have done much to offset this.

Evangelicals have an heroic heritage in the urban arena, one that must not be abandoned. The inheritance was weakened in the age of embattlement as evangelicals lost schools, missions, and societies to a liberalism that found certain basic tenets of Christianity to be an encumbrance to the performance of good. History has shown how bankrupt that movement was and what great need there now is for a genuine, biblically based social involvement, without which the deepest needs of man cannot be met. In an age when renewal is evident on every hand within the church let there also be a renewal of ministry to the centers of our civilization from which impulses emanate to shape the thinking and life of our nations.

Notes to Chapter 2

1 John H. Overton and Frederic Relton, *The English Church from the Accession of George I to the End of the 18th Century* (1906), p. 250.

2 R. N. Stromberg, *Religious Liberalism in 18th Century England* (1954), pp. 154f.

3 Cf. Henry Venn, *The Conversion of Sinners The Greatest Charity.*

4 David Owen, *English Philanthropy 1660-1960* (1964), p. 93.

5 H. Venn, *The Complete Duty of Man,* 5th edition, p. 194.

6 *Ibid.,* pp. 197, 199.

7 *The Good and Righteous King,* p. 22.

8 See Kathleen Heasman, *Evangelicals in Action.*

9 J. L. and B. Hammond, *The Town Labourer* (1917), pp. 225-228; W. D. Morris, *The Christian Origins of Social Revolt,* pp. 153-173.

10 Standish Meacham, *Henry Thornton of Clapham* (1964), pp. 26ff.

11 W. D. Morris, *op. cit.*, p. 158.

12 Hugh Watt, *Thomas Chalmers*, p. 62.

13 E. D. Bebb, *Nonconformity and Social and Economic Life 1660-1800* (1935), pp. 54f. See pp. 164f. for a catalog of the nonconformists' contributions to social reform.

14 Meacham, *op. cit.*, p. 138.

15 *Ibid.*, p. 139.

16 William Roberts, *Memoirs of the Life of Hannah More*, Vol. 2, p. 168.

17 John Venn, *Henry Venn*, p. 365.

18 E. M. Forster, *Marrianne Thornton 1787-1887*, p. 13.

19 F. J. Hurst, *History of Rationalism*, p. 310.

20 J. L. Patton, "Innere Mission," in *Hastings Encyclopedia of Religion and Ethics* (1908-27).

21 Cited by E. Hodder, *Life of Shaftesbury* (1886; repr. 1971), Vol. III, p. 421.

22 J. W. Bready, *Lord Shaftesbury and Social and Industrial Progress*. See also K. S. Latourette, *Christianity in a Revolutionary Age*, Vol. II, pp. 355ff.

23 D. L. Howard, *John Howard: Prison Reformer*, pp. 53ff.

24 Janet Whitney, *Elizabeth Fry*, p. 117.

25 See William Hannah, *Memoirs of Thomas Chalmers* (2 vols.).

26 A. F. Young and E. T. Ashton, *British Social Work in the 19th Century* (1956), p. 70.

27 See *Autobiography of Thomas Guthrie*, Vol. I.

28 See John Campbell, *Memoirs of David Nasmith* (1844).

29 See R. M. Offord (ed.), *Jerry McAuley* (1907); and C. F. H. Henry, *The Pacific Garden Mission*.

30 Samuel L. Loomis, *Modern Cities* (1887; repr. 1970), pp. 163-181.

31 Timothy Smith, *Revivalism and Social Reform* (1957), p. 167.

32 *Ibid.*, p. 163.

33 Quoted by Timothy Smith, *ibid.*, p. 164.

34 Meacham, *op. cit.*, p. 141.

35 Quoted by Ray C. Petry, *A History of Christianity*, Vol. I (1962), p. 20.

3: A THEOLOGY OF COMPASSION FOR THE CITY

by Ross Nelson

What follows is only an outline of the biblical basis for a theology of compassion and concern. To fill it out would require a more thorough analysis of the Scriptures and frequent appeal to cognate and correlative truths, especially from the behavioral sciences. Because of space limitations, our discussion is limited to biblical essentials. I believe that what God has said in his holy word can be clearly focused so as to cast bright light on the task of the Christian church in reaching the lost in the inner cities of America.

We shall discuss the biblical guidance for finding the will of God in human situations under five major headings: (1) the tragedy in the first family; (2) the contribution of the Mosaic law; (3) the supportive contribution of the prophets; (4) the teaching of Jesus in the Sermon on the Mount; and (5) the vital teachings of the apostles and New Testament writers.

ROSS NELSON is the assumed name of a Christian layman who has long been deeply involved in urban ministries. An evangelical social scientist, he is currently working in this field in Michigan.

Tragedy: The First Family

Genesis 4 records the murder of Abel by his brother Cain. When God sought to deal with him about it, his reply was insolent: "Am I my brother's keeper?"

The facts of this episode are well known: Abel brought a more excellent sacrifice than Cain; Cain's envy and hatred of his brother, whose works were righteous, resulted in cold-blooded murder; Cain denied responsibility, but was judged by God, who set a mark upon him and banished him. The point is that God expected not only a proper sacrifice from Cain, but also devotion and thanksgiving, with a submissive and worshipful heart, and fulfilment of his social responsibility toward his brother. God expected him to be his brother's keeper. Cain's insolent and angry reply throws back into God's face that which God had made clear was his duty.

This tragedy in the first family underlines a truth that God wants all men to understand, a truth implied throughout the Scriptures: *each man is his brother's keeper.* To please God, to worship him properly, is not only to bring an acceptable sacrifice in faith, coming with thanksgiving and honor and praise unto God, but also to assume the responsibility God gives us to care for our brother. These two responsibilities are correlative and cooperative. The command is not only to worship him, but, because we are men of faith who do worship, to care for our fellow man as our brother.

To the question of the rebellious murderer of Abel, the answer is affirmative, "Yes, we are our brother's keeper, and we cannot avoid this God-given responsibility!" A theology of Christian compassion and concern begins at this point. The evangelical Christian looks out on the whole human race and sees each man as his brother. This does not mean that he considers those who do not know Christ as Savior to be fellow members of God's redeemed family. But he recognizes all persons as God's creation, to be treated with brotherly concern. Before God he accepts his responsibility of compassion and concern. He is his brother's keeper.

Compassion and the Jewish Law

The Jewish law continues the teachings of early Genesis, particularly the emphatic principle that we are our brother's keeper. The Mosaic regulations point out specific things a person is to do to act on behalf of his brother. The first verses of Deuteronomy 22 are typical:

> You shall not see your brother's ox or his sheep go astray, and withhold your help from them; you shall take them back to your brother. And if he is not near you, or if you do not know him, you shall bring it home to your house, and it shall be with you until your brother seeks it; then you shall restore it to him. And so you shall do with his ass; so you shall do with his garment; so you shall do with any lost things of your brother's, which he loses and you find; you may not withhold your help. You shall not see your brother's ass or his ox fallen down by the way, and withhold

your help from them; you shall help him to lift them up again (Deut. 22:1-4).

The idea behind such rules is that one's brother is a fellow Jew, one who is of the same people and serves the same God, and is under the same Mosiac requirement. There are strong punishments for anyone who kidnaps a brother, and seeks to sell him as a slave (Deut. 24:7). The Jew was to lend to the Jew without interest, but he was permitted to charge interest for his loan to one who was not a Jew, a stranger (Deut. 23:19-20). If he fails to be brotherly in the lending of money, food, or anything else, God sees him and cannot bless him as he would if the person's conduct were right and proper.

The modern reader who looks at the Mosaic requirements will perhaps be shocked at the apparent severity of some of the punishments specified for wrongdoers in Israel. Compared to contemporary standards these prescriptions sound cruel indeed. Exodus 21:22-25 prescribes retaliation "eye for eye, tooth for tooth." In Deuteronomy 25:2 we read that a man is to be flogged (but not to receive more than forty stripes). Exodus 21:12-14 talks about cities of refuge and the avenger of blood: if a person inadvertently killed someone he had to flee for his life, for it was morally incumbent on the relatives of the dead person to chase and put to death the killer. The incorrigible son was to be stoned (Deut. 21:18-21); the virgin who was raped but did not cry out for help when it was near was to be stoned along with her accoster (Deut. 22:23-24); an illegitimate individual was not to enter into the congregation of the Lord and his progeny unto the tenth generation were likewise prohibited (Deut. 23:2).

Our purpose in this essay is not to address questions about the severity of these penalties. Two things can be said briefly. These punishments were part of an entire legal code given by God for a particular situation that is now part of history. And, second, with our limited viewpoints we are not in a proper position to call God into question. Humanly speaking, it may be difficult to say, "The Judge of all the earth will do right" and "He doeth all things well," when we cannot fully understand all God has done and is doing. But the person of true faith responds with the holy trembling of thanksgiving and reverence for God, the God of holiness, justice, and goodness, who is also the God of grace. Less than this acceptance shows a lack of true faith (Rom. 9:6-33). Our major interest here is that God does not nullify the principle that man is his brother's keeper in these specific legal requirements.

Specific instruction is given in the law about several classes of people: the poor, strangers, the fatherless and orphans, widows, bondservants and slaves, and Levites. In each case Moses, writing the requirements of the Lord to Israel, makes very clear the responsibilities of care and concern.

Deuteronomy 15:7-8 tells us, "If there is among you a poor man, one of your brethren . . . you shall not harden your heart or shut your hand against your poor brother, but you shall open your hand to him, and lend him sufficient for his need.... Another passage warns against trying to take advantage of a poor person through usury and using the bare necessities he might have as a pledge, creating further hardship for him (Exod. 22:25-27).

Obviously God's legal requirement was to behave graciously. The poor are called "the neighbor" and "the brother." Not only were the Israelites to remember that they were their brother's keeper, but also that God would bless them for discharging this responsibility properly. If they failed God himself would hear the cry of the oppressed person and assist, for he characterizes himself as "compassionate" (Exod. 22:27).

The parts of Israel's fields that were not reaped were to be left for the poor, as were the grapes of the vineyards (Lev. 19:9, 10; 23:22). Moses expands on this responsibility to provide sustenance for the unfortunate in Deuteronomy 24:19-22, concluding with the reminder that all the Israelites had been in similar states of dependency in Egypt.

Other unfortunate and perplexed individuals and families—the strangers, orphans, and widows — suffered economically and thus needed assistance from those whose needs were more than met. Further, the Lord wanted Israel to provide for those who had been slaves, and to free them with adequate means (Exod. 21:2-4; Deut. 15:12-15). The freed bondslave was not only to have capital to begin to live as a freedman, but also was under other conditions able to remain as the head of his family, with new status and position. No slave could be made to serve more than six years, if he were a man; as a result, the heads of families could not become a permanent slave caste.

A somewhat different arrangement was observed for women who were bondslaves. Exodus 21:7 requires that they were not to go out as the men-servants do. The woman bondslave was to be protected, in a culture where males were dominant and required to protect their wives and concubines (Exod. 21:8-11). Above all, the master was not free to sell her to a foreigner. If the bondwoman was married into the master's family she was to have the status of a daughter. Furthermore, she was to be adequately cared for (or freed if not adequately cared for).

Similarly, provision was made for slaves who loved their masters and wished to stay with them for life, providing mutual benefits (Exod. 21:5-6; Deut. 15:16-17). The Mosaic code prescribed requirements for both bondslaves and masters. It set guidelines for status and responsibility so that in a culture that perpetuated slavery, slavery was not extreme and excessive, nor was a permanent slave caste to be established. It provided a channel for genuine compassion and mutual concern. This is not to say that the law *caused* men to have true compassion for one another; I do not think that can be demonstrated. But the commandments did provide channels, in a stern and often cruel culture, where genuine compassion and concern could find ready expression within legal boundaries.

The offering of the first fruits and the requirement to tithe are mentioned in Deuteronomy 14 and 26. Full provision is made for the Levite, the stranger, the fatherless and the widow. The Levites as a tribe had not been given property for an inheritance to pass on to their children. Clearly, they were dependent on the tithes and offerings of God's people for their support.

We may summarize the Mosaic section of the Scripture by stating that the Lord demanded specific obedience to his commandments concerning those who need care and compassion. The law did not command compassion, but it did require adequate care and certainly pointed out the necessity for personal concern.

The Prophets

The writings of the prophets re-echo the teaching of the law. As Jeremiah warned Judah of the need to repent and turn back to God in the face of the Chaldean threat, he called for justice and compassion. If they wished to dwell in the land of their fathers they were to truly execute justice one with another . . . not oppress the alien, the fatherless or the widow, or shed innocent blood (Jer. 7:5-6). Habakkuk pronounced woe against "him who gets evil gain for his house" (2:9-10). He reiterates the theme that one must have compassion for his brother.

Denunciations of unrighteous behavior are legion throughout the prophets. Where men have distorted truth, broken ethical requirements, minimized moral responsibility, or taken unfair and wicked advantage of others, their behavior is thoroughly condemned and God's judgment pronounced on it. Both negatively and positively, the prophets declare that true compassion and concern for one's fellow man is the proper expression of godly living. The charge is to obey the high and holy will of God.

Space prevents us from quoting many of these prophetic passages, but one further example may be cited. Isaiah 5 records a song about the Lord's loving care in planting a vineyard that failed and brought forth wild grapes.

This chapter elaborates the sins of Israel, particularly the southern tribes of Judah, who not only failed to worship God with the genuine devotion pleasing to him, but oppressed the poor and needy, and treated their fellow men as merchandise, determined to profit by their unfair treatment of others. The grapes produced by the choicest vine were wild grapes with thorns and briers, so God was required to judge his own vineyard, his own people.

Covetousness and unholy acquisition of property (vs. 8), carnal passion and drunkenness (vs. 11), deception and distortion of honor and truth (vv. 20-22) receiving of bribes and taking away of the rights of the righteous (vs. 23), deliberate destruction of righteousness (vv. 24-25) — all these are specifically inveighed against. God pronounces unfailing judgment on them. Sadly, this judgment pertains to all his people. Collectively they have brought forth wild grapes, and so he pronounces judgment (vv. 5-7).

If we learn anything about a theology of compassion and concern from studying the prophets, it is that persistent disobedience and spiritual decay, moral laxity and blight force the covenant-keeping God to judge his people whom he loves. He poured out his wrath (Isa. 5:25) because of their failure both to worship him in spirit and truth and to manifest the behavior of proper concern and compassion for others.

While collective responsibility is clearly itemized by the prophets, and collective judgment is also promised, individual responsibility for full personal obedience to God is equally required. Micah put it succinctly:

> Will the Lord be pleased with thousands of rams, with ten thousands of rivers of oil? Shall I give my first-born for my transgression, the fruit of my body for the sin of my soul? He has showed you, O man, what is good; and what does the Lord require of you but to do justice, and to love kindness, and to walk humbly with your God? (6:7-8).

The tragedy is that there were so few individuals who truly loved God and had compassion for their fellow man that God was forced to judge the entire nation.

The Sermon on the Mount

In comparison with the law and the prophets, Jesus' Sermon on the Mount (Matthew 5-7; Luke 6) sets a standard of behavior that reaches beyond the requirements found in them. It is more than a presentation by Christ of supremely sensitive ethical relationships and spiritual duties to be discharged in relationship to both God and man. It demands a very different kind of person from what we find even among God's people in the Old Testament. Such thoroughly Christlike behavior requires a thoroughly changed being.

This socially sensitive, ethically exalted, and spiritually effective person is described in the passage that begins the sermon—often called the Beatitudes (Matt. 5:1-12). This person is poor in spirit, realizing his own spiritual bankruptcy and trusting God fully to provide him with deliverance and redemption. He may mourn due to the sorrow, perplexity, or problems he experiences (some perhaps in compassion for others), but the Lord assures us that he will be comforted. His meekness and preference for God's holy will in every circumstance lead Jesus to promise that he will inherit the earth. His hunger for righteousness will be satisfied; his mercy insures that he will receive the blessing of mercy. This person is pure in heart, possessed of inner integrity and genuine, unselfish love for God and man. He will be blessed with the most glorious fellowship of seeing God. This person is a peacemaker, who brings harmony and healing to others, blessings to people caught in tense and antagonizing social situations. As a reward he will be called a child of God by those around him. He may be persecuted for righteousness; his reward is the assurance that he has an inheritance in the kingdom of heaven.

The individual who is spiritually in tune with God and ethically and socially concerned for man is the "salt of the earth" and the "light of the world" (Matt. 5:13-16). As the salt, he helps preserve and heal his fellow men. As the light, he shines forth in all the world, glorifying his Father in heaven.

Such a person obeys the commandments, carries out the moral and spiritual requirements of the law, and teaches these obligations to others (Matt. 5:19). His righteousness is not born of external compulsion but internally by faith in the living Christ. The person who is in tune with God and effectively ministers to his fellow man does not just possess a *judicial* righteousness, conferred on him through the act of faith. Beyond this standing of justification, he demonstrates God's righteousness in his daily behavior. His living faith produces God-glorifying conduct; thus he serves his fellow man in the will of God. Such a man has faith at the root of his behavior. He manifests the fruit of both his faith and fellowship with God in his love and compassionate concern for his fellow man.

Consequently, such a person refrains not only from murder but also from being angry with his brother without a cause. He does not speak disparagingly of his brother. If there is a controversy between the two of them, when he goes to worship, he leaves his gift on the altar, and finds his brother to be reconciled with him. Only then does he worship his Lord and is he reconciled with his God. This person agrees with his adversary quickly. If he is sued at law and his coat is taken away, he lets his cloak go also. If he is compelled to go a mile with someone, he goes two miles. If he is struck on the right cheek, he turns the other. Above all, he loves his enemies and prays for his persecutors.

While ethical and spiritual behavior, seen in day-by-day social situations, is very important, the Sermon on the Mount presents us with demands for a higher type of person, on the whole, than did the Old Testament. Its requirements are, indeed, for behavior that would be impossible without the transforming work of Christ.

The New Testament

We can begin our consideration of this fifth major category of biblical evidence with Paul's words in Romans 12. Paul's emphasis is that one must become and be a godly person in order to manifest effective behavior before God and man. The mercy of God and the redeeming grace of Christ must bring about a genuine transformation in the life and personality if one is to be able to properly and consistently show godly compassion.

Beyond initial regeneration, Paul pleads that we not be conformed to this world, but rather be transformed by the renewal of our minds, that we may prove (in daily behavior) what is the will of God (Rom. 12:2). The several members of the body of Christ have an interrelated ministry. Their gifts differ, but they are to be used for the benefit of all and the glory of God.

The regenerated believer will love without pretense. His warmly affectionate relationship with others will show itself in brotherly love, in giving preference to his brother, in continuing prayer, in liberal distribution according to the needs of others, in hospitality.

Paul's letters are full of admonitions and exhortations about the behavior of the regenerated individual. In order to have godly compassion and deep concern for others, one must not only be born again, justified by faith, possessing the gift of divine righteousness. He must become ethically sensitive and socially aware. He must become a truly spiritual man in all that the word implies. He is to give glory to God as he serves his master in heaven, by serving his fellow man with a divinely engendered compassion and sincere concern.

Similar themes appear in other New Testament writers. The letters of John are well known for their emphasis on love as the inevitable accompaniment of knowing God. This love is not just a thought or a feeling. It is practical. James's short letter is full of exhortations not to make distinctions among persons or to despise the poor (2:1-9), to love our neighbor as ourselves (2:8-9), to control our tongues, to be without envy or strife, to seek wisdom from above, sowing the fruit of righteousness by being peacemakers or reconcilers (3:17-18), not to speak evil of one another (4:11), and not to hold grudges (5:9).

In the midst of his denunciation of spiritual wickedness and heterodoxy Jude points out that New Testament believers are to have compassion (vv. 17-21), to be so concerned for others that they may snatch them, as it were, out of the fire (vv. 22-23).

The apostle Peter, in his first epistle, points out the very high spiritual and ethical position the New Testament believer is to occupy. He quotes from levitical law, "You shall be holy, for I am holy" (1:16; Lev. 11:44). Such a holy person, such an ethical and socially sensitive person, will manifest honesty and demonstrate the integrity of his faith in good works. The result will be the glorification of God even by those who do not know him.

We could augment these few examples at length. The message is clear, however: the New Testament believer is to be socially and ethically sensitive. He is not only to enjoy fellowship with God through his new birth, but also to reflect that fellowship in his relationships with those around him. He is to be a person of heavenly wisdom, sweetness, grace, tenderness, and deep compassion and concern.

Summary Scriptures

From the tragedy of the first family we have pointed out the basic scriptural principle that men of faith are their brother's keeper. We saw that the Mosaic law made special requirements for the care of those classes of people in particular need. We pointed out the reinforcement of those requirements by the prophets, who called men of faith to "do justice, love kindness, and walk humbly before God." We discovered from the words of Christ in the Sermon on the Mount that those who serve God are a different kind of person from the ordinarily religious or secular. They must be ethically and socially sensitive, spiritually attuned to God and in fellowship with him. Clearly, what men are to *do* for their fellow man for God's glory is to stem from what they *are* as persons transformed by God's grace.

Two familiar parables of Jesus provide a summary statement of a theology of Christian compassion. First is the story of the rich man and the beggar Lazarus, for whom he showed no concern as he dined sumptuously. Tormented in the flames of hell after death, the rich man lifted up his eyes and saw Abraham with Lazarus in his bosom. He pleaded with Abraham to have mercy on him and send Lazarus to dip his finger in water to cool the rich man's parched tongue. Abraham denied the request, for, he said, the rich man had received good things in life, and Lazarus evil. Now the situation was reversed, and furthermore a great gulf was fixed between them (Luke 16:25-26).

Why was the rich man in torment? Why was he, conscious and in possession of his whole faculties, suffering intensely? In contrast, why was Lazarus comforted and blessed? Because Lazarus was a man of faith. He had nothing in his earthly life, but God honored his faith. The rich man was not a man of faith. No indication is given that he believed and trusted God. Since the Bible makes it plain that faith bears fruit, it seems clear that the rich man, who did not even invite Lazarus inside his gate nor make any adequate provision for him, did not have that faith. The wages of his sin, as Paul taught, was death.

The second parable is recorded in Luke 10. A lawyer questioned Jesus about eternal life; Jesus in turn asked him what the law said. The lawyer's summary met with Jesus' approval: first, one must thoroughly love God; and second, he must love his neighbor as himself.

But though the lawyer knew the need for such love, he did not love God or his neighbor thus. Seeking to justify himself, he asked a question similar in intent to Cain's: "Who is my neighbor?" In response, the Lord told the poignant and revealing story of the man victimized by robbers, passed by by the religious leaders, and finally helped by a Samaritan.

Here Jesus points out what it is to be one's brother's keeper. The Samaritan—that representative of a despised and mixed race, neither Jew nor Gentile—had compassion and expressed it in concrete brotherly concern. He bound up and anointed the victim's wounds; he set him on his own beast and took him to an inn where he provided for his future care. Thus he proved that he was a different kind of person from the priest and the Levite, religious as they undoubtedly were. The fruits of his concern and compassion were manifested in unabashed and unashamed mercy. The Samaritan was a man of ethical and social sensitivity, of spiritual stature.

The lawyer knew that the merciful man was the true neighbor. Jesus' pointed statement, "Go and do thou likewise," implies that if one completely loves God he will be transformed by God into a person of divine compassion and concern. Knowing the commandments is not enough. Saying one loves God is not enough. One must love others as himself.

Conclusion

What can the average evangelical Christian (aided by the Holy Spirit), who wants to be obedient to the biblical directives we have mentioned, do to reach the people of the inner city? What can the church of Jesus Christ do to practice the compassion which, we have seen, is expected of it?

Obviously, the first thing is to become sensitive to the Lord's command, "Go therefore and make disciples of all nations" (Matt. 28:19). Surely this includes the persons at our doors and the people of the inner city as well as those in foreign countries.

Second, we must reach people where they are, as they are, person to person. Those in the suburbs will not reach people in the inner city without going into the inner city, meeting those who live there, getting acquainted with them, coming to grips with their real needs and problems as genuinely interested, warm-hearted, empathetic, Spirit-enabled believers. There is no short-cut to compassion that avoids that sort of involvement. Christians can never gain the confidence of those in the city or bring the message of the risen Savior apart from doing what God clearly points out they must do — demonstrating that they are their brother's keeper.

What about the very real concern some Christians feel that they are exposing themselves to physical harm in the inner city? There is no denying that that is the case. But the Lord offers wisdom and grace to those who trust him.

The message of the Bible is clear. Christians must act as Christians. Christians who are convinced that the inner cities of our nation present a crying need for compassionate relief will want to take their place personally in making possible a vigorous and effective Christian response. The Christian's standards of success will not be those of the world. But the godly individual, filled with the Holy Spirit and the love of Christ, determined not to be discouraged, looking to the sovereign Lord to work in prepared hearts, will see results, because of his practical, loving concern. Grace will abound. It is on the strength of that promise that we must care, we must dare to obey the command of our Savior to go. Nothing less will do.

PART THREE:
CULTURE, CONFORMITY, AND CHRISTIANITY —
SOME HINDRANCES

INTRODUCTION

From the moment of birth an individual is exposed to the customs, language, life-style, and beliefs that make him a member of a particular culture and subculture. For the first part of life these perspectives and behaviors are transmitted through the powerful influence of parents. Later, in adolescence, some rebel and attempt to escape or alter their subcultural trappings as their world widens. Many simply continue on in the ways of the parents. Those who do rebel may succeed in getting rid of many of the effects of their socialization, but really only exchange one subculture for another.

Rather than deny that we are all acculturated in this way, even after we become Christians, we need to examine some of the powerful forces that have affected us as members of American society, so that we might move toward the implementation of Paul's charge in Romans 12:2: "Do not be conformed to this world but be transformed by the renewal of your mind." None of us is completely transformed into an absolute showcase of heaven when we come to know Christ. Although we become spiritually new creations, a lifelong work of sanctification remains for us. We frequently reflect the patterns and attitudes of both the surrounding secular culture and the evangelical subculture.[1] The evangelical subculture, we sometimes fail to realize, is not nearly as "heavenly" as we would like to believe. Often evangelicals attempt to find scriptural rationalizations for their adherence to the norms of secular society, while attacking "liberal" theologians for selective interpretation. Norms unique to the evangelical subculture are subtly attached to our interpretation of what the Christian should be like, though these norms may have little or no basis in the Scripture. One observer remarks that "the very heart of cultural evangelicalism is often fear, rather than the good news of forgiveness and love. Much of the cultural conformity and lack of inquisitiveness is a by-product of fear rather than reasoned conviction."[2]

The point is, are we aware of how we are shaped by the ungodly influences of our culture and subculture? When made aware of these "trappings" are we willing to take the steps necessary to obtain the purifying forgiveness of God and of men? Are we willing as believing Christians to actively shape our subculture, or do we passively allow it to shape us? If we fail to shape our culture and subculture in ways that please God, we will end up shaping our children in ways and perspectives that displease him. If our passive acceptance of cultural or subcultural mores means that persons are physically or psychologically destroyed, or that we care more about our own status than the welfare of others, or that we follow the call of convenience rather than the call of God, how can we expect to escape the judgment of the Father "who judges each one impartially" (I Pet. 1:17)?

Three such sets of cultural and subcultural influences that the majority of Christians have conformed to in our society are discussed in this section: Joseph Daniels talks clinically, then personally, about racism among evangelicals. Art Gish focuses on the social and economic trappings of middle-class culture that keep many Christians from involvement in the city. Myron Augsburger points out a number of ways in which Christians misuse Scripture in order to serve self-interest.

Prejudice and the Christian

Both historical accounts and contemporary research data give a sobering picture of the Christian community's mirroring—and at times leading—American racial prejudice.[3] Although much of the available information focuses on white-black relations, similar findings would no doubt result from a study of attitudes toward American Indian, Spanish-speaking, and Oriental minorities. There are, in addition, other forms of prejudice—religious prejudice and prejudice against the poor or less powerful—that infect the evangelical community.

Milton Rokeach found that "those expressing views unsympathetic to the black, the poor and the student-protest movement, and those who did welcome the church's involvement in political and social affairs uniformly valued salvation more than those taking a more compassionate stand on such issues. . . . Christians who valued salvation were not necessarily the same ones who valued *"forgiving."* [4] In contrast to Allport and Ross, who found that those who tend to use religion to serve some self-centered purpose are more prejudiced than those seeking religious experience as an end in itself, Rokeach failed to find any differentiation. Indeed, the religiously devout are "on the average more bigoted, more authoritarian, more dogmatic, and more anti-humanitarian than the less devout." [5] For those who worship and are supposed to identify with God "who is no respecter of persons" (Acts 10:34), and who has "broken down the dividing wall of hostility" (Eph. 2:14), which involved a great deal of ethnic prejudice, this should be shocking.

We preach Christ's love as the essence of the gospel. The central components of prejudice are fear, struggle for power, neuroticism/ego-insecurity, and hatred. That Christians should be afraid of and hate an entire race of people is incredible. If our prejudice stems from a struggle to maintain power or status or position, we are at the least failing to trust God and at the most emulating Lucifer before his fall. If our prejudice stems from insecurity, we need to learn new ways to make God's unconditional love and acceptance of us our emotionally *experienced* standard of self-acceptance.

Prejudice is not only vented in the overt, Ku Klux Klan type of terrorism, or even in the use of obscene racial epithets. It may come in the production of religious education literature that pictures story characters and Christ as invariably white and blue-eyed. It may come in a tacit fear that one's child might marry one of "them."

One final word—though a response of fear or caution is typical when a person is exposed to something strange, he quickly adapts to the object when regularly exposed. Perhaps one of the reasons prejudice has been maintained among Christians is that we have limited contact across races. The white middle-class person has moved to get away, and the minority person has learned to avoid the white person because of the frequent personal pain. In both cases there is the need for the persons to come into *constructive* contact with one another.

Social and Economic Hindrances

In recent years, the connection between prejudice and social and economic concerns has been drawn sharply. Rokeach found that equal status contacts between those of different races tend to reflect less racial hostility. On the other hand, a great deal of the reaction (including that of conservative Christians) to the racial unrest of the 1960s seemed to combine the fear of economic loss with underlying racial dislike.

As Gish points out, American Christians often sell out to the temptations of status and secular respectability and allow economic or property considerations to dictate their human relationships. Again the basic problem is not the *fact* that one is a member of a particular group or economic class. The question is, how far does the Christian cease to be salt because of these influences? To what extent does he actually help perpetuate ungodliness by adherence to secular standards of success?

> But those who desire to be rich fall into temptation, into a snare, into many senseless and hurtful desires that plunge men into ruin and destruction. For the love of money is the root of all evils; it is through this craving that some have wandered away from the faith and pierced their hearts with many pangs. But as for you, man of God, shun all this; aim at righteousness, godliness, faith, love, steadfastness, gentleness (I Tim. 6:9-11).

We may respond that we don't want to be *rich*, just to have what is our "right" as a result of hard work. Indeed, some seem to have imbibed so deeply of the Protestant work ethic that outward signs of material abundance compensate for the lack of genuine spiritual life.

Have the rugged individualism of American culture and the notion of laissez-faire been allowed to cushion our sense of responsibility for the brother in need? Are productivity and property more important than persons? Have we excused the frequent greed encouraged by economic competition and capitalism by confusing capitalism and freedom? Have we swallowed the world's criteria of success and supported them with some vague justification of "evidence of God's blessing"? Have we been so tuned to the work ethic that we feel justified in our lack of love for those who do not possess the skills or are not given the opportunity to work?

Why should theological conservatism be equated with political conservatism? Shouldn't all Christians be "liberal" in their concern for those in need? Can we justify noninvolvement in politics because it is a "dirty business"? Can we simply condone immorality in government—whether in the form of ignoring the needy or justifying law-breaking?

Gish considers these and related questions, and calls the American evangelical church to "submit all our social, political, and economic ideas to the test of biblical revelation and the final norm of Jesus Christ."

Theological Rationalizations

In the final essay of this section, Myron Augsburger comes to grips with the tendency of Christians to misuse Scripture, thus gaining authority to justify a faith of convenience and noninvolvement. Augsburger points out several areas of concern to evangelical ministry to the city. He calls for us to be humble before the Word, carefully weighing our interpretations in the light of scriptural context and the implications of Christ's life, not searching out prooftexts to prop up our bias. If the Christian accepts the Scripture as his authority, he must take special care to implement his understanding of Scripture in a life-style that reaches out to others who need Christ with an incarnated message of love.

Notes to Part Three: Introduction

1 It seems to me that there is enough similarity between various evangelical groups, both theologically and in terms of attitudes to be considered here, to consider them as one subculture. There are variations; and in a more technical sense we would have to speak of evangelical "subcultures."

2 James R. Dolby, "Cultural Evangelicalism: The Background for Personal Despair," *Journal of the American Scientific Affiliation,* September 1972, Vol. 24, No. 3, pp. 91-101.

3 Several books are valuable for historical perspective, including Charles Silberman's *Crisis in Black and White* (New York: Random House, 1964), and Woodward's *The Strange Career of Jim Crow* (New York: Oxford, 1966). Of special interest to the Christian will be Kyle Haselden's *The Racial Problem in Christian Perspective* (New York: Harper, 1959). For contemporary sociological data on religion and prejudice, see Milton Rokeach, "Faith, Hope and Bigotry," *Psychology Today,* April 1970, pp. 33-37, 58; Robert C. L. Brannon, "Gimme That Old-Time Racism," *Psychology Today,* April 1970, pp. 42-44; Gordon W. Allport and J. M. Ross, "Personal Religious Orientation and Prejudice," *Journal of Personality and Social Psychology,* 1967, 432-433; Rodney Stark, Bruce Foster, Charles Y. Glock, and Harold E. Quinley, *Wayward Shepherds: Prejudice & the Protestant Clergy* (New York: Harper, 1971).

4 Rokeach, *op. cit.,* p. 37.

5 *Ibid.,* p. 33.

4: RACISM AND THE EVANGELICAL

by Joseph Daniels

The Psychodynamics of Racism

Racism is imbedded deep within the life history of the individual and the history of mankind. The term "psychodynamics" refers to the systematized knowledge and theory of human behavior and its motivations. Psychodynamics contends that a person's total makeup and his probable reaction at any given moment are the product of past interaction between his specific genetic endowment and the environment, both animate and inanimate, in which he has been living from the time of his conception.

A child is born as free of racial prejudice as of political preference. The significant activities and needs of a human being are not determined by the

JOSEPH DANIELS is a neuro-psychiatrist in private practice in Bloomfield, New Jersey. In addition, he serves as a consultant to the East Orange public school system and to Victory House in Newark, and teaches psychiatry at New Jersey College of Medicine. He is a graduate of Lincoln University in Pennsylvania, and received the M.D. from Howard University Medical School in Washington, D.C. He is a member of the American Psychiatric Association, the Christian Medical Society, and the Christian Association for Psychological Studies. He is the author of several scholarly papers in the field of psychiatry.

amount of melanin in his skin. While the experience of the black person may differ, in a given society, from that of a white person, their physiological and psychological functions are the same.

> There is nothing reported in the literature or in the experience of any clinician . . . that suggests that black people *function* differently psychologically from anyone else. Black man's mental functioning is governed by the same *rules* as that of any other group of men. Psychological principles understood first in the study of white men are true no matter what the man's color.[1]

To understand racism, therefore, we must dig below the surface.

The influence of the child's early thought patterns stains his lifelong perspective on his fellow human being in ways of which he may not be conscious. Many Bible-believing, evangelical white Christians find it impossible to accept a black man into fellowship with them. Why? Let us look first at how the emotional effects, attitudes, and concepts of color in a child lead to racial prejudice.

As the child's sight and hearing develop, he is also developing his internal psychic mechanism. This happens through reflex behavior, associations, assimilations, and various psychic defense mechanisms. All these processes enable him to interpret the various images and concepts that will form part of his life. Significant adults in the child's life convey their thought patterns and their anxieties. There is an intermingling of concrete and abstract stimuli, and emotional and intellectual responses are formed.

The child of three or four becomes familiar with the color spectrum. While his eyes are interpreting and distinguishing colors, his ears are picking up everyday phrases like "pure and white," "black as sin," "yellow coward," "savage redskins." Such emotionally flavored word groupings portray colors as abstract qualities. In the primitive thought-patterns of the child's mind they become emotionally charged by the various methods of reinforcing present in the child's environment.

One of those methods of reinforcement is fear, which may be used to control the child's behavior. The child may be told, "if you're bad, the big black boogieman will get you." In this way the very color black can arouse a phobia — that is, fear attached to an object or situation that objectively is not a source of danger. The object or circumstance feared is something that can be avoided. For example, the child may fear his parents; but he is unable to avoid them. If he is told about the "big black boogieman," he is given an object of fear that he can avoid and repulse. The "black object" can later become the first black boy he meets in kindergarten.

I vividly recall one of the first poems I heard recited to me during my kindergarten days:

> God made the nigger;
> He made him in the night,
> He made him in a hurry,
> He forgot to paint him white.

The white kindergartner who recited this to me had already been programmed for a racist view of a fellow human being. To him color had by the age of five become a measure of a person's worth; and in his deception he attempted to make me an inferior creature of God.

The fantasy of white-good, black-bad, white-superior, black-inferior, has been maintained and preserved by our society with all the resources at its command. Christians and non-Christians alike have used phony "science" to perpetuate the fantasy. This method of brainwashing is seen in the following quotation from a genetics text:

> Before the abolition of slavery persons of mixed Negro and White were produced in very large quantities in the southern states. The best blood of the south flowed in the veins of Virginians and South Carolina slaves, and there is said to have been not a plantation in Louisiana on whose cotton fields there were not to be found the half-brothers, and half-sisters, the children of the grandchildren of the owners kept at work by the overseer's whip.[2]

What conclusion would you draw from this? By a process of mental distortions, the authors draw this one: "Naturally this extensive admixture of white blood has contributed to raise the intellectual level of the colored population." In other words, slaveowners who exploited the minds, bodies, and souls of fellow human beings, disobeying the laws of God and man, are portrayed as if their sins were a blessing.

But how can a white *Christian*, one who knows and believes the Bible, refuse to have fellowship with his black brother? This is accomplished through a mechanism called logic-tight compartments.

> The psychotic patient may live simultaneously in two related worlds—one of fantasy, and one of reality. One patient in his fantasy would own the United States Treasury and its contents; he built and controlled the hospital in which he lived, but had just lost the key to it. Almost daily he would hand his physician an order for a billion dollars, at the same time begging for some tobacco and that he be given parole of the grounds. . . . This coexistence of the consciousness of fantasy and the consciousness of reality is made possible by the mechanism of rationalization and its production of what is known as logic-tight compartments. Related ideas exist in each compartment undisturbed by those in the others, each group pursuing its course segregated from those which are incompatible by a barrier through which no reassuring or argument can force a passage.[3]

Logic-tight compartments produced by the defense mechanisms of rationalization and denial are not only found in the psychotic patient; they are also found in persons considered to be of sound mental health. By such a mechanism, a white, Bible-believing Christian can read I John 4:20 — "If anyone says 'I love God,' and hates his brother, he is a liar . . . " — and refuse to have fellowship with his black brother.

Society has been instrumental in planting the seeds of racism in concepts other than color. Words such as "high" and "low" are used to assign roles to people:

> High-type people are associated in the mind with the high part of the body, with the head, with thinking, with leadership, with what is taken in and believed and with food. Low-type people are associated with the lower body, with the bottom, with the perineum, with what is excluded and expelled. Lower parties are often trained or molded by upper parties and [regarded] as expendable, as reflected in military and other hierarchial organizations.[4]

A person's behavior is likely to be influenced by whether he is perceived, and in turn perceives himself, as "high type" or "low type," as one who should control or who should be controlled. The systematic manner in which the black man has been held in the "low" position perpetuates the fantasy that the black man is less human and less worthy than the white man, who makes laws to enforce this fantasy. This sense of paternalism of the white man to the black man is reflected not only in political areas, but also in the missionary efforts of the church.

Because society is programmed to reproduce white and not black power, black people in positions of control are difficult for whites to accept. In turn, forming a positive self-image is extremely difficult in the black community. Through word-concepts of color and of "high type" and "low type," the white child is, on the other hand, engendered with a sense of self-aggrandizement and control. Any challenge to his authority, whether violent or nonviolent, must be suppressed.

Perhaps the most important dynamic factor determining personality is a person's choice of a device to handle his fears and anxieties. Since the Garden of Eden man has used the defense mechanism of projection—finding a scapegoat. Society can also project repressed impulses onto an outside source when its members learn to project the same impulses to a given object or an idea. By this process, group members identify with people who are perceived as similar ("our kind") and trustworthy; they are associated with the "higher things of life," and thought of as right. Those who are different are to be regarded with suspicion. Their culture may be strange; their appearance is unlike that of group members. They are considered either wrong or inadequate and must be rejected. They must be kept out of the "in"-group. Even if the ideas of "in"-group members are delusions and fantasies, they are not recognized as such because all the members believe them and use their reason and their other faculties to support them.

To act out impulses of anger or hostility on other members of the group would interfere with society's sense of unity, so the "in"-group finds an outside object on which to project those impulses. For more than three hundred years, the black man has provided that scapegoat for the "in"-group of white American society. He was, as could plainly be seen, different, and it was a difference he could not hide. To the black man could be conveniently imputed all those repressed, forbidden impulses which human nature harbors. The forbidden sexual impulses, for example, were placed upon him, and that projection gave rise to further myths and fantasies.

A weak society, like a weak individual, is threatened by immature thinking processes. Instead of building its inner strength, it constructs outer defenses that delude it into thinking it is strong. The process of segregation is such an outer defense, and it has been harmful to the United States. Now the black man is saying to the white man, "I am no longer going to be your scapegoat." The young black child is not swallowing the poison that has tended to make him hate himself but is spitting it back into the faces of those whose forefathers fed it to his forefathers. Now that the psychological projections of the white man are not being accepted by the black man, white society is frantically searching for another scapegoat.

The Christian church has tended to maintain society's fantasies by presenting a false picture of the Christ of the Bible. It has tended to portray Jesus as Anglo-Saxon, blue-eyed, blond, Protestant (and, some add, Republican). As William E. Pannell writes in *My Friend the Enemy*, "this conservative brand of Christianity perpetuates the myth of white supremacy."

Underlying all injustices and the desire to dominate is the self-serving inner force that Freud called the id. The basic nature of man, which in theology we know as our sinful nature, cuts across all racial lines, and the black man as well as the white man is subject to this disease that perhaps more than any other cause leads one human being to dehumanize another. The Black Panthers — who refer to white policemen as pigs — have learned this lesson in dehumanization well. So have those whites who refer to blacks as monkeys or apes. When we deprive human beings of their humanity and soul, we can justify and rationalize anything we do to them. We can murder them, lynch them, or shoot them as easily as we shoot a squirrel or rabbit.

Perhaps the black man's use of the word "soul" is a reminder to himself and his white brother that he is a human, that he is a "living soul."

An Open Letter to White Christians

Although we have known each other for centuries, we have not truly known each other. I, the black man, feel I know more about you because I had to. My will to survive forced me to learn about you. I was forced to learn your ways of doing things, forced to accept your concepts and values, and yet denied the right to share them. From my youth I have heard the phrase "white is right," sometimes said in jest, but many times said with a sarcasm that can be detected only by the black man.

Do you really want to know me? I find I am skeptical—I doubt that you do. Perhaps this in itself reveals some of my own psychopathology. Both you and I are suffering from the effects of many years of the poisoning of racial prejudice.

If I express my feelings and thoughts, can you understand them? Much of your conception of me has an illogical basis, and the more I tell you about myself, the more you may use this against me. Yes, I mistrust you, because of the way you deceive yourself, and the way you have failed to look into your heart.

If I tell you that I have hostility and anger within me, how do you interpret those emotions? Do they make me a savage who will riot and burn your property? Do you ask yourself the cause of the hostility? I ask myself this question, and offer answers that at times satisfy me and at times do not. I too have become somewhat illogical, as I attempt to handle my frustrations.

No doubt some of my hostility is the outgrowth of remembering the degrading names of my youth. Could I really have accepted the reply my mother told me to give — "Sticks and stones may break my bones, but names will never hurt me"? You taught your children to hate me, and so they hurt me. When I struck out to hurt them back, I was punished by the white teacher. Can you understand the frustration of a black child caught in this situation and not knowing how to express what he feels in words? Observe his actions; they are the only way he can express his anger.

Lying somewhat deeper in this substratum of hostility are the names you made me call myself. Sometimes directly, sometimes subtly, you programmed into my early years a feeling of self-dislike, even self-hatred, and deep inferiority, so that I could not accept what God made me to be. I ask you, how does one get to know who or what he is when his society distorts what he is and tries to shape his life to prove this distortion? To the extent that a society hinders a person from developing to his God-given potential, it sins not only against that person but against God. It seems to me that our society is presently paying for the many years of wrongs done to the black man.

At times I am afraid of my anger and hostility because I don't know what form it will or should take, and I don't know if I will be able to hold it in check. Like Hamlet I ask myself "whether 'tis nobler in the mind to suffer the slings and arrows of outrageous fortune, or to take arms against a sea of troubles. . . . "

In my rational moments, I can understand that you are a product of your forefathers' teachings, and are not entirely to blame for your feelings toward me. But if you or I should pass feelings of racial hatred to our children, we stand condemned before God.

I, the black man, am beginning to see my children develop a sense of worth, and respect for their racial heritage, and this above all gives me hope for the future.

Why have you distorted the history books and deprived my forefathers of their place in history? Why don't you understand the need for my children to discover the roots of their racial heritage? If you can be honest with yourself as you answer these questions, then there is hope for my children and your children in the next decade.

Along with my feelings of anger and hostility, there is a strong sense of disappointment. This disappointment is felt most keenly toward those who had taught me of God's love for all mankind. It was your missionaries who came to my native land with a message of love and mercy. When you brought me to your country against my will, you distorted God's words to justify your evil acts. You are still doing this, and I am still forbidden to attend some of your evangelical colleges and churches, and to be your neighbor. Do you think heaven will be segregated too?

Closely connected with this feeling of disappointment is a feeling of sorrow. I am deeply sorry that you have been misled in your thinking about me these many years. We both are suffering from this. You have missed out on many of the benefits of what I could have contributed, and now the financial burden of the black man is disturbing to you. Since you have deprived me of the right to develop my mind and reach my God-given potential, you have had to help me support my family. Yet out of this perhaps will come a better value system. People are to be loved, not used. But now things are being loved, and people are being used. I feel that politicians usually do what is expedient, and that if Christians who know the love of God fail to do what is right and just, there is little hope for our country.

I have been referring to myself as the black man. But I still feel I have not been allowed to reach complete manhood. You have made me doubt my ability to compete with you intellectually, and you keep stunting this area of my life with inferior school systems. You cannot doubt my ability to compete with you physically, however — and you have used this to put a feather in your cap and money in your pockets.

It is as if my first hundred years in your country were my infancy. I was dependent upon you and I obeyed you; but I did not receive nourishment from you that would enrich me or help me to grow. I was like a foster child, not knowing my parentage and kept from knowing it. You as my foster parents used and abused me; you gave me no love, but your discipline was severe. I still remember those years. If your foster child cries out "I hate you," perhaps you can understand that he is expressing a feeling that he has been deeply wronged.

The second hundred years were my childhood. I grew into childhood despite the methods used to keep me an infant. I started to become aware of some of these methods. I saw more of the unfairness of your treatment of me. At times I would fight back, but for the most part I continued to play the role you assigned to me. I soon learned that when I would cry out for justice, the rules became stricter, the punishment more severe. During those second hundred years I was a "boy," and you constantly reminded me of that status.

Over the last hundred years, I progressed into the adolescent stage, and now I feel I am ready to emerge into adulthood. Don't call me "boy" any longer, because I will no longer accept that label. Haven't you seen the evidence of my growth? I no longer accept what you say as gospel truth, and I am not afraid to tell you. I am finding and recognizing my own identity and sense of worth. I desire to make it on my own, and I become disturbed when you tell me I'm rushing things—this process has been going on for *over three centuries* now. If God in his mercy allows the human race to exist, I shall achieve my full manhood in a few more years.

I am telling you these things because I do want you to know me. You have tried to observe me from afar while maintaining your myths and fantasies about me. I quote the following from a letter written by a young white person after a Christian conference where this problem was discussed:

> Almost every white person I know who has been raised with prejudice and has come out of it, has done so because of a warm relationship with some Negro. This happened to me when I was seventeen, and I worked for a wonderful Negro man, who was one of the first persons I ever really loved and admired. Those who have not had this kind of experience frequently complain that they are paralyzed in relating to those with the dark skin. If they try too hard, they create resentment by gushing and realize they aren't being very human. If they don't try, their old prejudices come out. They are unable to be friendly in a take-it-or-leave-it way.

The patterns of a lifetime are difficult to erase. Both you and I have blind spots. We are both indwelt with an innate depravity that, without the constraining power and love of Christ, can cause us to destroy ourselves as well as each other. We are both prone to anger, resentment, and hostility. Yet we both respond to love and acceptance and respect, and we both have the basic drives to live, to love, and to enjoy companionship. Our experiences are different, and I may consciously or unconsciously misinterpret your intentions initially, as you may misinterpret mine. Unfortunately, those of us in the older generation must learn again to give each other a chance, something we might have been willing to do when we were children if we had been allowed to.

I, the black man, suggest that you really get to know yourself. Evaluate your life experiences and see how they may have given you your views of the black man. The only real frontier we have on earth is the frontier of human relationships. Let us hope and trust that ultimately, as we have learned to release energy from the nucleus of the atom, we shall learn to release a greater energy from the nucleus of the soul. If that happens, it will enable us to love and to live together and enjoy the blessings of God that he intended us to share.

Your fellow human being and future friend,

The Black Man

Notes to Chapter 4

1 Wm. H. Grier and Price M. Cobb, *Black Rage* (1968), p. 129.

2 Baur, Fisher, Lenz, *Human Heredity* (3rd ed., 1931), p. 628.

3 Arthur P. Noyes, *Modern Clinical Psychology* (4th ed.), p. 62.

4 Charles Pinderhughes, in *Journal of the American Psychiatric Association,* May 1969, p. 1552.

5: WESTERN SOCIAL AND ECONOMIC INFLUENCES

by Arthur G. Gish

Evangelicals have talked much about the infallibility and inspiration of the Bible. When faced with the social and economic forces and values of Western society, however, they accord the Bible significantly less authority. The church has often accepted from the culture values that directly contradict the biblical message. In many instances the evangelical church has become so identified with culture that its gospel is little more than an expression of the culture. The world has more influence on the church than the church on the world.

This is disastrous both for the spiritual health of the church and for the world, which has not been presented with the radical saving message of the gospel. The failure of the church to struggle with the problems of urban society from a scriptural basis has prevented her from speaking with authority on the major issues. It has also precluded any corporate testimony. At least some of the suffering and chaos of the 1960s was caused by the church's failure to

ARTHUR GISH is a free lance writer living in Philadelphia. A member of the Church of the Brethren, he is a graduate of Bethany Theological Seminary. Much of his time is now spent speaking in churches and schools. He is the author of two books, **The New Left and Christian Radicalism** *(Eerdmans) and* **Beyond the Rat Race** *(Herald Press), an account of simplicity as a life-style.*

make its voice heard. What if the church had spoken more clearly on the issues of racism or war? Was there no word from the Lord that applied to such modern moral problems?

The church's passive internalizing of surrounding secular culture has resulted in a situation in which each church member follows the culture on most issues, rather than submitting his thinking to the light of Scripture. Everyone does what seems right in his own eyes. This makes unity in the church practically impossible, and, because there is no unity in the church, the church finds itself unable to reach out to most of the needs around it.

Lack of unity in the church means a further breakdown of the community already attacked by urbanization and industrialization. The church has not only accepted this, but has developed an individualistic theology to match the individualism of Western culture. Another contributor to this loss of community has been the increasing control of governmental, educational, and economic institutions over our lives. The desire for a small space of privacy is understandable, but this leaves little room for the church. An hour or two on Sunday morning as a spectator is about all most are willing to give. They do not want the church also breathing down their necks.

Participation in the life of the church has acquired a pattern of passive responses. The worshipers in most evangelical churches form a passive audience, reflecting the passivity of secular culture as encouraged by the mass media and large spectator businesses. The church for its part often encourages this approach to worship rather than genuine participation.

The movement of civilization from community to impersonal society has deeply affected the church. Individualism, competition, rationalism, and egoism are also part of the life of the church. Intimacy, love, and mutual support do not often characterize congregational life. More often than not, the church is a secondary group rather than a primary community. We are a group of strangers rather than a people who deeply share our lives with each other.

A fragmented church with an individualistic theology cannot preach the gospel in a way that is adequate to address the loss of identity, integrity, and purpose prevalent in Western society. The personal salvation intended only for an inner soul does not seem to have reached even our hearts, much less our lives. People have sought in drugs, the occult, materialism, and status what they should have been able to find in the church. That is no fault of the gospel: it is the fault of those who have reduced the gospel to something less than good news, to something that does not speak to the whole person in all situations of life.

Inroads of Secularism

While the evangelical church has been vocal in its opposition to secularism, its inroads have been deep. Throughout the church there is a deep crisis of faith in God. While God is given much lip service, the decisions of most Christians and of the church are influenced far more by social and economic considerations than by a deep sense of God's sovereignty. Money, technology, political considerations, and social class have more influence than the teachings of Jesus. These things are more real for us than is God. When we feel sick we call a doctor; when the power goes off we call the electric company. God is something to teach the children about on Sunday morning. He may even love me, but his sovereignty has little to do with the urban crisis.

Rather than being a people with a completely different orientation from the world's, we are basically the same as the world with a few peculiar theological affirmations added on. We are Americans and, by the way, also Christians. The flags in the front of our places of worship reflect our true allegiance. The American flag is in the place of honor and the Christian flag to the left of the speaker in a subordinate position. A watered-down state religion is quite attractive to many evangelicals. Many actually see America as the hope of the world and the bearer of salvation. Secularism has gotten through to us too.

One attempt to combat secularism has been to sharply distinguish between the sacred and secular. Unfortunately, the result has been a further stimulus to secularization. By denying any relation of the Christian faith to the secular, Christians have been encouraged to accept secular values rather than bring the secular under the judgment of the gospel. The claim that the church should not be concerned about "secular" issues has been in effect a call to accept conservative secular values.

The church has yielded to the temptation of status and respectability. Wanting to be an accepted part of society, it has made the compromises needed to exchange the role of prophet for becoming the chaplain (if not one of the pillars) of society. Because of its allegiance to the status quo, the church has not been able to utter the painful words of judgment that are needed. Often evangelicals are reduced to preaching sermons in the palace that say exactly what the king wants to hear. Even as our cities decay, we continue to support the status quo. We do not get very specific in our calls for repentance, if we mention the need for repentance at all.

True, evangelicals still maintain "sound doctrine," but could the words of Jesus apply to us?

> Woe to you, scribes and Pharisees, hypocrites! for you tithe mint and dill and cummin, and have neglected the weightier matters of the law, justice and mercy and faith; these you ought to have done, without neglecting the others. You blind guides, straining out a gnat and swallowing a camel! (Matt. 23:23-24).

Racial and Economic Oppression
We seem to have forgotten (tried to forget?) that Christ has broken down the dividing walls of hostility and brought reconciliation through the cross to those

who once were enemies (Eph. 2:14, 16). We have not only accepted racial, class, and social distinctions; we have often defended them in spite of clear New Testament teaching against making distinctions or showing partiality (e.g. James 2:1-7). We can attempt to build up our egos by putting others down, but God is hardly impressed by our attempts to justify ourselves (Rom. 3:28). Before God all of us are beggars. Why is it that evangelicals have been so slow in accepting cries for racial and social justice?

Somehow we have not heard the biblical emphasis on liberation. Other times we spiritualize it away. Moses' call to "let my people go" is never associated with Christ's purpose of "setting at liberty all who are oppressed" (Luke 4:18). Rather we have allied ourselves with those who are oppressing others and see God's judgment on the oppressed and not on the oppressors. Calls for freedom and social justice have too often been seen as threats to the Christian faith rather than as possibilities for proclaiming God's concern for the oppressed.

The church has accepted a work ethic that sees affluence and prosperity as signs of divine favor and misfortune or poverty as signs of divine disfavor. It was not difficult to conclude from this that the rich are good and the poor are evil. Since it is necessary for the evil people to be restrained, it seems natural to support the rich in their restraining the poor. The biblical message of God's concern for the poor never quite gets through. Even the common sinfulness of all humanity seems not to apply. But we do have a good excuse not to care for the poor (never mind the teaching that runs throughout the whole Bible that a major cause of poverty is exploitation by the rich; Amos 8:4-6; James 2:6).

People who supposedly believe in salvation by grace alone believe all poverty is caused by laziness and that people can lift themselves up by their own bootstraps if they try hard enough. This makes little economic or theological sense. In spite of the boasting of many people, we did not make it on our own strength and efforts, but only by the grace of God and help of countless people along the way. How can we expect others to make it on their own?

Even though the position of both Old and New Testaments on economics is unmistakably clear, the church has taught that our economic lives are a private matter. Usually the church accepts—often it blesses—the evils of capitalism. It fails to see how certain values and presuppositions of capitalism contradict the Christian faith. For example, God did not will that we each seek first our own self-interest and profit. He directed us to renounce our selfish and sinful will, seek first the kingdom of God, and serve the needs of our neighbor.

The Bible could not be clearer in its judgment on those who trample on the poor (Amos 2:7). We often praise them as blessed of God and even as great philanthropists. Then we elect them to city council, where they can further their interests and keep the poor "in their place." The command to care for the widows and fatherless and not to lay up treasures on earth cannot be dismissed. Jesus' story of the rich man and Lazarus (Luke 16:19-31) speaks directly to us. Indeed, Jesus mentions the subject of money and economics more often than any other subject in the four Gospels. How can we not take these teachings seriously?

If we bring our economic lives under the lordship of Christ, can we remain well integrated in our economic system? Where our treasure is, there will our heart be also. The effect of Mammon upon the church has been disastrous.

The church has repeatedly allowed the state to set the common goals of church and state, rather than make a clear choice between the lordship of Christ and Caesar as did the early Christians. While Romans 13 and I Peter 2 call the Christian not to overthrow the state with violence and recommend adherence to the law, nothing in the New Testament calls for unquestioned obedience to the state. There is no hint of pledging allegiance to Caesar.

We have unconsciously accepted the Enlightenment view of progress. Instead of seeing the state as under the judgment of God, we believe that we can have continual progress by working through it. There is no biblical basis for this optimism.

Too often the church has been ready to bless whatever the state does. Too often the church has bowed down before the idols of nationalism and the militarism that goes with it, even though they directly contradict New Testament teachings of suffering love, the cross, and the new life in Christ.

Most nonpacifist churches officially hold to some doctrine of the just war, but they never get around to ever declaring any war unjust. Consequently, the just war theory becomes a cheap support for any war or urban police action that arises. The church is comfortable accepting the expenditure of vast sums for war and larger police forces, even though this drains away resources that might have been used for the needs of people right next door to the church. We can accept cutting programs to aid the poor while increasing military spending.

We can take this one step further. The political philosophy most evangelicals hold directly affects their understanding of how to solve the problems of the city. More police power and show of force have been seen as the best way of solving social problems, rather than acts of Christian service and witness in the development of programs to meet people's needs. We would rather add a thousand more police to the public payroll than a thousand more teachers. We can more eagerly support programs of coercion or violence than programs of compassion. Jesus Christ seems to have little relevance to the city in the minds of many.

The church has also bought into the philosophy that property is more important than persons. We accept the idea of shooting a looter on sight. Many congregations reject programs of outreach and witness because they are more concerned about preserving church property than speaking to people's souls.

Our decisions and values seem to be more influenced by the fears of our society than by our confidence in God.

A Challenge to Complete Christianity

This recital of some of the failures of the church is not meant to negate the importance of the evangelical church, but to show some of the areas where we need to be more faithful. I believe that God's primary way of accomplishing his purposes in history *is* through his people. It *is* the church — not the state or bureaucratic institutions — that is the primary locus of God's action in the world. That means that the church has a crucial role in the city and it is imperative that we begin to follow our Lord rather than the social and economic pressures around us.

It is doubtful, however, that the church will make any significant witness to the city before we begin to submit all our social, political, and economic ideas to the test of biblical revelation and the final norm of Jesus Christ. Communities of faith must test the spirits and discern what is of God and what is not. When we begin again to check our values by God's standards, we can recover a corporate witness to society and be a sign to the world of hope and the coming of God's kingdom. When the church and the gospel begin to have more influence on our lives and decisions than does society, we will have a witness that cannot be ignored or dominated by any of the social or economic forces around us. We will be the light of the world and a city on the hill that cannot be hidden (Matt. 5:14). We will be demonstrating for the world what God's will is for all humanity as revealed in Jesus Christ.

6: THEOLOGICAL TWISTS

by Myron S. Augsburger

Theology is human reasoning about the meaning of faith. Man does not only think; he reflects on his thinking and reasons about its meaning and consistency. Man is a philosopher; and theology is a philosophy about faith.

But man's greatest uniqueness, his creation in the image of God, has been perverted by his self-centeredness. This affects his reasoning. The ability to reason, essential to our humanness, is also our greatest danger. We use the process of reasoning to rationalize in self-defense. We set up structures of thought that begin from premises we accept, which largely determine the outcome of our reasoning.

MYRON S. AUGSBURGER is president of Eastern Mennonite College and Seminary, Harrisonburg, Virginia, from which he also holds the A.B. and Th.B. degrees. He took a doctorate in theology from Union Theological Seminary in Richmond, Virginia. The author of seven books, he has conducted evangelistic crusades in Wilmington, Delaware; Salt Lake City; London, Ontario; Schenectady, New York, as well as ministries in Europe, the Middle East, India, Japan, and the Caribbean. He serves on numerous boards and committees in the Mennonite Church, and is active in the National Association of Evangelicals.

Kerygma

It is essential that we recognize the authority of the inspired Scripture as the basis for Christian reflection, otherwise we cannot adequately understand Jesus Christ, the "cornerstone" of our faith. However, it is expressly at this point that a basic problem appears in contemporary theology — whose Christ? A philosophical Christ, meaning basically an authentic personality, a self-awareness that includes ethical responsibility and love? Or the Jesus Christ of Nazareth, of the cross and of the empty tomb, who was and is the expression of true humanness, of authentic personhood, of love and ethical responsibility, and who as Lord is the person whose grace and presence transforms us? As Carl F. H. Henry has said, "The risen Christ demonstrates in His person the character of humanity God approves in the eternal order; His is the moral image to which all the people of God will ultimately be conformed."[1]

Here is the basic question of why we minister in the city. What do we have to offer? When Jonah was sent to Nineveh, a city that symbolized what Israel rejected, he was given God's plan: go and announce the word of the Lord. When the early church went from Jerusalem to the cities of the then-known world, it was to announce the *kerygma*, the good news of the gospel. The question is not, "Did they do more?" Where the gospel is authentically presented, deeds of love and compassion are present. The Christian's work in the city will involve the cup of cold water, *in the name of Christ*. It will involve the deeds of the Good Samaritan, and thereby express love with the *kerygma*.

It is no secret that much of liberal theology has lost this dimension and turned into a secular expression of Christian values without the lordship of the risen Christ. After the attempt to purge the Bible of "myths" unacceptable to modern, scientific man, as Oscar Cullmann has pointed out, it was a short step to the point where there was no saving act of God from beyond us.[2] What followed "demythologizing" was, of course, "dekerygmatizing," for in place of the "good news" of reconciliation with God has come a social reconciliation with our fellows in a community of self-authenticating persons. This theological mood in turn expressed itself in the depersonalization of God. Since, it was argued, we cannot adequately "think God," we must look on him as that ground of being which we realize in our own experience of self-authentication. Prayer is not talking with someone, but the exercise of self-actualization, which is enhanced by the symbols of one's particular religious tradition. For the Christian that is the language of prayer taught by Jesus; for others their own religious symbols accomplish the same.

Evangelical Christians ought not to be too glib in responding to this (admittedly brief and generalized) analysis. Before patting ourselves on the back because we have the *kerygma*, the good news, to offer, we should ask: *Is the kerygma obscured by our theological twists, our reasoning from premises that we assume to be biblical, but which in fact need to be laid open to the judgment of Christ and his word?* Do evangelicals, in their sensitivity to liberalism in theology, reject some valid insights from humanism? Do we, in our fear of the "social gospel," in fact identify with the materialism of our society? Does our self-interest lead to a blackout in the city set on a hill?

Myths

Evangelicals might well begin their own program of demythologizing, directed against some of the religious ideas that are commonly accepted though utterly without biblical foundation. One such myth is that *personal faith means individualism.* This view has promoted private piety and minimized the importance of the covenant community of new men and women in Christ. Personal faith is essential, but it is never private faith. We are reconciled to God with our brother; we are a part of a redeemed community. The congregation of believers is to function together in its community as a people of God. The idea of the invisible church must not keep us from seeing that the New Testament instructions are always to the church visible, the congregation as a loving, discipling, serving, witnessing brotherhood. This is an essential aspect of the character of the church as a healing community in our fractured society.

A second myth is that of *separation between the evangelistic and the social aspects of the gospel.* We have often created a false dichotomy, which disregards the teaching of Jesus that the first and second commandment together constitute the meaning of love. The evangelical is concerned about regeneration, the work of the Spirit in transforming lives, the experience of wholeness for each person. This is not without social implications. Man is a social being created in and for community with God and man. As a re-created person his social participation and concern attune themselves to God's will for society.

Another myth is that *conservative theology entails conservative political and social views.* This mistaken notion puts many evangelicals in a position of compromise, supporting in society and politics things that are incompatible with the kingdom of Christ. The other side of this error is that many evangelical college and university students become, as they are exposed to higher education, more liberal in their political and social concerns. Following this myth they assume incorrectly that they must become more liberal theologically. A conservative theology — one which holds that Christ is Lord, and that his will is expressed in his word and not in the processes of society — frees one to be quite open on social and political matters, always seeking God's best even for unbelieving man in society. Not to see this distinction is to fall prey to a cultural or civil religion.

A fourth myth is that *experiential faith is automatically emotionalism.* This is not to ignore the danger of emotionalism; but the brotherhood of believers should be an authenticating, exhorting community, which will inevitably lead to joy and freedom, not necessarily excess. Evangelicals have too often been uptight about the experience of others, finding it a ready source of division in the church. Especially in the city an authentic congregation must cope with a variety of cultures, which will require it to be flexible about differing religious experiences. The Swedish Lutheran theologian Krister Stendahl has warned of the artificial encouragements "interfering with the reality of the Spirit," but adds that "the flashlight voltage of the churches just isn't strong enough to beat sin and drugs; . . . a high voltage experience belongs to us all."[3]

Another myth is that *holding to the fundamentals of the faith means being a "Fundamentalist,"* with all the cultural trappings that go along with that. Much of the difference between evangelical groups is not because of more or less authentic commitments to the fundamentals of faith, but because of other theological perspectives. For example, there are many differences between evangelicals in the Anabaptist tradition and other churches which also trace their origins back to the Reformation in the sixteenth century. Merely to label one another as evangelical or not evangelical on the basis of these differences is clearly an unfair and unproductive approach.

One further evangelical myth is that *material benefits and "spirituality" go together.* This hinders us in several ways. First is the problem of materialism itself and what it does to dwarf one's spirit. When Jesus remarked that it is easier for a camel to go through the eye of a needle than for a rich man to enter the kingdom of heaven, he put his finger on the heart of the matter: the rich man in the present age has difficulty identifying himself with the true nature of the kingdom. Second, materialistic evangelicals have been guilty of ecological sins, using the resources of the world for their own advantage regardless of the cost to others, including future generations. Christians who are materially successful tend to look down at the poor and interpret their plight apart from the circumstances Christians help to create, as though the poor were lazy or incapable of management. Our compassion is thus often really condescension. In contrast, Acts 2 teaches us that what is mine belongs to the church if my brother has need.

Poverty is a basic problem in our society, especially in the city. Mark Hatfield, calling attention to the inequities in the distribution of wealth in American society, points to Ezekiel's words, "This was the iniquity of your sister Sodom: she and her daughters had pride of wealth and food in plenty, comfort, and ease, but did not aid the poor and needy" (Ezek. 16:49).[4] We need to repent and seek a social answer compatible with the gospel; we need to hear the cry of the poor and the downtrodden. Society itself needs to be led to repentance for its own health and for its future.

Twists

It is a religious tragedy when men use a doctrinal or theological stance to dodge moral and spiritual responsibilities. Our failure to live as disciples of

Christ is exposed in the words attributed to G. K. Chesterton: "The Christian ideal has not been tried and found wanting; it has been found difficult and not tried."

The good news of the gospel is that God loves the world and sent Christ to die for it. Believers are seed sown into the field, the world. The city is today the heart of the population of the world. The early church grew in the cities, the major centers of population, culture, and trade. The disciples saw the city as the key to the expansion of the Christian church, for here faith could be shared and proved in the arena of life. The world expects to see in those who believe the qualities of a redeemed life — the kind of understanding Jesus showed the woman at the well, the acceptance that he gave to the woman of the street who wept over his feet in Simon's house, the compassion of the Good Samaritan. Salvation means that God makes us a new people moving among others to achieve his purpose. The converted city-dweller does not simply "whistle in the ghetto" happy in his new assurance of salvation. Rather he prays that the God who makes everything work together for good for those that love him will by the Holy Spirit help people in sin, trapped in economic systems that destroy them, and estranged from those about them.

Believing and doing are inseparable, for believing is identifying with Jesus' way of life. Evangelism is precisely this: presenting Jesus Christ in life and word so that faith in him becomes a clear option. But life in Christ does not automatically solve one's problems or transform social situations. It does give the believer new resources to bring to the problem, among which is his new community of Christian brothers. Certainly we help our brothers in the ghetto face its pressures and the problem of being "trapped" by them, but we also help him change them.

Before rushing to accuse secular urban man of living an artificially contrived life, we must learn to recognize the artificiality of our own attitude toward Christian doctrine. No commitment to eighteenth- or nineteenth-century interpretations of Scripture can absolve us from twentieth-century responsibility. We must learn to see how our patterns of thought determine the present structure of our doctrine, how our cultural conditioning, bias and prejudice are read into the Scripture, hiding or even perverting its message to us. Let us look at a number of theological twists that evangelicals often apply to the Bible, and thereby alter its message.

"Go Into All the World"

The Great Commission (Matt. 28:19-20) is usually read with the stress on "Go ye therefore into all the world." As a result many Christians live with the compulsion to go to other countries to spread their faith and fail to share it with equally needy persons about them. Missionaries are sent to Africa, but persons about us are avoided. Others live with a legalistic constraint to be "going" to persons to *talk about* the gospel and miss the freedom and joy of a witness that comes by *living* the gospel.

Actually the Great Commission could be better translated from the Greek, "While going about in your personal world make disciples of all men." The thrust is on the authority of the risen Christ to create a new people of God by commissioning each believer to disciple others, and to do this in the authentic life experiences that come through our occupation. The gospel is best communicated to people who know us well enough to see its effects in our lives, people in our cultural group.[5]

Disciples share a "covenant community" as the fellowship in which brotherhood is expressed and maturity of faith is promoted. Making disciples is far more than an evangelistic solicitation of a "commitment to Christ." The total life of the believing community is one of giving and receiving rebuke, encouraging each other in grace, and exercising the ministry of forgiveness and reconciliation according to the ideas Jesus sets forth in Matthew 18. In an urban context where fragmentation is a way of life, it is even more crucial for discipling to be continuous interaction, deciding together about the "Jesus way" in particular situations. Discipleship as a code of ready-made answers will not last long in the city.

"There Will Always Be Poverty"

"Blessed are the poor," Christ said (Luke 6:20); but his commands to minister to the poor (Matt. 25:34-40) are often negated by Christians who quote his statement, "the poor you have always with you" (Mark 14:7). Jesus does not say that just because the poor are blessed we should all be poor, nor does he mean that since there will always be poverty we should not minister to poor people. Actually, the statement quoted from Mark is made in a setting of correcting the hypocrisy of speaking to a good concern so as to bypass another good act. Strange that some evangelicals would, in effect, commit the same error as Judas by raising this quotation as a way of escaping the implications of other of Christ's teachings to minister to the poor.

Such bad theology often comes from fear of the "Social Gospel," which reached its peak in the early part of this century. The problem, as is often said, was that there was too much "social" and not enough "gospel." But evangelical Christians need to recognize that the gospel has social implications. Let us beware of words of the gospel without its works.

In today's urban situation Christians must understand the complexity of the city and learn about the differences between inner-city, middle-city, and outer-city dwellers. The inner-city dweller has pressures unique to his situation. Today it is often the black community that is in the inner city, which adds the issue of race to that of poverty.[6] This calls for a spirit of Christian brotherhood if we are to take Christ's call to mission seriously.

When Jesus told the story of the Good Samaritan, he was answering the lawyer's question "Who is my neighbor?" The lawyer wanted to pass judgment on whether others counted as neighbors. Jesus flipped the lawyer's question around. The question was not "Who is my neighbor?" but "Are you willing to be a neighbor?" That is the issue – being neighborly.

The Curse of Canaan

Numerous Scriptures are wrenched out of their context to generalize a position regarding race. Racial differences are not a problem but a privilege for the true Christian, since they witness the uniqueness and essence of the image of God in man, and to that true humanness which is not defined by the pigment of the skin. The early church at Antioch was, as reported in Acts 13, a biracial church. In the Old Testament Moses and David took wives across racial lines.

But many evangelicals perpetuate the misreading of Scripture, that God's curse on Noah's son resulted in a black race with a resultant curse of servanthood. Careful study of the Scripture leaves that interpretation unsupported. The account in Genesis 9 does not say the curse is associated in any way with race. Nor may one interpret that text in isolation from the total unfolding revelation of Scripture. One must read Genesis 9 alongside of Paul's words in Acts 17:26, that God has "made from one every nation of men." In view of the many references in the New Testament calling us to love for all men and equality in God's grace, where there is "neither Greek nor Jew, barbarian, Scythian, bond or free," it is doubly strange that some Christians give up their humanity for racism.

What a tragedy that Gandhi, as a young man in South Africa, went to church but was turned down because of the color of his skin. It has been said that Gandhi rejected not Christ but the perverted picture of Christ that he was given. He never became a Christian as a result, because he thereafter regarded Christianity as Western, and he was first of all an Indian.

Perpetual Conflict

Jesus said, "You will hear of wars and rumors of wars" (Matt. 24:6). Many evangelicals use this verse as an excuse to neglect concern for peace. But in the same passage (vs. 12) Jesus talks about the multiplication of wickedness and the coldness of people's love. Yet few would argue on that ground that we should not preach against personal sins and call people to revival. Similarly, while war is a fact of human sinfulness we should not give up working for peace.

The Christian has a higher calling than earthly clashes over economic and political matters. Jesus' statement that "there will be wars" is a part of his judgment of the world, not a word that excuses the Christian from his higher calling as an "ambassador for Christ."[7] We are members of the global kingdom of Christ, a bond of fellowship with blood-bought brothers in other lands. The citizens of a country that is an enemy of my own are not my personal enemies. They also stand under God as persons to whom I am sent as an ambassador of

Christ. I am called to win this "enemy" to be my brother in Christ. No one who is truly evangelical can cut off a loving attempt to win all for whom Christ died because of a mere national hostility. We wrestle against the prince of darkness, who uses war to thwart the extension of love. But when we were his enemies Christ died for us.

The city is often a scene of conflict and tension between peoples whose geographical closeness does not indicate any other kind of community. Psychologists have shown that tame rats can be turned into killers just by increasing the number in a cage. The same tension happens among peoples where population explosion and living conditions give them the feeling of being trapped. Here the ministry of reconciliation, of creating a caring-community of brothers is most relevant.

The Sermon on the Mount

The Sermon on the Mount is rejected by some evangelicals as inapplicable for us today, to be relegated to a future, post-church age. This is a theological twist, not a clear word from the Lord. Its inconsistency is exposed by the appearance of the essence of the sermon in Luke, who was not writing primarily for Jews in interpreting the Kingdom of God, and of its basic teachings in Paul's epistles.

If one reads the Sermon on the Mount without theological bias it is clear that Jesus has given us what someone has called the Christian's working philosophy of life. While dealing with motive, and thereby the "deeper life" of the Christian, the Sermon on the Mount deals expressly with the social dimensions of the gospel.[8]

This sermon has a unique relevance and penetrating correction for the church at work in urban society. Jesus deals with the importance and value of *all* persons. He answers the problems of materialism and affluence by elevating the human and spiritual level of life. He exposes pretense and phoniness and calls for sincerity. He moves us beyond deed to motive, beyond ritual to genuine love. He calls us to priorities for action that liberate us from exclusive pietism for compassionate piety. He frees us from the tyranny of the status quo morality and from a merely socially acceptable ethic by calling us to live by his lordship.

Separating from Sinners

A difficult theological issue to resolve is the principle of separation from those who follow heresy. Paul clearly pronounces a curse on any who preach a gospel other than salvation in Christ (Gal. 1). John writes that we are not to receive as guests those who do not abide in the doctrine of Christ, and if we bid such people Godspeed we partake in their evil deeds (II John 9-11). The intent of these passages is clearly the integrity of our witness to the gospel of Christ. Evangelicals often go beyond these passages to make decisions of fellowship on the basis, not of the gospel of Christ, but of their own secondary systems of theology.

We must be careful that our emphasis on separation from sin does not separate us from people. We are "in the world but not of the world." As Ellul says, "as long as the city continues, God's people are protected, protected against Babylon's sin. They can live there without necessarily being seduced."[9]

People of different theological persuasion can work together to share the witness of Christ. In an urban setting this is very important. The appropriate model is not that of an ecumenical bureaucracy, in which full identification washes out the unique contribution of each group, but the model of cooperation, where each group shares its strengths, and thus increases the impact of all, avoids duplication and competition, and convinces the unsaved world that we actually care more about ministering to them than promoting our own cause.

When one of the disciples criticized a non-disciple for casting out demons in Jesus' name, Jesus replied, "Do not forbid him; for he that is not against you is for you" (Luke 9:49-50). Or recall Paul's words: "Some indeed preach Christ from envy and rivalry, but others from good will. . . . whether in pretense or in truth, Christ is proclaimed and in that I rejoice" (Phil. 1:15, 18). We need the discernment of the Spirit to know where we can relate to others for the total "Christianizing" of the thought of a community or city without compromising the gospel. Arbitrary and judgmental categorizations are not adequate. There is no biblical basis for the refusal of a Calvinist and Arminian to cooperate, or for "nonpeace church" evangelicals to back away from "peace church" evangelicals. We may not lightly turn our backs on a common meeting ground of evangelical faith and commitment to the risen Lord.

Romans 13

Another major problem is what to do with the teaching of Romans 13 that existing authority is ordained of God. Many evangelicals take this verse and let the powers that be practically determine their platform of behavior. They overlook the fact that if the powers are ordained of God then God is still above the powers. There are occasions for saying with the apostles that we ought to obey God rather than men (Acts 4:19). As evangelicals committed to the lordship of Christ we stand first of all as citizens of the kingdom of heaven. We cannot afford to compromise the lordship of Christ by provincializing Christianity, or domesticating or Americanizing the message of our Savior, thereby subverting the communication of the gospel.

Deification of political power has historically limited the church in its ministry of reconciliation. Evangelicals today need to clarify this issue in relation to the moral and social issues confronting us now and to prepare our youth to stand for Christ in future days of compromise.

The "God and country" emphasis needs to be converted to a biblical philosophy of being "strangers and pilgrims here" in an awareness of Jesus' words that his kingship is not of this world (John 18:36).

Summary

My analysis of these several issues has come from my own theological perspective. But each of us who believes the Bible to be fully inspired must be humble before this Word, the only sure guide for faith and life. Over and beyond the question of how we think is the major issue of how we live. Believing is doing, it is behaving our beliefs in love and wisdom.

The Holy Spirit is here to guide us into all truth. If we are closed to him, he will carry on Christ's work through others and we will be the losers. With his discernment we can serve our age in the spirit of Christ. We are co-laborers, building the kingdom of Christ. When the kingdoms of this world are fallen we will still say "Hallelujah!" for our security is in him and his eternal kingdom.

Notes to Chapter 6

1 *World Vision,* Jan. 1974, p. 17.

2 Cf. Oscar Cullmann, *Salvation in History* (London: SCM, 1967).

3 Quoted in *Gospel Herald,* Feb. 26, 1974, p. 191.

4 Quoted by Hatfield, "Repentance, Politics, and Power," *The Post-American,* Jan. 1974, p. 7.

5 See Donald A. McGavran, "The Dimensions of World Evangelism," paper prepared for the International Congress on Evangelism, July 1974, section III.

6 Vern Miller, *The City* (Scottdale, Pa.: Herald, 1970), pp. 13-18.

7 Jacques Ellul, *The Meaning of the City,* pp. 80-81.

8 See Myron Augsburger, *The Expanded Life* (Nashville: Abingdon, 1972).

9 Ellul, *op. cit.,* p. 79.

PART FOUR:
LOOKING IN NEW DIRECTIONS —
URBAN AWARENESS AND EDUCATION

INTRODUCTION

Much of the lack of urban involvement among evangelicals stems from lack of information and misinformation. John Alexander begins this section by pointing out some of the major prerequisites for developing communications that will change minds and engage evangelicals in serious urban ministry. The following chapters present models of education for evangelical minority leadership, Christian undergraduate education, and seminary education for pastors and Christian "professionals."

It seems unlikely that those already heavily enculturated and set in their non-urban life concerns will become directly involved, although they can become importantly involved in the supportive ministries of funding, prayer, and encouragement. In order to develop the quality leadership and human resources needed to meet the massive challenges of urban ministry, those willing to become directly involved must be shown the need. For this Christian education has a major responsibility.

Most of those attending Christian colleges and seminaries today come out of a relatively monolithic culture. They must become aware that the world is larger than their background might suggest and that urban centers provide fantastic challenges to their limited cultural perspective. Minority persons must also have the opportunity for formal education and for cross-cultural, interpersonal exchange with the dominant community if the cooperation and understanding essential to urban missions are to be gained.

The development of urban awareness will come through the knowledgeable use of communication, prophetic voices, and the integral inclusion of urban programs in Christian education. The development of evangelical urban leadership, minority and majority, must involve direct exposure to the conditions and people of the city, as well as the opportunity for interracial, inter-ethnic, and intercultural exchange.

Urban Awareness

Although somewhat pessimistic about changing attitudes, especially through the use of mass communication, John Alexander points out how knowledge of the components of the communication process can channel the broader concerns of the evangelical community into specific concern for the city. It is necessary to know about the interaction of audience, message, and media and to have a well-defined plan if communication about the city is to begin affecting evangelical consciousness—and conscience.

Except for an occasional article, few evangelical periodicals address the needs of those in the city or of others in society who suffer oppression. Few sermons by evangelical preachers devote themselves to such issues. Instead of seeing these needs as a matter of basic Christian moral concern, preachers often regard them as "political" matters. So they go back to preaching frequently tepid, socially irrelevant, and almost totally inner-directed sermons.

Perhaps the development of urban awareness will require some form of evangelical coalition to form publishing and speaking outlets. But many evangelicals will be reached only if the word comes more regularly from editors of established Christian periodicals who begin to see these concerns as part of Christian responsibility.

Urban Education

Meanwhile, definite steps can be taken in Christian educational institutions to bring the city and its needs into the consciousness of Christian young people, who will then become leaders and disciples to communicate Christ to today's world. For some colleges a serious address to the provision of healthy, systematic minority education may mean risking loss of constituency.

The educational programs needed will involve direct experience with the city and its life, as well as reflective study. Curriculum innovations will be necessary to open up these long-neglected areas, e.g., cross-cultural programs and courses such as "urban missions."

Ronald Sider describes and analyzes the possibilities of the Messiah College Philadelphia program, which is unique in its attachment to a major urban university, innovative summer programming, and separate urban campus segment of the college's board. An urban campus like this could be the setting for exciting possibilities: an evangelical center for urban studies, a comprehensive program of cross-cultural experiences, a model for maximum college-community interaction, missionary preparation,[1] an evangelical center on race relations, and a truly multi-racial college, perhaps providing the sort of constructive development of minority leadership necessary.

Chicago's Urban Life Center is not a college, but it does have cooperative credit arrangements with several surrounding colleges. Its focus is more on field experiences and interpersonal exchange than the Messiah or Westmont programs, and the "students" are integral participants in the directions taken by the Center. Rather than emphasizing the usual fixed college curriculum, it provides for self-directed learning that can be applied in urban and nonurban cultural and governmental settings. Although it started out as an educational center for suburban whites, it has become a center for *exchange* between suburban whites and urban dwellers, including minority students.

On the west coast, Westmont College's San Francisco Urban Program seeks to integrate analytical and reflective learning with that gained from a 24-hour-per-week city agency placement or field projects. Students in the program spend one semester in the city, with their regular tuition being applied there. The program is an interdisciplinary one, and has also begun to involve students from several other colleges.

Finally, Don Dayton and Burton Nelson consider the direction that evangelical seminaries must go if they are to become relevant in twentieth- and twenty-first-century urban America. Seminaries must break out of traditional curricula to the extent that these simply allow seminarians to remain ghettoized. If the gospel is to be perceived as relevant by the cosmopolitan contemporary urban world, seminaries must provide the systematic opportunity for their students to deal with people from different classes, races, and economic backgrounds. They must learn more than theology in an elitist institution. They must learn to "take the other person's point of view" (Philippians 2:4, Phillips), to understand and appreciate those outside of their own cultural background. Dayton and Nelson present models for such seminary training. Besides educating their students, seminaries can expose ordinary Christian laymen to the theological, educational, and human concerns pertinent to the city.

Minority Leadership

Finally, Bill Pannell considers the kinds of minority leadership that must be developed if evangelical urban ministry is to be adequate. He stresses the need for quality *education* rather than specialized training programs if minority Christians are to be able to lead in the kind of problem-solving needed. He then calls for minority leadership in several spheres pertinent to the city: medical, political, and psychological, as well as more sophisticated theological lay leadership.

Pannell analyzes the nature of the Christian college in contemporary America as basically destructive of this much-needed minority leadership. He is direct in pointing out the negative effects that insensitive white, middle-class Christian education can have on minority students. But he does not write off these colleges, and suggests some healthy variations that could be developed.

As urban centers become increasingly populated by minority persons, this kind of vital minority leadership will be essential if the gospel is to be perceived as more than the white man's "thing."

Note to Part Four: Introduction

1 One must be very cautious, however. The central-city resident must not be seen as someone to be practiced on. This will only arouse intense resentment. There does seem to be value, however, in thinking of a period of urban internship as a prerequisite to overseas missionary activity. The candidate's ability to cope with and positively relate to a cross-cultural setting could be better assessed. Also, our missionary societies might begin to interest more minority candidates who would have a better chance of establishing overseas relationships in certain settings, and who are essential to any home urban mission efforts.

7: MAKING PEOPLE AWARE
by John F. Alexander

Most evangelicals seem scarcely aware of the suffering in our cities. What they know about the city is pollution, crime, and concrete. And that keeps most of them out.

How can evangelicals be made aware of urban needs and opportunities? How can the evangelical community be changed so that it can serve the central city?

The research done on change is frustrating. People rarely change; and when they do, mass media almost never have much to do with it. Most people's attitudes are about the same as their parents'. Nine out of ten contemporary students claim the same political party as their parents.[1] If their political views do change, it is often because their economic status and other self-interest factors have also changed. Our abilities at selective perception, distortion, and

JOHN F. ALEXANDER is editor of **The Other Side,** *a national magazine seeking to activate Christian social concern. He holds the B.A. and M.A. degrees in philosophy and psychology from Oxford University; the master's degree in philosophy of religion from Trinity Evangelical Divinity School; and is a Ph.D. candidate at Northwestern University. For five years he taught philosophy at Wheaton College.*

self-deception are so great that we seem able to hold on to almost any belief, providing we learned it at our mother's knee. Consider what frequently happens when a psychotherapist, a highly trained agent of change, works for an extended period of time with a person who wants to change badly enough to pay for it: the very thing that would have happened if the person had had no professional help.[2]

Many reasonable people conclude from this that trying to change people's attitudes toward the city is hopeless. All we can do, they say, is to shape our own children so that their attitudes toward the city will be better. My own experience (perhaps it is only my ability at self-deception) has made me mildly hopeful that we can do more than that.

But if we are to do more, we must first face how difficult it is to change people. We must not harbor illusions about coming up with a master plan to change the basic attitudes of evangelicals toward the city. We may imagine that if only we got our message out people would believe it. But the likelihood is that they would not even notice it.

If we are to bring change, we must develop modest and realistic plans based on a careful study of communication. In considering communication it will be convenient to divide it into three parts: the message, the audience, and the medium.[3]

The Message

We may imagine that our message is that evangelicals must change drastically and get deeply involved in the city. But — at least initially — we should have a more modest message. We should simply advise evangelicals about getting involved in the city in ways they already understand. Instead of trying to change them we can meet them where they are and try to channel their action. We can be "facilitators" with suggestions on what they can do.

Here we should learn from Madison Avenue. Advertisers know that it is easier to cater to "needs" that people already have than it is to produce new "needs" in them. Similarly, telling an evangelical that the social structures of the city must be completely transformed will be a waste of effort if he is relatively satisfied with our social structures. If we tell the same person about an urban family without food, he is much more likely to act. A related goal is to draw together those already concerned about the city, not to change them but to channel them. By conferences, books, and magazines, people could be brought together to learn from each other and work out concerted action programs.

Eventually, though, we shall want to try to change people. What will our message be then? We may think that our message is certain facts about the city and the Bible. There is a tendency to imagine that communication is planting facts in a person's head, rather like transferring bits of information from one computer to another. But what we want to communicate is not primarily facts but changed attitudes, increased sensitivity, effective action. Of course, facts are not unimportant. A social worker ignorant of the facts about welfare would have limited ability to work with the poor; a pastor unaware of the biblical teaching relevant to urban problems would be paralyzed in the city. But still the facts themselves are secondary; anyone can quickly acquire the facts once he is sensitive to urban needs and motivated to act.

The West has a deeply ingrained tendency to treat everything intellectually. Aristotle defined man as the rational animal. Descartes said, "I think; therefore I am." So we keep slipping into the idea that our message is a cognitive, factual discourse; and we must remind ourselves again and again that our goal is not "head knowledge" but action and change. We must not assume that exposing people to facts will change them.

Man is an emotional animal as much as he is a rational animal. The reason evangelicals are inactive in the city has more to do with emotions and attitudes than it does with ignorance of facts. But evangelical communication has usually followed the secular, cognitive model. The centerpiece of evangelical communication is probably the sermon, and, at least in middle-class churches, sermons are often didactic discourses explaining some position or interpreting the cognitive side of some verse. Unlike Christ's or Isaiah's sermons, most of our sermons are hard to distinguish from classroom lectures. Our publications are similar: our magazines are collections of essays, and our books are extended essays. Consider how evangelicals have tried to communicate about poverty, racism, and the city. On such topics we have written hundreds of learned treatises, but no novels, very little poetry, few short stories, even fewer allegories, little humor,[4] practically no songs, and only a few photo essays or movies. Do we really believe that two-hundred-page essays are the way to produce change?

If we want to make people sensitive to human suffering, let us show human suffering. If we want men secure enough to face facts that will contradict cherished beliefs, let us provide the emotional support of friendship. If we are after people who can accept different cultures, let us bring them eyeball-to-eyeball with different cultures till they realize what is biblical and what is cultural. If we want changed attitudes, we will have to display changed attitudes. If the goal is action, we had better be full of action suggestions.

The Audience

Communicators usually spend more time on their message than they do on their audience. But we cannot get our message accepted unless we know what our audience already believes, what their prejudices are, what media they are exposed to, and the like. It is no use giving the same political message in the same package to black militants and to members of the John Birch Society.

The problem can be illustrated by imagining what happens if we decide to publish a magazine carrying essays explaining how Christ would deal with the city. Right away we have limited ourselves to a very small audience. A lot of people read very little. Of those who do read, few read essays, and practically no one reads essays on theology and politics. Among those who read such essays, some will be offended if the theology is evangelical and others will be offended if the politics is liberal.

Notice that we must either adjust our audience to our message, or adjust our message to our audience. Both are appropriate at different times. If we are committed to a particular project, say raising money for low-cost housing, then we should select our audience accordingly. Or if we have a given audience, we should make our message one which may require them to change, but which will not outrage them completely. For example, there are few evangelicals who cannot quickly see the need to help with evangelism in the city. So, go to work on that. We may not immediately get them to finance some area of work that we think is most needed at the moment, but we should be able to get them to finance the work *they* think is best.

Medium

The third component of communication is the medium. The most important consideration here is learning to use many media. No single medium reaches a wide enough audience. With the possible exception of the comic page and very popular television programs, few media reach even a sizable minority of the population. Furthermore, encountering something in more than one medium greatly increases the impact. Reading something in a book and seeing it in a movie has much more impact than reading it twice or seeing it in two movies.

We must free ourselves from construing the communication media too narrowly. Besides getting our message out in essays and lectures, we can consider novels, comic books, parables, guerrilla theater, drama, folk music, poetry, underground newspapers, jokes, cassettes, TV, radio, press services, newspaper columns, movies, coffee klatches, actions that get news coverage, short stories, records, children's books, letters to the editor, public demonstrations, private conversation over the back fence or dinner table, newsletters, quizzes, paintings, calling in on talk shows, annotated Bibles, small group encounter sessions, floats in parades, public conferences, college texts, Sunday school classes, billboards, leaflets, bumper stickers, adult fellowships, posters, film strips, direct mail, door-to-door visiting, press releases, coffee houses, and so on.[5]

As we think of using the various media, we have to be imaginative. It is discouraging to see how badly Christians use new media. Much Christian television broadcasting simply reproduces what is done elsewhere: a church service on television, using none of the special effects possible in television. If we want to preach a sermon about race relations on television, we can at least show stills that bring some of the problems to life.

Another point is that we need to match our media to our audience. If we want to reach white evangelical pastors, a journal and the existing books on race are probably effective. To reach the average member of a suburban church, however, that approach is very limited. We may need a Sunday School quarterly, a conference, and some movies. If we are after ghetto residents, more down-to-earth methods may be required. A public nonverbal demonstration may have to be primary, accompanied by vigorous outreach in the schools and community organizations.

Our media must also match our message. Essays are reasonably effective to dispense facts. So are quizzes, posters, novels, and other things. But if we want to make people more sensitive to each other, encounter groups and short stories full of feeling make more sense. If we are trying to get people to act, parables, examples, and extended personal contact become much more important.

A final point about media is that in an important sense the medium *is* the message.[6] A journal of theological essays is unlikely to produce much more than theological dispute, even if the essays are on theology of action for the city and the readers are all urban evangelicals. But a magazine full of action has a good chance of producing action. Similarly if our main approach is sermons urging action and people never see us acting, they will be more struck by our medium (talking) than by our message (action). By contrast, if the medium we choose is a footwashing ceremony at city hall, action will almost inevitably follow.

An Example

Let us look at an imaginary example. Suppose your suburban community is about to have a referendum on whether to allow construction of low-cost housing. There is an elder in your church who is reasonably open and compassionate, but inclined to oppose low-cost housing on the ground that it might lower property values and increase taxes. In addition, he feels there is no reason poor people cannot just live in the city where (he supposes) they are probably happier anyway.

How do you approach such a person in order to change his position to support the housing? How do you keep him fron wandering off on one of the thousand different paths he might see to avoid change?

1) Get quite clear on your goal and be sure it is a reasonable one. In this case that is easily accomplished. You know that you want him to vote in favor of low-cost housing, and you know that he is not fanatically opposed to it.

2) From now on make sure your communication with him is, within reasonable limits, tailored to that goal. Do not get sidetracked onto issues that might be red flags for him.

3) Consider carefully *who* should talk to him. Central to communication is the credibility of the communicator.[7] You can communicate effectively only

if the other person trusts you. Your message may be logical, lucid, and kind, and you may be a responsible citizen, but if he sees you as an unreliable radical, you might as well go home.

4) Know what you are talking about. Be prepared to tell him the facts about property values, taxes, the shortage of housing in the city, biblical teachings about helping your brother even if it is costly.

5) Try to figure out his problems and deal with them before he raises them. That will give him confidence in you and it forces you to think about your "audience" as well as your message. (This is expecially important in mass media where the one-way nature of the communication prevents dealing with the audience problems in any other way.) By the same token, do not say things which are needlessly offensive. Again, knowing your audience is critical.

6) Use the Bible as much as possible. This is crucial. Your elder accepts Scripture as his authority; so use it. Challenge him to be consistently biblical.

7) Try to reach him emotionally. Make the plight of poor people trapped in the ghetto live for him, as it really is. Let him be aware that these are real children trapped by terrible schools, or threatened by rats in their houses.

8) Remember you are not debating him. You are trying to make him aware of the need and to persuade him. Annoyance and anger will not help. Don't let him rile you, and don't be condescending.

9) Emphasize points of agreement. Try to accept what he says as often as possible. Work from his framework, not yours. Try to get him to agree with you without challenging his whole way of life. Right now you are trying to get him to vote for low-cost housing, not join a Christian commune. Meet him where he is, not where you think he should be.

10) If what he says is inconsistent, be tactful. It is probably worth making him realize the contradiction, but do it by asking a quiet question that allows him some room rather than forcing him to admit he was wrong or unreasonable.

11) Whenever possible it is a good idea to take the position of a learner. Ask leading questions. That deals with the problem of arguments and condescension, and you might even learn something.

12) At some point, ask him what the alternative is. When he is faced with the reality of having to produce solutions, he may see the wisdom of your solution.

13) Answer what bothers him, not what he says bothers him. Often people will ask questions or make remarks which are not quite appropriate or which are not as important as they seem to think. Then you have to figure out what is really eating them.

Getting the elder to vote for low-cost housing will not be easy, but it should be possible if you are reasonable, thoughtful and gentle.

The Prophetic Role

One aspect of communication which I have not mentioned so far is the role of the prophet. My advice has been rather like "winning friends and influencing people." But another approach also has validity. Speak the truth, and let the audience respond as it will.

A number of things must be said here. First, and most important, the men of God in the Bible were almost always prophetic rather than diplomatic. If people were offended by what the men of God said, it was up to the people to repent. Consider Christ's attacks on the Pharisees, John the Baptist's bluntness with Herod (Matt. 14:3-11), and Paul's attacks on the Corinthians (II Cor. 10-12) and on the Galatian heretics (Gal. 1:6-10; 5:12). The Old Testament provides endless examples of blunt saints: Ezekiel was always calling the Israelites whores (ch. 16 and 23), and when the king told Amos to be quiet Amos replied, "Your wife shall be a harlot" (Amos 7:12-17). Then there is Daniel who insisted on praying publicly to Jehovah (Dan. 6), Moses with Pharaoh, Elijah with Ahab (I Kings 18 and 21), Abijah (I Kings 14:10), Micah (I Kings 22), and the prophet known only as "this mad fellow" (II Kings 9:11).

Evangelicals have not taken these biblical precedents for the prophetic seriously. Perhaps we have become too conformed to this world by becoming mild-mannered "organization men." Those of us who accept Scripture as our authority can say without question that we should have more prophets and fewer diplomats.

Second, once again we need to use more than one medium. We need both prophets and diplomats. In II Kings 18 there is diplomatic Obadiah as well as fearless Elijah. Both groups should accept and respect each other.

Third, the prophet must still speak to his audience. He may offend them, but at least he must make sure they know what he means. There is no point in even a prophet addressing Spanish-speaking people in English. If people are going to be upset, the prophet should make sure that they are offended by the right things. When Stephen spoke to the Jews, he knew his audience and spoke to them in a way they understood. In fact, they understood so well that they killed him (Acts 6 and 7).

Fourth, the prophet must be careful to speak redemptively. He cannot be on an ego trip or working out his own problems. He must be trying to help. Similarly, the diplomat must be careful that he is not just protecting his own skin, that there are some things he will not compromise, that his "tact" does not undermine his own integrity and honesty, and that he is not using people for some other end (to return to the case we discussed, talking to the elder just for his vote, without concern for his welfare).

Finally, the practical importance of the prophet should not be underestimated. The truth is not all that easy to find, and someone must sort out what it is. If you are too concerned about your audience and are always adjusting your message to suit them, it is very hard to keep your message clear.

Furthermore, really substantial changes seem to come most often from men who are seriously out of step with their times and are usually quite blunt about it. Think about Jesus, Luther, Galileo, Paine, Marx, Freud, Darwin. None of them was in tune with his audience, and none of them had a diplomatic bone in his body. But they are the men who have produced change.[8]

The Place of the Church

What we want is profound change in people so they will act to heal the city. To produce basic change, we need more than mass media. We need to be more drastic than that. We need prophets. And we need a total, coordinated program. We need a way of making men into disciples of the living God. In short, we need a church.

This is not the place to spell out the New Testament concept of the church in detail, but let me make a few suggestions. It is composed of people who have been born again, that is, of people who recognize the viciousness and pointlessness of their way of life, reject it, and ask God to forgive and change them. Such people are open to change.

Following the New Testament pattern, they meet together often (nearly every day) to talk about their problems, to encourage each other, to share what they discover about God, and to pray. They are so committed to each other that when one of them does something wrong, another tells him about it, instead of boiling inside and telling someone else. They like each other enough to give each other a sense of security, which makes them more able to face bad things about themselves, to change, and to act on the awareness.

There are elders to whom the people are responsible and who are responsible to see to it that all these things happen. All of the people study the Bible continually, and together they help each other face what it really means for them.

That kind of church would produce change. And action. I do not know of any scientific studies showing that it would produce change, but it would. It turned the Roman Empire upside down. And it would solve the problems of our cities.

Notes to Chapter 7

1 David S. Sullivan, "Children, Adults, and Racism," *The Other Side,* VII (Jan.-Feb. 1971), p. 10.

2 O. Hobart Mowrer, *Crisis in Psychiatry and Religion* (New York: Van Nostrand Reinhold, 1961). For a slightly more positive view, see H. Eysenk, "The Effects of Psychotherapy: an Evaluation," *Journal of Abnormal and Social Psychology,* 1952, pp. 319-324.

3 I am heavily indebted to the writers of the January-February 1971 issue of *The Other Side* on attitude change, both for their articles and for their many conversations with me. See especially the articles "Children, Adults and

Racism" by Dr. David S. Sullivan; "Changing Institutions" by Dr. Benjamin Sprunger; "Mass Communications and Social Change" by Joel Belz.

4 A notable exception is *The Little White Book on Race* by Judi Culbertson and Patti Bard (Philadelphia: Lippincott, 1970).

5 See Arthur G. Gish, "Evangelism Reconsidered," Tract 11 of the Brethren Action Movement, reprinted in *The Other Side,* VIII, 2 (March-April 1972), pp. 20, 36-38.

6 Marshall McLuhan, *Understanding Media: The Extensions of Man* (New York: McGraw-Hill, 1964), chapter 1.

7 C. I. Hovland and W. Weiss, "The Influence of Source Creditability on Communication Effectiveness," *Public Opinion Quarterly,* XV (1951), pp. 635-650.

8 For a more detailed treatment of the prophetic role, see my "Madison Avenue Jesus," *The Other Side,* VIII (Sept.-Oct. 1972), pp. 2-3, 56-58.

8: THE MESSIAH URBAN SATELLITE CAMPUS

by Ronald J. Sider

Messiah College has two campuses: one in the rolling hills of mid-Pennsylvania, the other in the heart of the black community of North Philadelphia. In order to strengthen the Christian liberal arts college by expanding the academic, cultural, and cross-cultural opportunities available within the context of the Christian college, a satellite campus was established on the edge of the Temple University campus. This cooperative program, begun in fall 1968, was the first such arrangement between a church-related college and a secular, state university in the United States.[1]

Messiah's Philadelphia campus combines many of the strengths of the

---

RONALD J. SIDER is Associate Professor and Dean at the Philadelphia Campus of Messiah College. He is a graduate of Waterloo Lutheran University in Ontario, and holds the Ph.D. in history from Yale. He coordinated the 1973 Thanksgiving Workshop on Evangelicals and Social Concern, and is chairman of the expanded committee, Evangelicals for Social Action. His articles have appeared in **Journal of Theological Studies, Mennonite Quarterly Review, HIS, Scottish Journal of Theology** *and* **Christianity Today.** *He has edited* **The Chicago Declaration** *(Creation House, 1974) and written* **Andreas Bodenstein von Karlstadt** *(Brill, 1974).*

large, public university with the advantages of the Christian liberal arts college. Juniors and seniors in Philadelphia take three or four courses a semester from Temple University faculty. The university considers them full-time students and grants them all the associated privileges. Students thus have the opportunity to gain depth within their major discipline by taking courses from a broad spectrum of professors with different methodological approaches. Students who want a major that the small liberal arts college cannot afford to offer spend two years at the Philadelphia campus, taking specialized courses at the university and general education courses at the college, and graduate with a degree from Messiah College. Because of this cooperative program, Messiah can offer over 45 majors, more than any other Christian college in the United States. Since the state university provides the more expensive educational services, the Christian "cluster college" can spend its limited resources on person-centered programs and activities directly related to its distinctive goals as a Christian college.

Carl Henry has lamented the fact that Christian colleges have too often "provided a sanctuary from secular ideas and ideals rather than confronting and disputing the tide of contemporary unbelief or giving modern man an explanation of his predicament based on biblical premises."[2] When faculty and students constantly rub shoulders with secular colleagues, such isolation is difficult. The cluster college model enables students to experience the full force of contemporary critiques of Christianity (and it lets the state pay the agnostic professors!). Yet this model also remains thoroughly Christian.

Through resident Christian faculty, regular chapel, small residential units, and Christian fellow-students, the Philadelphia campus retains the advantages of the Christian college. Each student must take a course each semester from Messiah's Philadelphia faculty. These team-taught, interdisciplinary courses offer help in relating Christian faith to the powerful forces of modern thought and society. They provide biblical foundations for social action and help nurture the informal, intimate Christian community in which brothers and sisters play, study, learn and change together.

The environment of Messiah's Philadelphia campus is not only the secular academic community represented by the university, but also the excitement and confrontation of the black inner city. Such a setting is ideal for "consciousness raising." Church and society today desperately need a new generation of young people with the courage to confront racism, structural injustice, and the still festering urban crisis. But the change of values required for this confrontation will seldom come from learned discussions and assigned readings carried out in academic settings safely isolated from both black persons and the urban ghetto. Students are most likely to adopt new ideas and values when they have first-hand, experiential encounters with new situations and different cultures and also enjoy a supportive community of caring persons and regular, informal contact with faculty.

Messiah's Philadelphia campus strives to be one such setting. Inner-city life offers first-hand contact with the tragic results of institutionalized evil. Articulate black speakers in class and chapel, new acquaintances from other cultures in the university, and attendance at black and Puerto Rican churches all help to open up new vistas of cross-cultural understanding and appreciation. A course on Christianity and Contemporary Problems deals with racism, poverty, rich and poor nations, militarism and the role of the church in social problems. As a part of this course, almost all students engage in "community involvement" — tutoring, recreation clubs, assisting in inner-city classrooms, working in political campaigns. Careful orientation on the subtleties of paternalism is crucial. An urban practicum offers the possibility of more extensive involvement in an inner-city school, social agency, or church.

To meet the need for Christian community, about forty students, staff, and resident faculty members and their families reside in seven rowhouses. The community is informal, intimate, and Christian. Students on work-study are in charge of food service. Classes are sometimes held in living rooms, and students have constant opportunities for informal exchange with faculty members. There are early morning prayer meetings and evening Bible studies in student rooms.

The first task of "concerned" whites, blacks insist, is to help their white brothers overcome their prejudice. The Philadelphia campus is an ideal location for taking this demand seriously. Students have presented the play *The Man Nobody Saw* at approximately two dozen churches. Weekend seminars on racism for churchmen from the constituencies of the college have also proved to be a useful approach. After four or five speakers, lively discussion in small groups, and attendance at a black worship service, new attitudes sometimes slowly emerge. In the large minority communities of big cities live many persons who can contribute greatly to seminars on racism. These sessions have shown that sharp confrontation and vigorous honesty can be instruments of the risen Lord, who still is in the business of converting the worst of sinners like white evangelical racists.

It is possible, in the face of all these resources, for the attack on racism to forget a fundamental of evangelical theology: that knowledge is not virtue, that Christians need more than just sociological and historical information about their corporate sins—racial and otherwise. We also need the radical, transforming activity of the Spirit. The supernatural presence of God comes after much prayer. If evangelical "activists" have overcome the activism-pietism dichotomy at the theoretical level, they still have a good deal to learn in practice. All the programs suggested must be immersed in prayer; then piety must be demonstrated in salient action.

Most of the students at the Philadelphia campus are from Messiah's Grantham campus. A significant number, however, have come for a semester or year as visiting students from other Christian colleges (e.g. Eastern Mennonite College, Taylor University, Elizabethtown College). Thus the advantages of this new model of cooperation between a Christian college and a public university are available to students in Christian liberal arts colleges across the country.

An Evangelical Center for Urban Studies. A serious hindrance for evangelicals concerned with the city is the desperate lack of thoroughly trained personnel. We need a few centers for training a core of thoroughly committed evangelical urbanologists. Messiah College's location in North Philadelphia is ideal for this task. Its cooperative program with Temple University makes available undergraduate majors in urban studies and urban recreation. Courses on the city are also offered in Temple's political science, education, economics, sociology, and history departments.

A summer seminar on urban problems (begun in 1972) was a step in the direction of becoming a center for the training of evangelical urbanologists. Under the direction of a black activist professor from the city, students from different colleges and universities have listened to a broad spectrum of guest lecturers and read current literature to analyze the effectiveness of various current models of urban ministry. Work-study jobs with inner-city agencies provide the students necessary summer income and valuable practical insight.

White students in the program have been a minority. The result has been an intense, sometimes painful, but extremely valuable summer-long, black-white exchange. There were times when people shouted angrily at each other, but they also prayed together. As the young black evangelicals became more aware of their identity, and as both blacks and whites became more honest about their feelings, there was sharp debate and disagreement about how to demonstrate visibly the oneness of the multiracial body of Christ. Surely any program meant to develop sensitive and evangelical urban specialists will require that they communicate honestly across racial lines on critical issues.

As the program has developed, new courses have been added to the original course on "Models of Christian Ministry in the City." Students in the summer seminar may now take a course on evangelism in the metropolis and the urban practicum. At the same time, students eligible for summer work-study through their home college can work for about eleven weeks in some inner-city agency. Others may choose to do volunteer work. Still others may take a full academic load by choosing one or all of the above courses plus one or several courses in urban studies offered at Temple University.

A Comprehensive Program of Cross-Cultural Experiences. A huge metropolis such as Philadelphia, with its large black and Puerto Rican communities, as well as smaller Chinese, Japanese, and other ethnic communities, offers as many opportunities for cross-cultural learning as a "semester abroad" in Korea, France, or Haiti, and offers them for much less money. But since the setting *seems* more familiar, it is easy to miss the genuinely distinct cultures at one's doorstep in the large city.

Offered as intensive term courses in January and May, two four-hour cross-cultural courses are an alternative to the college's traditional language requirement. Students study the history, sociology, politics, and religious experience of the culture (the first two courses developed are on black culture and Puerto Rican culture) through theoretical methods (reading and lectures) and experiential techniques (visits to restaurants, churches, homes, and businesses in the culture under study). After a ten-day orientation to the culture, the students spend two weeks living with a family from the culture and working in a school, social agency, church, or business in that community.

The initial experience in these cross-cultural courses suggests that they will be a far more effective tool for introducing students to other cultural traditions than the traditional required language courses.

Community Relations. How does Messiah College relate to its inner-city black neighbors? Since Temple, like most urban universities, has not always been a good neighbor to the surrounding black community, Messiah decided, after some initial groping and orientation, to enter into direct negotiations with the black community to develop a mutually acceptable plan for expansion that would benefit both college and community. The college has agreed to sponsor a camping program every summer for a hundred inner-city youth and assist the community in the renovation of community housing as the college takes over nearby rowhouses for its own expansion. The college has also applied for and received federal funds (Title I) to run an Adult Education Program for the community. In 1973-74, this program enabled paid community planners to develop and offer courses in three areas: How to Relate to City Hall; Consumer Education; and The Health Care Delivery System. At the same time, the college has also made a genuine effort to become multiracial. At the Philadelphia campus, the college now is multiracial at every level—students, faculty, staff, administration and Board of Trustees.

In many ways an inner-city campus of a Christian college is more attractive to minority students than the typical Christian college. At the inner-city campus, black students are usually close to their home church or some similar black congregation. Numerous black cultural events are at the doorstep. Because of the large minority population in the city, black students do not experience the same degree of loneliness and alienation they often feel in largely white Christian colleges located in suburban or rural settings.

Some Possibilities for the Future

An inner-city Christian college campus can be an exciting link between the joys, insights, and needs of the inner city and the deficiencies and resources of evangelicals in suburban and rural areas. A brief sketch of some of the possibilities will suggest the extent of the challenge and the opportunity.

A Model for Maximum College-Community Interaction. If a fundamental objective is to maximize cross-cultural experiences, then the physical facilities must be so arranged that college and community encounter each other as often and as comfortably as possible. One way to foster such interaction would be to scatter several small clusters of college buildings, for about fifty students each, throughout a largely residential, owner-occupied minority community. The daily interaction thus encouraged would permit numerous cross-cultural learning possibilities—for example, host family arrangements in community homes, or joint college-community cooperation in lobbying for action by city hall, or married students' renting rooms from an elderly, widowed homeowner.

In the light of present black-white relations, it is possible that the presence of even a relatively small number of white students would substantially harm the emergence of black self-consciousness and identity in the community. If a scheme like that suggested above were to be tried today, it would require the college, first, clearly to understand that the white students are learners and not teachers; second, to negotiate in advance its presence and expansion with the community; third, to increase the number of minority students it serves; and fourth, to contribute significantly to community needs as the community requests and directs assistance.

Possibilities for cooperation would be numerous if the college decided that being an urban college entails substantial financial and staff involvement and cooperation with the community on a basis of genuine equality. An Adult Education Program, a college preparatory program for community youth, nursery schools, recreation programs—all could be developed on a cooperative basis.

None of this will work if it is based on a secret hope by paternalistic white liberals that black people will, with this sort of help, eventually adopt white standards. Those involved must agree that black culture is a different culture of *equal* value and that it ought to retain its distinctive characteristics. The assumption is that in a pluralistic society, blacks and whites cannot live together in peace in the long run without genuine interaction between the races. Should not evangelicals take the lead in promoting genuine interracial interaction, which happens only on the other side of a confession of racism and a determination to change by whites, and a vigorous assertion of self-identity and black consciousness by blacks? Evangelicals, after all, know that the Spirit, who will ultimately create one glorious multiracial body in the kingdom, is now at work removing the hostile barriers we erect between men. It is only realistic to admit that the dynamics of white racism and black separatism in our society could preclude the ultimate success of this model of maximum college-community interaction. That is hardly sufficient reason not to try.

A New Location and Model for Missionary Preparation. An inner-city campus cooperating with a large public university might prove to be an excellent location to prepare missionaries for tomorrow. To immerse the future missionary in a culture completely different from his own would lessen his cultural shock in future arenas of service.

Sessions with young black evangelicals whose personal struggles in the United States have taught them about Western cultural imperialism would whittle away at cultural and racial prejudice. Available courses in the anthropology, history, sociology, political science, and religion of almost every part of the world could teach missionaries a great deal about the culture of their area of service before they arrive on the field. In many cases, they could also learn the required language. Since mission agencies increasingly require highly skilled missionary technologists, future missionaries might want to major in areas like engineering technology, radio-television-film, journalism, business administration, medical technology, which are usually unavailable at smaller schools. Courses in biblical studies and the history of missions (taught by a missiologist) would round out the undergraduate program of missionary preparation.

One couple on the way to an African assignment spent a semester at Messiah's Philadelphia campus taking specialized courses in hospital administration at the university and a seminar on cross-cultural learning at Messiah. Orientation programs for church agencies sending voluntary service personnel into American settings have also been conducted.

An Evangelical Center on Race Relations. One of the most painful things for any honest evangelical to face is the correlation of conservative theology with racial prejudice.[3] New journals such as *The Other Side* and *Inside* offer one avenue to change attitudes. Others are desperately needed, and perhaps a center on race relations, located in a major urban complex, would be such an avenue. An evangelical college campus in the inner city could be the site for this. Aided perhaps by a church agency or foundation to supply staff and funding, a comprehensive educational program on race relations by evangelicals for evangelicals could be established. Weekend exposure seminars for specific groups of churchmen (key leaders, youth groups, Sunday School classes) would be one major focus of activity. New films and plays might be developed. Sunday programs could be produced for teams of students to take to churches. Current work on evangelical literature (especially Sunday School material) could be encouraged and guided in conferences and seminars.

A Truly Multiracial College. Most evangelical colleges have recently made token efforts, at least, to add minority students. Some have made significant progress. But all are still *white* colleges. Again it must be said that discussion about an "integrated" Christian college dare not be on the silent assumption that blacks ought to be given the privilege to learn superior white customs. The only basis for the dream of a multiracial college is the Pauline vision of one multiracial body of Christ that supersedes all human commitments to class, race, or nation. The church has not been faithful to Paul's revelation. But perhaps it is not too much to hope and pray that God may yet grant evangelicals the grace and guts to implement the divine revelation they cherish.

How might an urban satellite campus enable a Christian college to give flesh to such a vision? Obviously, the college would have to decide to have more than token minority representation in the student body, faculty, administration, and board of trustees. Perhaps evangelical foundations would fund a major college preparatory program for youth in black and Puerto Rican evangelical urban churches. A concerted effort would be needed to find minority faculty and assist them through graduate studies.

The urban campus would be the ideal location for the extensive orientation programs on race-relations which would be required for white students as the number of minority students increased. Curricular changes would be numerous. Perhaps the only way to change the attitudes of faculty, staff, and administration sufficiently to make life endurable for minority students in the early stages would be a comprehensive program of exposure to minority culture and history for all college personnel. Would an evangelical college have the courage to require that all faculty, administrators, and staff spend at least a week every two years in a carefully planned program of exposure to minority culture? The urban campus would have excellent resources available for this.

There would be questions from the traditional constituency and, alas, changes in it. But is it too much to hope that there are also many evangelical parents who would like their children to attend a college that gives flesh to the biblical view of the body of Christ?

Maybe it is impossible. But perhaps the radical, regenerating power of the resurrected Lord Jesus will so remake a few groups of very imperfect men that we can have here and there a visible witness to the world that the Pauline vision of one body of Christ is not pious chatter or wistful illusion but the surest truth about God's future.

Notes to Chapter 8

1 Conrad Grebel College (Mennonite) at the University of Waterloo in Canada is similar at many points. Messiah's Philadelphia Campus resulted from discussion among Dr. Ernest Boyer, a member of Messiah's Board of Trustees and now Chancellor of the State University of New York, Dr. Albert Meyer of Goshen College, and President D. Ray Hostetter of Messiah. For recent discussions of the concept of the cluster college, see Jerry G. Gaff, *The Cluster College* (San Francisco: Jassey-Bass Inc., 1970); John W. Snyder, "Why Not a Christian College on a University Campus?", *Christianity Today*, XI (1967), 494-99; and Ronald Sider, "Christian Cluster Colleges – Off to a Good Start," *Christianity Today*, XVIII (May 24, 1974), pp. 12-16.

2 C.F.H. Henry, "The Need for a Christian University," *Christianity Today*, XI (1967), 487.

3 After sociological study of the connection between religious faith and prejudice, Milton Rokeach concluded: "Those who place a high value on salvation are conservatives anxious to maintain the status quo and unsympathetic to the black and the poor." "Faith, Hope and Bigotry," *Psychology Today*, April 1970, p. 58.

9: THE URBAN LIFE CENTER

by Eunice and Donald Schatz and Lucille Dayton

The Urban Life Center was born one evening in spring 1970 as a result of deepening concern over evangelical apathy about social injustice, racism, militarism, and materialism. A small group of people in the Chicago area, including eight or nine restless college students, agreed that the place to begin in working for change was with the young. College students seemed ready to challenge materialistic values in the Christian community, to take the risks of conscientious objection to the war, to work and live among minorities in order to feel the heat of oppression and discrimination.

Some of the group described an idea for an urban center where students

EUNICE and DONALD SCHATZ and LUCILLE SIDER DAYTON are all members of the staff of the Urban Life Center in Chicago—the Schatzes as co-directors, Mrs. Dayton as assistant director. Eunice Schatz holds master's degrees in sociology from the University of Chicago and in Christian education from Wheaton; Donald Schatz is an artist and poet, and holds the B.G.S. degree (art) from Roosevelt University. Lucille Dayton has the M.A.R. from Yale Divinity School and M.S. in student personnel from the University of Kentucky. For three years she has had staff responsibility for the Urban Ministry Program for Seminarians (UMPS) in Chicago.

might live for a term, grappling with some of society's problems firsthand. There was consensus that an urban location was essential, because the city is the point of convergence of society's strains and tensions and also its cultural and creative force.

A building was found in the Hyde Park area of Chicago near the University of Chicago—a church no longer in use with a recently remodeled educational unit convertible to living space with minor alterations. Accreditation through Roosevelt University was secured (students would transfer into Roosevelt for the term, then transfer back to their schools of origin); and one of the original founding group agreed to take on the responsibility of coordination of the Center, living—with his family—at the Center with students.

And so, in September 1970, the first group of students (mostly from nearby Trinity and Wheaton Colleges) moved in and the Urban Life Center officially began its first term just six months after the birth of the original idea!

Many important changes have occurred during the Center's brief history, but these are best described in connection with an explanation of its basic philosophy. What follows is a description of the costs and risks of attaining one's ideals, the realism of failure as well as success in trying to put together a creative institution along distinctive lines.

Distinctives[1]

1. Residential Education. The founding group's choice of developing a residential community at "the Church" building was first seen as one option among several. Over the years, however, despite some extremely painful experiences, the Center has become increasingly committed to this model. Two important modifications developed through experience.

In the first place, an educational center, with its typically high level of activity and constantly changing group, cannot rely on the long-term commitments needed for a true commune. So the Center changed the concept and name of the living unit after nine months to "co-op," suggesting that the group lives together, shares work and expenses, and has some kind of common group life. (The co-op is quite different from a dormitory situation in the amount of interdependence required.)

Secondly, after the shift from commune to co-op, there was still a need for minimal definition of limits. "Ground rules" had been omitted from the original plan on the assumption that Christian students living together would share common values and assumptions, and that consensus would occur rather naturally. But the heterogeneity that became important to the Center (inclusion of urban blacks as well as suburban whites, and students with no Christian commitment as well as Christian students) produced a substantial number of clashes of values. During the third year minimal ground rules were established to prevent behavior detrimental to a healthy growing experience. The residential coordinators have also taken major responsibility to help the group work through conflicts in values and life-styles.

There are at least two important reasons for continuing with the residential model. First of all, education 24 hours a day multiplies the impact of the experience immeasurably. Students invariably report that the co-op living experience contributes more to their growth than any other aspect of the program. To make this experience substantive, care has been taken to insure that the residential coordinators are well qualified professionally and academically, and well informed about the academic content of the curriculum (sometimes taking part in the actual teaching); and a course dealing with group living skills is offered for credit each term. Secondly, the co-op living group becomes a microcosm of the larger society, since there is variety of ethnic background, sex, academic majors, schools, and religious belief. This complicates the living; but it also enriches it.

2. Experience-oriented Learning. Traditional academic curricula focus on "book learning." If such formal intellectual learning is to take hold of the student it must be supplemented by direct experience in which he takes responsibility for his own decisions and their consequences or sees this process in action through people he meets. Recognizing this, the Center concentrates heavily on experiences and people as learning resources, which is appropriate in an environment that is richly endowed with both. Interestingly, the outcome of that kind of concentration has not been a reduction in student enthusiasm for intellectual content.

The Center's resource people are those within the urban community. Professionals and academics are included, but there are also persons of rather ordinary status whose lives are interwoven with the fabric of Chicago's history and politics, its ethnic struggles, its art and music and theater. Some of these resource people are persons in poverty, whose surroundings are blighted and misery-laden, but who have learned to cope with amazing courage and tenacity, even giving to neighbors in greater need. They are teachers of students in a "school" foreign to most sons and daughters of affluent suburban parents.

Experience often comes through commitment to a regular responsibility within an urban agency or institution. Field trips and brief observations are not enough to bring abstract theory to life. Only by entering into an organization's struggles on a day-to-day basis, participating in its actions, and living with its monotony as well as its glamour, can a person achieve a realistic and concrete picture. For social work and education majors, field experience may be the core of the curriculum at the Center; for others, it is one part of a total immersion in Chicago. Because Chicago's culture and politics are so obvious— demanding attention and analysis—special effort must be made to help students transfer their new political and aesthetic awareness to the more familiar scene of their own college campus or home town. But, in a way, this is the point: not to see Chicago as an oddity, but as a concentrated reflection of common processes at work wherever men and women congregate.

3. Self-directed Learning. Those who founded the Center did not realize all the implications of their choice of self-directed learning in an urban educational experiment. Eventually the Center staff came to see itself passing through a recognizable pattern of development characteristic of many innovative educational programs.

The first phase of this pattern is captivation with the notions of freedom and informality and with the reduction of authoritarian teacher roles. This is followed by a letdown for both teachers and students. Apathy, boredom, disillusionment, and finally frustration arise from the feeling on the part of each that the other isn't doing what he is "supposed to." After a cathartic gripe session, there is a gradual movement to some limited structure with wide-ranging options for student choice and creativity. A genuine partnership develops between teachers and students, who work out a relevant learning and growth situation, full of struggles and misunderstandings as well as "peak" experiences.

Many educational experiments fold at phase three. That the Center did not is due to an incredible amount of persistence in trying to fully test the philosophy of education being used. Severe financial crises made the situation seem doubly traumatic at times, but lack of funding may have insured that the *only* basis for continuance was a sound educational philosophy and program, since there was no way to depend on automatic income.

To encourage self-directed learning, each student is required to develop his own goals and learning plan for the term. This includes more than academic goals; it involves personal changes he is striving toward—new attitudes and behaviors he is attempting to develop. Such a wide-ranging plan has to be very personal and flexible; and students are permitted to change it in consultation with staff if circumstances indicate. Within the living situation, students learn that it is essential to take responsibility in order to survive. This includes both physical survival and the more difficult area of human relationships—learning to trust and be open instead of playing games.

The process of evaluation is also part of the student's responsibility, including the development of criteria for letter grades where these are required by his school. Learning to handle evaluation constructively and objectively in an atmosphere of cooperation—as opposed to competition—visibly increases the student's self-confidence.

So far there is little information about the performance of Center students when they return to their campuses with large classes and more highly structured situations involving less experiential learning. A substantial number of students have left school temporarily after their term at the Urban Life Center, but this coincides with an apparent national trend to de-emphasize the four-year post-high school higher education plan in favor of a more relevant concept of lifelong education, with periodic "stopping out" experiences.

4. Student Participation. In the beginning, it was stated that a distinguishing mark of this new institution would be an egalitarian decision-making process. The constitution at the time of incorporation indicated that up to half of the governing board might be composed of students—a provision that still stands.

Even before the school term began, however, there were signs that some board members were more "equal" than others. Student interest visibly flagged during the lengthy meetings where fund-raising and legal matters were discussed. A strong desire to make all decisions by consensus produced typical strains in a group that was new to working together and struggling to formulate clearly the objectives and design of something not yet born.

It soon became apparent that student interest in participation and decision-making was largely confined to matters affecting the living situation and the curriculum. Accordingly, such a distinction was made. Full-fledged board members came to be defined as those persons willing to take on the *full* responsibilities of the Center. Inevitably this precipitated the issue of student power; for where responsibility lies, there also lies authority. It proved difficult for the adults, who were fairly sophisticated in using power and willing to take the responsibility that goes along with authority, to share these with younger persons meaningfully. Likewise, students unused to being treated as adults and expected to become autonomous learners had to learn how to relate to adults as persons rather than as authority figures.

An educational experiment that tries to share power in this manner faces the issue with difficulty and strain. Yet is is an element almost always lacking from the college campus, and absolutely essential for the full maturing of persons. Therefore the Center has continued to struggle with it.

5. Interdisciplinary Curriculum. If the student's experience in the city is to be interpreted meaningfully, it cannot be through the insights of one academic discipline alone. In the arts the Center's interdisciplinary perspective is most obvious. At the insistence of an artist on the staff, the program increasingly came to emphasize exposure to cultural perspectives and to the positive aspects of the avant-garde in music, poetry, art, and theater.

The expansion of the capacities of the senses (for example in receiving impressions in the highly stimulating urban environment), the appreciation of things as ends in themselves rather than always as sociological means, the development of an understanding of timelessness, and the encouragement of "mosaic" rather than purely linear and scientific thinking enhance the practical concerns of the rest of the program.

6. Diversity. Once in the city, it soon became clear that the suburban focus of the Center would result in a white suburban enclave and perpetuation of suburban ghetto thinking. Simultaneously, some educational needs of urban students came to the attention of the board, and a few such students were accepted the first year. Now there is a studied effort to include students who need a highly individualized educational program to ease their entry into college after the typically inadequate education received in the Chicago public schools.

The fact that some of the urban students are black adds yet another dimension to the Center. With forty percent of its population black, Chicago is still the most intensely segregated city in the country, and it is common for blacks never to get to know a white person on a personal basis. Likewise, many white suburban students have never become intimately acquainted with blacks on the latter's home turf. The Center brings the two groups together in an environment less hostile than the city at large, and one conducive to developing mutual understanding.

There is diversity of religious belief as well. Some are not Christians at all. Even those who are reflect varying orientations. The student from the small Christian college discovers quickly that the language cherished back on his campus to express Christianity is simply not understood in the city. The urban student finds that his everyday language is foreign and sometimes offensive to the suburban student. In the intimacy of the co-op, this inevitably leads to vigorous exchange and testing of everyone's beliefs. This is threatening for those who have felt secure in a more homogeneous group, but it has led to a deeper understanding of Christian faith and values.

The board reflects a similar diversity. More than a third represent ethnic groups. Half are female. Most of the board members identify themselves as Christians, but a few do not. All have committed themselves to work toward the Center's goals. The educational backgrounds of board members vary. Some have college degrees in subjects like sociology, art, religion, literature, administration, psychology and psychotherapy, education, library science. Other board members are self-educated. Some have long years of experience within an urban setting. They bring fresh approaches and insights, different from those of the "schooled" members, but equally as important. This intentional diversity contributes to the integration that the student needs when maturing in all areas of his life.

7. Students as Learners, Rather than Trainees for Urban Mission. The question is often asked: "Does the Urban Life Center prepare students for serving in the city?" While it is hoped that some students will consider this option, the primary focus is to provide a broad education for the student.

The suburban student often approaches the city with negative impressions based on what he has read of its crime, corruption and crowding. The Center does not ignore these problems, but it tries to expose the student to the city's beauties and assets as well. Chicago is a marvelous example of the city's extremes. It is in Chicago that the principle of nuclear fission was finally unveiled; yet its public school system is notoriously inept. Chicago is unique among Great Lakes ports for preserving its lakefront; yet its urban renewal policies—duplicated in virtually every major urban area—have thrust thousands from their homes and created miles of vacant lots awaiting the grasp of greedy land developers who are politically favored. The Civic Center's Picasso sculpture is world-famous; so is Chicago's crime syndicate.

Even more important is the Center's emphasis on the interdependence of suburb and city. Decisions made in the suburbs about open housing or a new expressway vitally affect the city's poor. Raising students' consciousness is the beginning of change in decision-makers of the future, many of whom will live in suburbs.

8. *Independent Organization.* The Urban Life Center has no organic affiliation with any one campus or consortium. The disadvantages of this are obvious: a large amount of time is spent in working out programs with ten administrations and their faculties, recruiting students from ten schools, and working with several different academic calendars.[2] The irregularity of support and uncertainty of students each term cause both financial and psychological insecurity. But the Center feels that the freedom for experimentation that independence affords and the diversity it provides in students outweigh the disadvantages.

9. *Christian Context.* The constitution of the Center says that its activities take place "within a Christian context." No phrase has been more thoroughly discussed, although it is nowhere formally defined. For those board members who so identify themselves, being a Christian means an acceptance of biblical authority and of the identification of Jesus Christ as Lord and Savior. The way this is worked out in specific beliefs and conduct varies from member to member. Some of the board members come out of the evangelical Protestant tradition. Though they are critical of the rigidity and lack of social responsibility that have sometimes characterized this tradition, they maintain its basic beliefs.

A variety of beliefs and religious practices is represented in the residents also. For the student accustomed to a more specific delineation of beliefs and behavior, this new freedom is painful. Even the minimum rules governing co-op behavior are based on the healthy functioning of the group rather than on religious principles. The Center staff feels this freedom is necessary for the student to discover those things most central to his faith. To experiment and even to fail is part of the process of maturing as a Christian.

Limitations

It has been observed that the Center tends to attract a certain kind of student—aggressive, independent, and somewhat adventuresome. Such students create an exciting group, but this leaves the Center open to the charge of serving "preprogrammed successes" and failing to reach those who might profit from the experience the most.

A second limitation is size. The house can accommodate ten or twelve students for an extended period of time (weekend experiences can involve many more). Future plans are to add one or two more residences as needs require. But as long as the Center maintains its philosophy of maximum interaction between students and staff, and as long as it remains independent of any one college or consortium and is limited in funding, it will probably remain relatively small.

A third limitation relates to finances. College budgets are extremely tight, and administrators are reluctant to part with tuition money for off-campus education, no matter how attractively innovative the project may appear. By relying solely on a percentage of tuition for faculty salaries, the Center is pursuing a course that continues to make it necessary for its staff to support themselves through part-time outside employment. In order to continue, supplemental financial support will have to be obtained.

This is the "skeleton" of the Urban Life Center story. To flesh it out would require talking personally to students who have spent time at the Center and who could describe their own personal alternation of turmoil and ecstasy, stretching and shrinking, apathy and discovery.

Notes to Chapter 9

1 None of these eight characteristics is in itself unique to the Urban Life Center, but *together* they distinguish this model of alternative education.

2 Anderson, Spring Arbor, Wheaton, Greenville, Adrian, Goshen, and Trinity Colleges and Taylor University have all had students at the Center for a term or more. Trinity Christian and Marion Colleges are in the process of developing a liaison with the Center. Students from all these schools have participated in short-term (weekend) experiences.

10: THE WESTMONT URBAN SEMESTER

by Ronald M. Enroth

In recent years colleges and universities have been engaged in a search for new directions. This quest is the result of financial pressures, periodic review of calendar and curricular matters, consideration of governance patterns, and the recognition for greater flexibility in the enterprise of education, especially with regard to innovative and experimental approaches to learning.

One of the most widely discussed new directions is the community-as-campus concept, the "college without walls" program, which seeks to relate traditional classroom learning to actual field experience or, in more extreme experiments, attempts completely to supplant conventional academic experience. The more radical of these efforts at undergraduate reform have abandoned the classrooom altogether, eliminated examinations, grades, and

RONALD M. ENROTH is chairman of the sociology department at Westmont College, Santa Barbara, California. He is a graduate of Houghton College; and has the Ph.D. from the University of Kentucky. A member of the American Sociological Association, American Scientific Association, and American Academy of Arts and Sciences, he is co-author of two books – **The Jesus People: Old Time Religion in the Age of Aquarius** *and* **The Gay Church,** *both published by Eerdmans.*

required courses, and in some instances have replaced professors with nondegree holding lay persons who supervise student field activities. More typical, however, are programs involving course work, internship or practicum, and independent study.

Students in Christian colleges also are demanding more relevant and meaningful educational experiences. Christian educators often use commencement exercises and academic convocations to remind their audiences that evangelical colleges seek to prepare young people for the complexities and uncertainties of modern urban society. This platform rhetoric, often expressed from a suburban or rural campus, seems a bit unrealistic when one surveys the curriculum of a typical Christian college. Few of them have pioneered in bold and innovative methodologies for coming to grips with the dynamic and much discussed "real world out there." Christian colleges and seminaries need to "step out of the half-world of white, Western, rural, peaceful and beautiful living to provide learning, participation and leadership experiences in the other half of the world that is non-white, non-western, non-Christian, urban, violent and ugly."[1]

Although some urbanologists have suggested that a new kind of national urban society is emerging which is increasingly independent of the city,[2] most observers agree that the large metropolitan center continues to function as the primary medium for transmitting the form, content, and ethos of contemporary culture. Despite the crucial role cities have played in history, many Americans—evangelicals included—have displayed a bias against urban life. Attitudes toward the "wicked city" are manifested in our political structure, in our art and literature, and perhaps even in the flight of the church from the inner city to the suburbs. "It is almost as if God had abandoned the city or never had anything to do with it."[3]

What is needed, as David McKenna has noted, is a change in attitude toward the city: "We need to realize that the city is still the rich resource for shaping men and determining the direction of the world."[4]

With the dual objectives of providing alternative and vital educational experiences for Christian college students and exposing them to the multiple needs and potential of the megalopolis, Westmont College launched a pilot program in San Francisco in spring 1971. The initial project has since developed into a full-fledged Urban Program involving twenty or thirty students a semester. Students have been placed in a living laboratory, a multi-faceted classroom without walls, and the results to date have been significant. The purpose of this essay is to describe this internship program, present the observations of some students who have participated in it, and suggest the potential this kind of program has for Christian higher education and, ultimately, the larger Christian and secular world.

Westmont is located in what its catalog describes as "one of the choice campus settings on the West Coast in the Montecito area of Santa Barbara."

Santa Barbara's "delightful climate and old Spanish culture add to its charm as a college setting." To this idyllic campus in affluent Southern California come hundreds of middle- and upper middle-class college students, not unlike their counterparts on Christian campuses across the country. For the most part they are WASPs—White, Anglo-Suburban-Puritans. Many drive sports cars and display the other familiar possessions of the privileged and the affluent. Some participate in the college's study abroad program and make the always fashionable pilgrimages to Europe and Great Britain.

More recently, however, Westmont students have made a journey to not-too-distant San Francisco, there to discover worlds previously quite unknown to them. As one student wrote, "I am certain that no one could continue to think in the same narrow groove after seeing people and situations that have been taboo in my sheltered, conservative, evangelical world. The students who experienced San Francisco now have a responsibility to those persons we encountered and to those in our own peer groups, families, and friends to communicate the problems, to break down the stereotypes, to help in small ways to bring the two 'worlds' together."

The Westmont Urban Program is designed to place mature students directly in responsible human-involvement situations in a variety of settings throughout San Francisco. The emphasis is on field learning, with the students serving on a volunteer basis in actual on-the-job situations. The total program consists of a minimum of twenty-four hours per week in field placements (usually six hours a day, four days a week) plus twice-weekly evening seminars in Urban Studies. Full academic credit is given for the field activity and the seminar, and most students are engaged in some form of independent study as well, usually a project related to their field placement or some other facet of the urban environment of interest to them. The Urban Studies Seminar serves as the integrating academic component of the program and provides the forum in which guest speakers and resource persons can enrich the learning experience of the whole group.

Students in the program must meet certain basic academic prerequisites. They are selected on the basis of emotional maturity, interest in the objectives of the program, and academic ability. Participants represent a variety of academic majors, although the behavioral sciences predominate. As the program continues to develop, it will undoubtedly become increasingly interdisciplinary in nature.

Students may select one or more field placements from among dozens of opportunities represented by diverse agencies and organizations throughout the city. Following an initial week of exposure to the possibilities, students are given specific agency assignments in view of their vocational goals, academic preparation, and interests. Some placements are specifically preprofessional in nature, providing invaluable experience prior to graduate study or other advanced training. Other placements provide more general learning experiences and might even be described as "exploratory" for those students whose vocational and career plans have not yet crystalized.

The diversity of field activities is one of the highlights of the program. Students gain experience in a variety of settings including social service agencies, consumer fraud units, mental health facilities, hospitals and clinics, minority group programs, legal assistance organizations, police and probation programs, tutoring programs, homes for delinquent girls, immigrant services, senior citizen programs, and a variety of ministries associated with churches and other religious organizations. When students informally interact at the end of the day over dinner, they frequently compare notes from that day's experiences "on the job." The opportunity that such discussion affords for informal learning is obvious.

The Urban Program is centered at Lone Mountain College, near downtown San Francisco. Westmont leases the necessary facilities from Lone Mountain, and two field instructors are housed with the students there. Faculty from the Santa Barbara campus are occasional visitors to the San Francisco site. Students are required to use public transportation to and from work. The use of private cars is greatly restricted so that students can more nearly approximate the situation of many city-dwellers who must rely exclusively on mass transit. Daily use of a bus or cable car is a new experience for many freeway-oriented college students. Waiting for a bus on a street corner can be an education in itself, as some students have discovered.

Much of the learning in an off-campus program is involvement learning, confrontation learning, participatory learning. It represents an attempt to effect a linkage between conventional classroom learning and the type of learning that occurs through encounter and real life involvement. Sometimes the element of serendipity is present in such experiential education—students discover that surprising things happen in cities. "The best learning happens by surprise; it is very different from the normal process of deliberate education. By watching young children happening to learn, it is still possible to sense what learning might be."[5]

Exposure to the many subcultures of San Francisco is meant to increase students' understanding of diverse life-styles and of the social, economic, and other forces affecting the lives of ethnic groups and members of the underclass of our society. All participants in the Program are required to keep a daily journal or log of their experiences. These entries often indicate that such learning is going on: "At the Golden Phoenix restaurant in Chinatown I felt just a tiny wave of what it is like to be black in white America, only I was white in Chinese America." "Today I found myself swimming in an ebony sea for the first time in my life."

The Urban Program has also sensitized students to the spiritual needs of the city. Some have had to confront and question the nature of their own commitment to Christ. Others have reevaluated their concept of the role of the church in the inner city. One student expressed it this way:

My experience in San Francisco has been invaluable. Not only have I been able to learn a lot about power structures, welfare policies, communities, and education, but I have been able to mesh it all together and somehow come out a stronger person because of it. I think all of us have really had to reevaluate where we are putting our "Christian" emphasis— on rhetoric or deed.

Another student described an experience that altered his thinking:

The Reverend Don Stuart [known as the "Night Minister of San Francisco"] took me down the streets of the Tenderloin at 3:00 in the morning and introduced me to young hustlers who were trying to pick up enough money from older men in order to survive. He showed me the pimps, and we talked to the prostitutes. I met Mark, a pusher, and Al, a pornographic art dealer, and a 15 year old girl who was "trying to find a date." We housed, fed, and listened to a score of vagabonds and transients and felt the sorrow of having to turn away an equal number.

Then the Night Minister turned and made a statement that made me re-think, re-make, and re-vitalize my entire concept of Christianity: "If these people don't know that I love them now, then no amount of verbalizing can ever do it." He was aiming, of course, at my evangelical heart; and he hit dead center.

Still another student expressed her concern for spiritual needs in this manner:

I am thankful I had the opportunity to go to San Francisco—to find what I thought sociology books over-exaggerate to be greatly under-exaggerated. When seen in real life, it hurts; not as bearable as a book or a film. But I am thankful for the pain too, because once felt, I know I can never pretend I do not know what is going on in the world outside Westmont's walls. . . . I learned about people and I learned about life—what it's really all about. As a Christian I have more than just an ear to listen with, a mouth to talk with, and a heart to feel with. I have a love to give. It is my obligation as Christ's witness to share his wonderful love with all people, but especially with the rejected and the neglected.

The Urban Program represents a highly successful model of extension of the traditional academic experience into a new and exciting dimension of living-learning. Perhaps more important, though, are the implications for evangelical action in the urban environment that such a program suggests. "When a 'new' scene is related to our interests, we may learn something. When it is compelling, we may enter it to change it by our actions or to join with others."[6]

Let us hope that experiences like this internship are so "compelling" that they result in decisions on the part of many young people to penetrate the areas of need—both as lay persons and as trained, sensitive professionals—in the urban centers of the nation and the world. Such programs provide opportunities for discovering vocational and Christian service options not always visible to the typical undergraduate student. They could easily become the springboard for increased participation by evangelicals in key leadership roles in American society. That we have come up short in such areas is obvious. "To control a city, you need to penetrate the educational system, the government, the labor force, the mass media, the minorities and the youth. Yet, these are the very areas from which we flee and then look back to indict them as 'evangelical wastelands.' "[7]

Christian colleges need to acknowledge what David McKenna has courageously asserted — that they are educating students to live in only half a world, that many sectors of contemporary society are closed to students in evangelical schools, and that steps must be taken to insure that students will have opportunity to learn about the conflicts of the other half of the world and to participate in those unexplored worlds as part of their collegiate experience.[8]

A brief word of caution is, however, in order. Evangelical colleges, in their attempt to keep pace with the changing educational scene, must not overlook the weaknesses associated with many so-called "experimental" endeavors. A recent report indicates that experimental programs represent a mixed bag. Some have been disasters in terms of academic content and integrity.[9] The Westmont experience has attested to the fact that innovative programs are not without their headaches. Such programs must be permitted to evolve, to adapt to unanticipated circumstances and events, to be refined and revised over a period of time.

Internship programs represent exciting opportunities for increased cooperation and interaction among Christian institutions of higher education. Perhaps through an organization such as the Christian College Consortium there can be developed an evangelical equivalent of the well-known Union for Experimenting Colleges and Universities, originator of UWW, the University Without Walls.

Notes to Chapter 10

1 David L. McKenna, "Educating for Half a World," *Eternity* (June 1968), p. 25.

2 Melvin M. Webber, "The Post-City Age," *Daedalus* (Fall 1968), p. 1092.

3 David L. McKenna, "Our Twentieth Century Target—A City," in *The Urban Crisis,* ed. David L. McKenna (Grand Rapids: Zondervan, 1969), p. 20.

4 *Ibid.*

5 Stephen Carr and Kevin Lynch, "Where Learning Happens," *Daedalus* (Fall 1968), p. 1277.

6 *Ibid.*

7 McKenna, *The Urban Crisis, loc. cit.,* p. 27.

8 McKenna, in *Eternity, loc. cit.,* p. 12.

9 Herbert London, "University Without Walls: Reform or Rip-Off?" *Saturday Review,* September 16, 1972, pp. 62-65.

11: THE THEOLOGICAL SEMINARY AND THE CITY

by Donald W. Dayton and F. Burton Nelson

A graduating seminary senior, asked to evaluate his theological education, responded that he felt well prepared — to meet the needs of the nineteenth-century church. While harsh, such a judgment is applicable to all too many

DONALD W. DAYTON and F. BURTON NELSON are on the staff of North Park Theological Seminary in Chicago. Dayton serves as director of Mellander Library, while pursuing graduate study in Christian theology and theological ethics at the University of Chicago Divinity School. A member of the Wesleyan Church, he has worked with inner-city ministries of various denominations in New York and New Haven, has served two years on the faculty of the Urban Ministries Program for Seminarians, and is the chairman of the commission of social action of the Christian Holiness Association. He is a regular contributor to **Christian Century, Christianity Today,** *and* **Library Journal.** *F. Burton Nelson holds the doctorate from Northwestern University in Christian ethics. He has served as a pastor of Evangelical Covenant churches in urban areas for more than a decade, and also served that denomination in various capacities relating to urban ministry. He has also been assistant director of Urban Ministries Program for Seminarians (UMPS) in Chicago.*

seminaries. Particularly in America, the intertwined forces of urbanization and industrialization are the great new social facts of the last century. Urbanization is perhaps the most inexorable social force at work in today's world. More than six of every ten Americans live in metropolitan areas with populations of more than 200,000, and this percentage is increasing. Yet, these facts are still to be fully faced by most seminaries.

The attitudes of ministers, especially Protestant ministers, toward the city have tended to be quite negative. As cities grew during the late nineteenth century, they wrote books whose titles reveal their concern: *The City: Its Sins and Sorrows* (1869) and *Evils of the City* (1898). At the 1900 General Conference of the Methodist Episcopal Church the bishops expressed themselves in the following words:

> The American city is a conglomerate of all races, nations, tongues, customs, and political ideas; and by this fact, and that of an easily obtainable citizenship, it is the menace of the American State and Church. To penetrate this alien mass by an evangelical religion is as difficult as it is imperative.

Today such statements are no longer openly expressed in seminary halls and classrooms, but one cannot avoid the impression that they lie very near to the surface. The seminary, however, has no choice but to face squarely the fact that the social context of ministry is and will increasingly be the city.

But the church and the seminary must go beyond recognizing urbanization as a fact of life and affirm that their Lord commissions them to be involved in the life of the city. It is clear from the Scriptures that the church has a special mission of proclamation and service to the poor and the oppressed. This concern is evident throughout the Bible, but particularly in the Psalms, the Prophets, and the Gospels (see, for example, Jesus' own statement of his mission, based on Isaiah, in Luke 4:18-19). It is in the cities that the poor and the oppressed are found in the greatest concentration.

It is liberating to discover that an anti-urban bias is more the product of American Protestantism and its cultural conditioning than of Scripture. In fact, the Bible is quite oriented to cities; though, of course, it does not anticipate the quantity and intensity of the problems of the modern industrialized city. One has only to consider the place of Jerusalem in the Old and New Testaments and the fact that for both the eschatological hope was expressed in terms of a heavenly *city,* the "New Jerusalem." Early Christianity was in many ways an urban phenomenon. Under Paul's leadership Christianity took its first roots in the great urban centers of the Roman Empire. Paul's epistles reveal that the world with which he dealt had striking parallels to our own in terms of pluralism, breakdown of morality and established patterns of life, skepticism, syncretism, and the like.

Raising "Urban Consciousness" in the Seminary

Unfortunately, strong psychological and sociological forces militate against the seminary's efforts to meet today's challenges. Seminaries, like church-related colleges, have often been founded in rural locations precisely to avoid the city and its problems. Those that have an urban location are often anxious to escape to more desirable surroundings.

Like the churches they serve, seminaries are powerfully bound to tradition and slow to change. This is particularly true among the more conservative seminaries where curriculum experimentation and change are often resisted as steps toward liberalism. Their faculty members, usually the product of long years of academic training in elite institutions, are locked into cushioned academic and professional life-styles and cut off from the real suffering and life-styles of urban inhabitants. The students are often the product of very narrow experiences. They are likely to have been carefully sheltered and nurtured in the church and its activities, are likely to have gone to a denominational college, and reflect in many other ways the efforts made to shield them from urban culture and its problems. Most seminary students grew up in middle-class homes (or, if not, are well on their way to establishing one) and lack understanding of other, especially lower, classes.

Finally, churches and denominational officials often bring forces to bear that prevent the seminarian from developing in ways that would enable him to minister effectively in the urban context. He is often subtly discouraged from creative experimentation and is pressured to be "success" and "growth" conscious rather than "mission" oriented.

These forces are extremely difficult to resist. The sustained effort required to counteract them must originate with the faculty and administration. Only carefully formulated goals and determined implementation of them will enable the seminary to keep on course. Faculty members should aggressively seek arenas of service that expose them to the needs of the city and to varieties of cultural and ethnic expression, both within and outside the church. Faculty members in all fields would profit from exposure to urban action training. Sabbaticals should be expended not only in research, travel, and mission service, but also in ways that permit the faculty member to serve and interact with the problems of urban life and various forms of social change activity.

Seminary students also need broader experience. Aristotle doubted whether moral philosophy could be taught to the young because they lack the one indispensable ingredient—sustained experience of life. There is a similar problem in theological education. Just as students are advised to seek variety in their pretheological undergraduate education, they should be encouraged to seek out varieties of experiences in work, cultural contact, travel, etc. The seminary can provide and encourage a greater variety of field work experiences. Students may learn much of value for future ministry by exposure to social service agencies, government programs and political campaigns, factories and labor unions. Seminaries should become more tolerant of the student who wishes to drop out of school for a while to gain wider experience in these areas. Such a step does not necessarily indicate a weak sense of call, and seminary is a much more convenient time for such experimentation than after entry into the pastorate.

Some seminaries attempt to build such experiences into the seminary program itself. Arrangements have been made for a "live-in" experience in prison that enables a student to understand correctional institutions from within. Students living in a slum tenement gain a much deeper understanding of ghetto life and its housing struggles. The Urban Ministries Program for Seminarians in Chicago uses the "rock-bottom plunge," developed by the Urban Training Center. The student is allowed $1.50 a day and sent out to live on the streets of Chicago for several days. He may beg, sleep overnight in a rescue mission (and thereby experience Christian charity from the underside), stay in a flophouse, try to find work, and in other ways experience the life of the outcast. Depending on the kindness and friendship of a skid row "bum" can give the seminary student a new self-understanding and awareness of other people. Such experiences can shake him loose from cultural patterns and free him for more genuine self-giving service.

Another way the seminary can broaden its own experience of the urban world and pluralistic society is self-consciously to cultivate racial, ethnic, and cultural diversity in both faculty and student body. This is much more difficult than it sounds. Most seminary constituencies are so culturally monolithic that it is difficult to find appropriate faculty and students to bring cultural diversity. And often, when such persons are found, they are so socialized to the patterns of that particular community that they only nominally contribute to cultural diversity. But it is important to have those in the seminary classroom whose different backgrounds enable them to call into question easy assumptions that are so often fallen into.

Adequate attention to the demands of urban mission will alter the curriculum of most seminaries, for seminarians need to understand the forces of urbanization and industrialization that shape the society in which they will serve. Urban sociology and history become important areas of study. If this sort of work is provided by arrangement with a local university, seminarians may pursue the questions with those who approach the same material from other perspectives. But just as important as expanding the curriculum into these areas is reshaping existing courses so that questions relating to urban mission may arise. Biblical studies might examine the biblical view of the city, or the Bible's concern for justice and the poor. Church history could include some attention to earlier efforts (the "Inner Mission," the Salvation Army, the "social gospel") to minister to the needs of the city. Theology classes might look at Christian patterns of speaking in terms of whether nineteenth-century cultural patterns are meaningful any longer in an urban context.

Some may react against such changes, arguing that the classical disciplines of biblical studies, history, and theology have already been diluted too much under the impact of the rise of the social sciences. Modifications to allow more awareness of the needs of urban society are often seen as just another step in the degeneration of "solid" theological education. But if such changes are carefully planned, precisely the opposite takes place. The classical studies are revitalized. Students come to the classical disciplines with their usual thought patterns shaken. New and existentially felt questions propel the student into Bible, history, and theology with new force. Theological education becomes an exciting process of search and reformulation rather than another period of arid classroom experience that must be endured before one can begin his ministry.

A final implication of this perspective for theological study is a reaffirmation of its character as "education" rather than "training." Too often, when the "professional" aspect of seminary work is emphasized, the impression conveyed is that such study is intended to impart the "skills" necessary for the "practice" of the ministry. The danger in this is that the student is being "trained" for a particular time-bound form of the ministry that may soon be obsolete. Theological education will always be concerned to some extent with the impartation of "skills," but it must also seek to reach beyond that for the development of the theological self. Students must learn to "do theology"—to be able to think theologically not only about themselves, but also about the variety of other persons and situations that they will encounter in today's changing and culturally diverse urbanized world.

Some Models

There is an increasing awareness, then, that seminary classroom work in the traditional vein must be supplemented by direct experience and involvement. To read about the black experience is one thing; to participate in the church's mission in a black ghetto situation is quite another. To amass a mountain of statistics about poverty in our national life today is one thing; to live on Skid Row and communicate with flesh and blood persons is very different.

In the past ten years this approach to theological education has been gathering momentum. Several models have emerged. One is the establishment of satellite campuses in metropolitan areas. A group of students lives on location in a large city for a month or longer, confronting the massive problems of urban society and working through the implications of these for the church and its ministry. Another approach is through field education and internship in urban churches, often for an entire year. The local congregation or agency becomes the context for the student's "doing theology," offering time and opportunity to reflect on what God is doing in the city. Or students may participate in specific programs located near the seminary. One example of this is tutoring in a literacy program for persons unable to speak English (estimated to be at least a half-million in Chicago). A fourth approach is working in industrial mission projects. The student works at a factory or shop job and periodically meets with peers and resource persons to share biblical and theological reflections.

One of the most creative approaches to the whole task of educating for urban ministry is the action training center. Over twenty centers have developed in the United States in recent years, among them the Urban Training Center for Christian Mission (UTC) in Chicago; Metropolitan Urban Service Training Facility (MUST) in New York; Center of Metropolitan Mission In-Service Training (COMMIT) in Los Angeles; Clergy Internship Program (CIP) in Cleveland; and the West Coast Urban Training Center in San Francisco.

In several of these programs relationships with seminaries have been established in order to provide resources for ministry in the city. The oldest is UTC. Started by eight denominations in 1963, UTC has pioneered in the sharpening of the church's ministry in the city. Among the persons who have benefited by the short- and long-term courses are numerous seminarians from across the country. The "plunge" has introduced them to Skid Row and other unique urban mission frontiers. Through seminars, "live-ins," work situations, and constant dialogue, the participants have emerged with a broadened conception of what the city is all about, together with a mode of theologizing about what has been heard and seen.

Another pioneering center has been MUST. Seminary students and others who have shared in this intense program have been given "a guided exposure to the structures and issues that confront the New York metropolitan area." Joint programs with Union Theological Seminary and New York Theological Seminary have enabled students to be involved in urban education, in the struggle for racial justice, and in day-to-day relationships with the poor.

Another model of seminary education for urban mission has been UMPS—the Urban Ministries Program for Seminarians in Chicago. This program was launched in 1970, under a grant from the Lilly Endowment, by seven evangelical seminaries. Dr. Gilbert James, an urban sociologist on the faculty of Asbury Theological Seminary (one of the seven), has been the major force behind its development. A base group of about thirty seminary students has participated each summer, the majority of them from the cooperating seminaries.

The program has consisted of four major phases:

1. The Plunge. Under the guidance of the Urban Training Center, the students spend several days and nights in selected areas — Skid Row, racially mixed areas, ethnic concentrations — with a mininum of money in the pocket.

2. Urban Studies. For several days and evenings, scattered throughout the eleven-week program, the students participate in concentrated urban studies. Included are lectures and diverse forms of input from urban specialists and informed persons on the meaning of ministry in the city. The titles of these sessions give a clue to their contents: "How to Read a City"; "The History of Chicago"; "A Black Perspective on Chicago"; "Politics in Chicago"; "How to Love the City"; "The Bible and the City." Throughout the summer, the students grapple with such books as Mike Royke's *The Autobiography of Malcolm X;* James Cone's *A Black Theology of Liberation;* George Webber's *God's Colony in Man's World;* Jacques Ellul's *The Meaning of the City;* Lyle Shaller's *The Change Agent;* and David Mains' *Full Circle: The Creative Church for Today's Society*

3. Ministry Assignments. Each student participates in an approved work assignment for almost two months, ordinarily living in the same neighborhood where he is working and relating to the needs of the community. In addition to churches in central city areas, work assignments have included such agencies as the Lawndale Mental Health Center, the Jane Addams Center, the Urban Life Center, Operation PUSH, and the Salvation Army Emergency Lodge.

4. Small Group Seminars. Students belong to small groups of seven or eight persons to consider new dimensions of ministry, to explore the church's relationship to the world, and to grow in self-understanding. These sessions become basic opportunities to ask probing theological and biblical questions in the context of the raw material fed to them daily in the urban setting.

Seminaries, the Urban Mission, and the Churches

It has become increasingly clear in the past decade that seminaries are responsible for more than the preparation of tomorrow's ministers. They are servants of the churches in providing services for the ordained ministry and the laity as well. If the urban mission of the church of Jesus Christ is to be taken seriously, seminaries must make resources for a more effective and relevant ministry available to congregations and clergymen. This is happening in part now, but responsible obedience to Christ calls for much more.

Continuing education for ministers and laymen is one must. Although many seminaries have seen the imperative of providing continuing education, financial resources and planning have for the most part been immensely limited. A pastor-in-residence program, which would enable a parish pastor to spend several weeks—preferably a whole term—on a seminary campus, is a possibility. The "retreat" for reflection and theological dialogue, already familiar in the seminary context, could be moved from its setting beside a beautiful lake amid sprawling elms, to the inner city—in the heart of glaring human need. Faculty members of seminaries and other resource persons could be enlisted as catalysts.

Seminaries could also provide the stimulus for lay-clergy conferences in which the leadership of the congregations in the metropolitan area are convened to celebrate God's mission in the city and to draft strategies of approach.

The demands of the urban mission are too great to be left in the hands of a minority of faculty members. The theologian, the church historian, the biblical scholar, the professor of pastoral care, the teacher of evangelism, the teacher of preaching, the Christian educator—all of these professionals have a part to play in the urbanizing of seminary education. The 1970s demand updating all across the spectrum of theological education.

12: DEVELOPING
EVANGELICAL MINORITY LEADERSHIP

by William E. Pannell

Solomon asserted that there was "nothing new under the sun," and while he didn't have modern educational theories in mind, his insight is applicable. He knew the limits of education (see Eccl. 1:12-17), but of course knew nothing of the modern educators' abundance of opinions about its nature or importance. Of course, he knew nothing about public education as Americans know it and certainly nothing of "Christian education" as evangelicals conceive and practice it.

Education is in trouble—at least if one is to believe those most responsible for the education industry. At no point is it more vulnerable to criticism than when it touches the lives of the so-called minority members of society. The issues at this point are complicated, but generally they focus on

WILLIAM E. PANNELL is an evangelist and vice president of Tom Skinner Associates, Inc. He is a graduate of Fort Wayne Bible College, and the author of **My Friend, The Enemy** *(Word Books), as well as numerous articles published in such periodicals as* **Eternity, His, The Other Side,** *and* **Journal of the American Scientific Association.** *Much of his involvement with Skinner Associates involves campus ministries directed at black university students in the southeast.*

the questions of quality education and equal opportunity for all in its pursuit.

Historically, Americans have paid lip-service to the notions that equality of opportunity is the essence of American life and that this equality is best displayed in our school system. This premise is still widely accepted. But something went awry rather early in the game; and, beset with problems ranging from educational philosophy to money and racism, the education of minority students has come up short in both quality and opportunity.

Recently the findings of James S. Coleman and Christopher Jencks have suggested that these historic concerns may be irrelevant anyhow. Their studies, the center of a raging storm in educational circles, seem to demonstrate that it makes little difference what is taught in schools. The determining factors bearing on quality in American society are found in society, not in the classroom. Family stability, the social and economic background of the family, the right connections, and just plain good luck are more determinative of quality education than pupil-to-teacher ratio and the racial mix at school.

So the battle rages. "New solutions" come off the presses daily. Meanwhile, the "small questions" persist and the little people are none the wiser about why Johnny can't read. Of course, it may be that whether he reads or not is irrelevant, since it seems that not too many educators can agree on what is worth reading. And if education is merely utilitarian, it may be argued that the age of technology may have made reading obsolete anyway. After all, machines do not need English Literature.

Training and Education

At issue is whether or not we intend to train minorities or educate them. (Of course, this is true of majority young people as well.) Robert Hutchins, former president of the University of Chicago, says of education that

it is a process of civilization. To this end it aims at intellectual development. It excludes indoctrination. Educated people may also be trained and trained people may be educated, but the two objects can be confused only at the risk of failure to achieve one or both. Since training is usually easier, and more easily measurable, than education, it is usually education that suffers from the effort to combine them.[1]

What minority leaders need is a first-rate education. This must be combined with training, but education is fundamental. In this sense, members of a minority group need the same tools of learning, the same exposure to the larger world of ideas and peoples, the same understanding of their cultural traditions as any other group. In fact, I would argue that leadership among minority people has the greater need.

The kind of education I mean is a general, broad-based exposure to the fundamentals of truth that have endured through the ages and come to form the basis of modern civilization. Only such an education can provide the perspective necessary to an understanding of the relationship that great ideas have with one another. Martin Luther King, Jr., found a relationship between Gandhi's perception of truth and Christ's, and he upset America's social life for all time. Learning, like life itself, is a study in relationships, and leaders in the minority culture must understand this connection. Their survival depends upon it.

This may sound elitist, but our entire educational system reeks with anti-intellectualism. This is a luxury that minority leaders cannot afford. And if that education is to be found in a "Christian School," the demand for quality is even greater, for the Christian's entire life is a matter of excellence. I am impressed by Will D. Campbell's understanding of the necessary scope of that excellence.

> Look for success. . . not in Christian Colleges because they call themselves Christian. Look for success in a student here, a "call to discipleship" yonder, an insight there from a teacher which makes it impossible to "study" war or racism or the New Testament and come away the same person, impossible to study physics or chemistry and not dedicate one's career to opposing their enslavement to the horrors of twentieth-century technological inhumanity, impossible to study money and banking and come away lighthearted at what our economics have done to those who originally had property rights to the land which supports us so richly, and to those whom we purchased as chattel and continue to treat as such. Look for success not where "Christ," but a Socratic Christian, is in the classroom — that is a teacher who will put *everything* under question and accept nothing at face value (especially himself and his discipline), not for the hell of it or because he is possessed of a demon, but because the cross and the resurrection put everything under question yesterday, today, forever. *Everything.*[2]

The realities of minority-majority relations in America suggest that two fundamental questions must be raised if minority education is to succeed: What kind of leadership is needed as defined by minority needs, and in what kind of learning situation can this leadership be developed best?

What Kind of Leadership?

There must be a leadership that is sophisticated in its understanding of the relationship between culture and biblical principles. Can a person be poor, for instance, and still be a Christian, or are conditions of poverty an indication that a person is in violation of an ethic that requires him to prosper in order to be certified in the kingdom? Or does one have to be middle-class in order to be significant? There must be a greater exposure to the insights supplied by cultural anthropology, so that minority leaders can more accurately perceive the distinctives between cultures in America. The myth of the melting pot must be exploded if ethnic groups are to accept themselves as valid. This in turn will allow a greater freedom to respect other groups.

There must also be leadership that understands the psychological relationship between inadequate self-esteem and powerlessness; men and women who understand that in America the name of the game is power in both human relationships and in politics and economics; both intra-culturally and cross-culturally. These people must also be able to deal with this reality in theological perspective.

Minorities also need leadership that understands how the American political system really works. We must produce leaders trained in law and political science whose roots are still in the neighborhood. We need Christian men and women who not only know corporate law, but who also know how to deal with crooked cops, realtors, and the board of education. We need Christian leaders who know the value of voter registration drives and how to do them.

Since minorities suffer disproportionate medical needs, there is a great need for leadership that could bring health care to neighborhoods in the name of the Great Physician. Only 229 blacks were graduated from America's 108 medical schools in 1972. There is only one black doctor per 2,800 blacks compared to five white doctors per 2,800 whites. The full range of health care needs cries out for Christian participation. Minority peoples need something comparable to medical missionaries here at home, especially in our major urban centers.

Then, of course, there is still the need for church-related leadership. The black community, like its white counterpart in the South, is Christ-haunted, to borrow from Flannery O'Connor. The pastor is still the center of the religious establishment and generally wields power out of all proportion to his skill in many areas of community life. Because he is spread so thin, and because of the nature of the system in which he operates, he frequently succumbs to the secularizing tendencies of society. To counter these tendencies, leadership for the churches in minority cultures must be more theologically sophisticated than ever. They need to be thoroughly familiar with the Scriptures and must know how to preach the Word intelligibly. But their training must not divorce them from the feel of their culture. Their preaching must be faithful to the text of Scripture and the texture of the culture. Hence, a good exposure to social psychology and cultural anthropology might prove beneficial alongside theological perspectives. Spiritual leadership in the context of the church must be spiritual in nature. Much more emphasis must be given to the cultivation of the holy life.

The tendency of minority leadership is simply to emulate the majority style and practice. It is evident that this style is largely bankrupt of spiritual integrity. Wholesome self-determination in the social arena must be supported by spiritual leadership that refuses to imitate decadent majority standards of religious life.

The list of minority needs is endless, and the initial question is still unanswered. I have only set forth what form leadership will take; in what areas it will operate. What it *is,* I have not yet stated—and for good reason. There seems to be no clear answer to the question. Is leadership an acquired skill or an accident of genetics, a quality conferred at birth? These are important questions, which are not readily or definitively answerable. A study of the literature that attempts to record recent American political life reveals that while the country has leaders, they do not always lead. Or they do not lead rightly. Simply to mention Vietnam or Watergate is to cite the ultimate expressions of our leadership dilemma.

Further indications of this search for definition is the current rash of management seminars sponsored by the evangelical church and denominational agencies. Led by the Harvard Business School and such stellar organizations as the American Management Association, a growing number of religious executives are being exposed to the disciplines of leadership responsibilities. The evangelical, who usually arrives a bit late, has finally caught on. Crippled for years by the inability of strong charismatic leaders to manage their leadership, evangelical organizations are now making management training a must for their executives. Edward Dayton, Director of Missions Advanced Research and Communications Center (MARC), states that "there exists a need for a continuous training for the leadership of Christian organizations."

What Is the Best Training Ground?

Significantly, this kind of training is happening outside established evangelical schools. Quite apart from its content, this factor brings up a second important question related to minority training: In what setting can this talent be trained best? My answer to this question is tentative at best, but reflects much thought and many hours of conversation with minority students at a good sampling of existing Christian colleges and seminaries. I have concluded that evangelical schools as they now exist are inadequate to train minority leaders effectively.

In the first place, these schools are not committed to train minority leaders. They represent middle- to upper-middle-class subcultural values and life-styles to which most minority members cannot or choose not to relate. Furthermore, their locations reflect one aspect of this subcultural mindset; they are either in the suburbs or nearby rural areas. Their mood is anti-city, a historic middle-class attitude. Too, evangelical theology as taught in these schools seems inadequate to the urban task. No one has as yet articulated a theological perspective on the city that would equip evangelicals to operate there as wily serpents. Minorities, whose life-style has been honed to razor-sharp sensitivities through exposure to urban realities, tend to view the atmosphere of an evangelical campus as make-believe, where make-believe whites try to absorb a make-believe theology for a fantasy world.

Of even greater importance is the question as to just how Christian these "Christian Schools" are. Will D. Campbell puts this issue in sharp and painful focus when discussing the relationship between education and social reform.

Charging that education as a whole has sold out to the "system," Campbell asks:

> Where are the Christian Colleges in all of this? Where they have always been, led by Caesar and his educational institutions and bureaucracies, except that in most cases we were early to segregate racially, in order to be relevant to our people, and late to desegregate because we had to preserve "unity"; and because of the strength of our conviction that our intentions are of the highest and purest quality, we are the last to understand that integration is, in fact, another way to "control" them.[3]

This is hard to take, but this is precisely the way minorities view the scene. Campbell continues on target:

> Whom does the Christian college serve? Whom do Caesar's colleges serve? The same people and precious few others. Certainly not the victims of Caesar's educational Gestapos, for these are "high risk." . . . For which among the present-day colleges has been more anxious about the dodges and deceits called "quality education" and "academic excellence" than the Christian liberal arts college? Which among them has been more anxious about accreditation than the Christian liberal arts college, even though it meant a service to Caesar and a denial of service to Christ? Which among the colleges has ignored more effectively than the Christian liberal arts college the stranger lying bloody in the ditch (cf. Luke 10:29ff.), the victim of the very educational system which now denies him? . . . Our Christian colleges speak for mammon, not for God. . . . Our Christian colleges serve themselves and not Christ when they explain in the most pained tones that they have only so "many" resources and that these must be allocated on the basis of priorities. And what and who are the priorities? Ourselves. Middle and upper income Christian Americans. And these are the priorities set by Caesar and not by Christ.[4]

Strong denials would be forthcoming from the leaders of such Christian schools, but the fact is that this is precisely the way these places are perceived and experienced by minorities. These schools exist for "our own" and are intended to keep "our own" system — Christian or political — intact. Rather than being agents of social change, they are conservative of things as they have been. The atmosphere is psychologically crippling for many minorities also, making it difficult for them to be themselves. "And what about the black man's blackness, the red man's redness, etc., in education today? It is a 'problem' that requires a solution: those who are different because of skin color or 'cultural deprivation' are made into 'white' in public institutions under the rubric of democracy, in Christian institutions under the rubric of brotherhood."[5]

In spite of these negative issues — and they are real issues — there are some major advantages in such institutions. They still offer much that can be helpful to minority students. This is especially true of the Bible departments. Since most students are biblically illiterate, this contribution is of fundamental importance. Furthermore, it is of great importance that such schools be exposed to varied ethnic and cultural inputs. White young people are culturally deprived and so are white faculty members and administrators. The presence of minority persons could be the cultural salvation of these places.

One possibility in relation to Christian liberal arts colleges is a sophisticated system of satellite schools where minority students can train in their own environment. These should be related to the parent school in such a way as to require that some part of the student's training be spent on the parent site. This is important since there is much cultural overlap in American society which calls for a leadership which is at home cross-culturally. Christian discipleship requires of students that they seek to be agents of reconciliation, and college is a good place to begin. Even if the place is called Christian.

Perhaps a better model would be that of a Christian training center in close proximity to a major secular university. This would certainly allow for a much more relaxed social context and provide a sharper focus for Christian discipleship. Removed from the cultural entrapment of evangelical religion, minority leaders could more effectively grapple with the theological issues that bear directly on this survival situation. Furthermore, such students could continue to live in their own communities, a factor crucial to the maintenance of social contact. Often a prolonged absence from one's "neighborhood" results in a different re-entry and a consequent frustration in communication.

The purpose of such a Christian center would be to strengthen the believers in the biblical perspectives related to the kingdom of God, to develop rationale and strategies for evangelism, to sharpen perspectives on community needs from within the community, and to develop strategies to meet those needs.

Course work toward a degree would be taken at the university, with theological studies at the center. Faculty for the latter could be supplied by local pastors and laymen augmented by visiting professors from accredited schools of theology. Additional perspectives on community issues could be supplied by guest lecturers from a broad spectrum within the area.

Specificity in programming is difficult. We do not have many good models. What we need is research by top-flight Christian scholars that will inform our schools about specific minority leadership needs and how they can best be met. It may be, for instance, that a school of mission like that at Fuller Theological Seminary could provide insight from its extensive research on training methods abroad.[6] Another possibility is an urban center on the order of the successful learning center at L'Abri in Switzerland. The advantage of this model is the potential for building a model of Christian *koinonia* as a necessary antidote to the impersonality of the urban culture. This approach could also tie the course content with already available curricula of the university or a nearby Christian college.

Whatever alternative is selected, minority training must provide leaders who are "at home" with themselves; people who are satisfied with God's choice of them as they are; people who see their culture for what it is under the scrutiny of God's word — neither better nor worse than anyone else's. This training would also give students the tools with which to deal with social problems, domestic, educational, political, and the like. It would provide a way of looking at the world and being able, in that expanded context, to trace those principles that affirm man's common humanity.

Notes to Chapter 12

1 Robert M. Hutchins, "The Schools Must Stay," *The Center Magazine,* Jan.-Feb. 1973, p. 16.

2 Will D. Campbell, *The Failure and the Hope, Essays of Southern Churchmen* (Grand Rapids: Eerdmans, 1972), p. 258.

3 *Ibid.,* pp. 252f.

4 *Ibid.,* p. 253.

5 *Ibid.,* p. 251.

6 Ralph R. Covell and C. Peter Wagner, *An Extension Seminary Primer* (South Pasadena, Cal.: William Carey Library, 1971). This is merely an introduction to training alternatives. Its value is that it assists North Americans in under-standing the nature of cross-cultural problems. Of special interest is Chapter 14 on the Third World. I perceive similar objections would be raised among minorities here if training-education were perceived as below accepted academic standards.

PART FIVE:
THE CHURCH IN THE URBAN COMMUNITY —
PERSPECTIVES AND CHALLENGES

INTRODUCTION

Just as the individual is affected by his surrounding culture, so the urban church is influenced by the community in which it resides. Decisions about methods of outreach and forms of worship are inevitably affected by the urban context. Where people have a diversity of backgrounds, and where the very human composition is constantly changing, is it enough to assure ourselves that since we have one God and one message, we need one method to get it across?

This section deals with four special concerns of the urban church— changing neighborhoods; multi-cultural ministry; urban community; and urban evangelism.

Changing Neighborhoods: Renewal or Retreat?
Arthur Whitaker points out the extent of the exodus by white evangelicals from the city in the past twenty years, while Larry Krause describes the difficulties and decisions faced by one church that decided to stay even though its constituency was moving out and its surrounding neighborhood was changing racially, socially, and economically.

Typically, a church's decision to leave the city is preceded by the move

131

of its members from the church neighborhood. Affluence and mobility make it possible for people to move to "better" areas, farther and farther away from the urban center. At first most members maintain loyalty to the church in the city, but the long drive begins to wear after a while. With a continuing energy shortage, this situation will no doubt be aggravated. If enough members move out, sentiment builds for moving "our" church out where the members live rather than driving all that way. The new housing developments that characterize many suburbs promise opportunity for further growth, so the church's "outreach" can continue.

In this apparently reasonable line of argument, a few questions never get asked. Why did the members move out in the first place? Surely not to find "wide open spaces"—real estate developers have taken care of that. Why the obvious correlation between the church's moving and the coming of those of a different race to the neighborhood? And what about the notion that this is "our" church, so it ought to move out to where "we" live? Does the church have a ministry to the setting in which it is placed, or is it to focus totally on the desires of its members? Are the churches simply reflecting a lack of such community ministry and the triumph of fear when they excuse their move because "some windows keep getting smashed"? Do we really believe that "God did not give us a spirit of timidity but a spirit of power and love and self-control" (II Tim. 1:7)?

These questions are most relevant to white congregations, but the vacuums created for the black middle class make it likely that they too must ask similar questions. Should they move or stay and find new ways to minister to those in the poorer sections of the city?

The church that decides to stay in the city will find itself depending on God in new ways. It will find itself asking God for wisdom (James 1:5) rather than just doing things the habitual way. Its very existence and effectiveness will depend not only on personal piety but on a sense of community that leads believers to encourage each other and work together. Not all churches that remain in the city are automatically renewed and dynamic; not all churches that move out are not. If the remaining church is serious about its mission, as it is more likely to be because of the choices it faces and the complex decisions it makes, it will become renewed. The retreating church frequently seems to lack the necessary faith for such genuine renewal, although it may have the resources and input of enough solid saints to field an active program.

The church whose congregation is largely commuter and whose outreach into its neighborhood is small or nonexistent has at least four options. It may decide to remain and minister to its constituency without community outreach. It may add some members to the church, but those added will be of similar racial and economic backgrounds, and if there is no other evangelical body in the community, the surrounding area is left essentially devoid of the gospel. A second option is to try various outreach programs while retaining the basic orientation to the commuters. This may work well for a while, but if Larry Krause's analysis is correct the commuters will soon start dropping out because of the emphasis on the community, especially if the people of the community differ from those in the initial body. On the other hand, it might be possible to find enough communality of style to develop a truly heterogeneous congregation. Third, the church may decide to move and simply sell its property. An evangelical congregation would surely be responsible to insure that the buying church is a genuinely evangelical body that can minister to the people of the community. It it can't insure this, it might develop a "mission" church in cooperation with remaining evangelicals. The final option is perhaps the most radical: significant numbers of the congregation can decide to move back into the area and learn to identify with, communicate with, be friends with, and relate Christ neighbor to neighbor.

The church that remains in a changing neighborhood will undoubtedly have to find new ways to minister, and will have to take steps to become a truly community, or neighborhood, church. How much it needs to change will depend on how similar the new members of the community, if racially different, are in educational or economic backgrounds. In any case, different ethnic groups have different perspectives and have learned to meet their own needs in different ways. These perspectives, patterns of need, styles of expression, and preferences must be seriously assessed by any church that moves from relative homogeneity to heterogeneity (whether the heterogeneity being introduced is racial, cultural, economic, or educational).[1]

Multi-cultural Ministry: Concepts of the Church

Missions strategist Donald McGavran emphasizes homogeneity as an important means of facilitating church growth.[2] The urban church, however, will find, if it seeks to reach out, that it is faced with a great deal of heterogeneity. In this section Larry Krause and Frank Leeds provide valuable insights into how a church can cope with diversity among its members. Both write from the perspective of multi-ethnic, multi-racial congregations that have attempted to find some unifying intracongregational experiences. Krause is very sensitive to social and psychological factors important to individual identity and security in his argument for the homogeneous church. Leeds shows an equally keen sense of psychological and anthropological awareness, combining it with hopefulness, in arguing for a pluralistic church. Krause's congregation is one historically more ethnic (though he indicates that the homogeneity need not be along ethnic lines).

It is probable that Leeds and Krause are not as far apart as they initially seem. Both point to the need for the urban church to be experimental enough to develop an inner community that satisfies the spiritual, psychological and cultural needs of the members. This is a critical point of concern for urban ministry. For while providing the inner community of support, the church is also faced with the command to disciple and with a surrounding heterogeneous urban community.

Much more analysis and clarification need to be conducted to find the critical, defining points at which different styles of support, expression, and communication are necessary to meet member needs. It is very likely, for example, that a racially diverse congregation, relatively similar in economic and educational backgrounds, may be very mutually satisfied. At this point the congregation would be racially heterogeneous, but culturally homogeneous.[3]

To what extent does difference in primary language erect an insurmountable barrier for the simultaneous meeting of spiritual/personal needs? At how many critical social-psychological points can members vary and still have their spiritual needs met in one congregation? To simply say that in Christ we are all one and we don't need to consider culture would seem to neglect the spiritual and social-psychological unity of the person.

The goal, never to be lost sight of, is the production of a fellowship of believers who understand themselves and those in the surrounding community, who are flexible and innovative, and who can fashion a meeting place where unity flourishes in diversity.

Understanding Urban Community

It is imperative for the urban "missionary" to understand the urban community. Arthur Whitaker brings out several of its characteristics as he considers differences in the conceptions of time, the nature of the family, and the transience of urban community.

The urban community is constantly changing. People move; highways wipe out a small neighborhood; buildings are erected and then torn down. I learned quickly as superintendent of an inner-city Sunday School that if I didn't want to spend a fortune on new address cards, I would have to put addresses in pencil. Stable relationships such as are essential to support and encourage mature Christian living are frequently impossible. Alternative inter-church support systems must be developed.

As Whitaker points out, the difference in family constellations in an urban setting can initially be confusing, but the confusion has to be mastered if broken and single parent families are to be met with the relevant gospel.

In addition, we need to learn about what is rewarding and interesting to each person, to develop curricula and preach sermons that are perceived as pertinent to the city-dweller. For many city-dwellers life revolves around action; and words may do little more than bore. Awareness of that will force us to become flexible and experimental in the church. As long as the church remains dynamic and reaches into the community it will not be able to get set in its ways.

For many city-dwellers, a sense of worthlessness is ingrained. The way they have been treated at school or by prospective employers, their dealings with bureaucrats and civic officials lead many city-dwellers to think that they can make no difference anyway. This may result in difficulty for the church that tries to motivate its members to take positions of responsibility or leadership. Similarly, thousands of people in the city, especially the elderly or infirm, live lonely and isolated lives. The church has a major opportunity to incarnate Christ's love to these. Simple, practical steps could be taken to reach out to these people.

The urban church is a place where the individual must be important. In the midst of anonymity and fragmentation and powerlessness, the urban church has the ministry to provide a place of belonging and importance. A community of interdependent, loving, communicating, caring Christians can be one of the most attractive places in the city for all of those feeling the isolation of urban life.

In understanding these features of urban life, and in providing a many-faceted witness for Christ through the ministry of compassion, the urban church will be looked to for leadership by the urban community. It can truly become a provider of life both in the directions it charts for the community and in its sharing of Christ with individuals.

Urban Evangelism: A Credible Witness

In the concluding chapter of this section, E. V. Hill examines some of the various ways the salvation message of Christ can be communicated most effectively to the city-dweller.

Hill stresses adequate training and commissioning of persons from neighborhoods. Through a description of the World Christian Training Center (WCTC) program in Watts, he provokes us to consider the fruitful coordination of personal evangelism, a training program, and the ministry of the local church.

Perhaps more than anywhere else, the central city calls for Christians to evangelize through action as well as verbal proclamation. Witnessing must not be stereotyped and limited. We must be willing to demonstrate Christ in lives of compassion and know how to articulate the gospel. Unless we are able to identify sufficiently with people to understand their needs and to communicate in forms that speak to them, I am afraid the gospel will fall on deaf ears. This is one of the exciting aspects of the WCTC program—people who are neighbors share neighbor to neighbor.

In its concern for ministering to the whole person, the urban church must not overlook its responsibility to face people directly with their spiritual destiny. The urban evangelical must be bold yet discerning; evangelistic but not compulsive about a form of evangelism; concerned about a person's eternal destiny but equally concerned about his earthly experience. The task is to reconcile men with God, and then men with men.

Notes to Part Five: Introduction

1 Historically the church has been a community institution and has been relevant to those around it. Those around it have generally been highly similar. With the mobile society this is no longer true, and herein lies the problem with many white churches who finally decide to move out. It is easier to choose a church of similar persons than it is to stay in a community that is becoming more diverse and fashion a cross-cultural outreach. The most frequent decision has been to move the church into a community with people around it that are similar to those in the church, and to where many of the original members have moved. The church then has lost the geographical mission (God called it to that area) and becomes a church of cultural mission (if the members move the church moves).

2 Donald McGavran, *Understanding Church Growth* (Grand Rapids: William B. Eerdmans, 1969).

3 For a much needed beginning discussion of the question of integration in the church as a complex spiritual, racial and cultural problem see *The Other Side,* January-February 1974. The focus in this issue is primarily racial, but I would hope that cultural differences, associated with race or not, might be more intensively examined by urban evangelicals in the future.

13: LESSONS FROM AN URBAN CHURCH
IN TRANSITION
by Larry Krause

The two main hallmarks of our era, says Harvey Cox, are the rise of urban civilization and the collapse of traditional religion.[1] No doubt these two realities, urbanization and secularization, are setting in motion forces that create some of the most serious challenges the Christian church has ever faced. The institutional structures and the theological formulations of the church are being confronted with the contemporary world's imposing demand, "Adapt or perish!"

Change is an essential dimension of reality. That the church has existed for nearly twenty centuries is evidence of its ability to make the adjustments demanded by the continuing process of life and history. Our times are no different. If the church is to survive, it must adapt to the new realities of urbanization and secularization.

LARRY KRAUSE is special director of information at American Baptist Seminary of the West in Covina, California. He is a graduate of Westmont College, and holds the master's degree in religious studies from the American Baptist Seminary of the West. For two years he was director of urban ministries at First Covenant Church, which is located in downtown Los Angeles.

But if this transition is inevitable, it is no less traumatic. There are two reasons for this. First, although change is not new to the church, the accelerated rates of change in our day are confronting it (and all of society) with what Alvin Toffler calls "a massive adaptational breakdown."[2] The shattering stress and disorientation induced by subjecting individuals and institutions to too much change in too short a time is what Toffler calls "future shock." Second, as a religious institution, the church plays a role in society of preserving tradition and affirming the common culture. In our day the church's adaptational stress is compounded by a growing identity crisis. Confronted by the challenges of urbanization and secularization, it must come to terms with what its role will be in the new secular urban world which is emerging: will it affirm it, or will it resist it?

One of the most crucial arenas of this confrontation is the local church, especially the local church in the heart of the modern metropolis. Nowhere else do the radical implications of urbanization and secularization come to bear so forcefully on the church. The local congregation in the midst of the urban scene faces two crucial sets of questions: (1) what institutional forms can it create to reach its urban community? and (2) how can it adapt and deliver its message to urban secular man while staying true to that message?

This essay will focus on the experience of one local congregation (we shall call it Central City Church) in the heart of a large American metropolis. From its encounter with the secular city come two lessons helpful for the church in general and for other local urban congregations in particular. In light of these lessons we shall consider the local church and its role in the city.

The first lesson is that, because the identity of individuals is socially and culturally fashioned, most persons will not voluntarily join a religious fellowship unless that fellowship affirms their personal and social identity. The second lesson is that most people join a congregation *primarily* to have their own personal needs met; and unless their needs are met, they are not likely to commit themselves to serving others.

Personal Identity and Religious Fellowship

Central City Church was founded in the late nineteenth-century by Europeans who came to the United States as part of the century of European immigration that ended substantially with World War I. The primary need of these new arrivals was getting economically established in the new culture. However, it was important to have a secure base from which to move into the new society. Therefore, according to Will Herberg, a major concern was the preservation of their wonted way of life—and American cities saw the emergence of the ethnic neighborhoods.[3] This attempt to anchor their identity was facilitated by transplanting their churches. The ethnic churches were established not only to worship God, but also to provide a meaningful center of life. They functioned as places for social fellowship and personal identity for a people living in a strange cultural context.

Few ethnics joined "American" churches, for they could not identify sufficiently with their American brothers-in-Christ, and American Christians in turn ignored or rejected their ethnic brothers both by refusing to allow foreign language subdivisions in their churches, and by moving out to new neighborhoods as the newcomers moved into the old ones.

Central City Church remained strictly an ethnic church for over forty years, when its European language finally gave way to English. However, because the members were white northern Europeans, their identities were gradually being "Americanized," a process that particularly affected their children. In the 1930s and 1940s Central City Church became a white, middle-class American church, and its ministry affirmed the members in that new identity. To be sure, their ethnic heritage was not forgotten, but the church reflected the new social and cultural context more than it did the transplanted ethnic culture of its first generation.

The next two decades illustrated even more dramatically the close relationship between socially and culturally oriented personal identity and religious fellowship. During the 1950s and 1960s the community around the church began to change drastically. Increasing industrialization brought a flood of nonwhite and lower-class immigrants into the neighborhood around Central City Church. White middle-class Americans — including many members of Central City Church — moved to the suburbs. Gibson Winter summarizes this phenomenon:

> The story of the metropolitan churches from 1870 to 1950 is the record of a desperate struggle for survival in the midst of rapid change. The average tenure of Protestant churches during this period was slightly over a score of years. The metropolitan struggle for homogeneous neighborhoods infected the churches so that the intrusion of outsiders usually meant the collapse of both the neighborhood and the local religious groups.[4]

Many churches left the central city. Some folded. But a number of factors made it possible for Central City Church to remain relatively strong even in the middle and later sixties. There was still a significant number of members whose identity was deeply rooted in the church and its ethnic traditions. By and large these were older members; but due to the intricate network of family relationships that evolved with two generations of inner-group marrying, many young families remained tied to the congregation. This made it possible for the church to maintain a program for the whole family. Another important factor was that the church was located just a block away from an exit ramp off the main central city freeway, making access to the church relatively easy.

Even so, the location of the church began to have its effect. For younger families, activities were increasing in their suburban communities, and the trips downtown for the church programs became more arduous. Besides, in many suburban communities there were thriving churches to which Central City Church had given birth. This made for an easy transition to new congregations where old friends and relatives already attended. As the children became teenagers, parents felt that involvement in a local church was especially important. Thus, more and more families left the church. This resulted in a diminishing in both size and fervor of the programs of the church — which led in turn to more families leaving, thus creating a downward spiral of the congregation.

It is important to note that during this whole period the life of the church revolved around its homogeneous, white middle-class congregation. No significant efforts were made to draw in new members from the lower-class, racially mixed community in which it was located. However, when a congregation begins to diminish in size, it begins to think about reversing this trend and trying to recruit new members. The logical area for recruitment, of course, is the immediate neighborhood. So, in the mid-1960s Central City Church began to look outward into its local community. The most significant development of its local outreach, the forming of a Latin American congregation, once again illustrates the fundamental truth of our first lesson.

After a neighborhood analysis, the church discovered that many of the people in its immediate community had recently immigrated from Central and South America. The pastoral staff encouraged the congregation to become a servant church, to reach out and minister to these needy newcomers—for had not their ancestors been in the same situation just two generations before? From pulpit and lectern to talk sessions and the printed page, the congregation was called to reflect the *diversity in unity* implied in the New Testament's image of the body of Christ. In face of the temptation to follow the exodus to the suburbs the church was challenged to stay and extend God's redemptive power where it was. The congregation of Central City Church voted to develop an outreach to the Latin Americans in its community. They added to the pastoral staff a former missionary to Bolivia, who began immediately to develop a Latin congregation. This congregation grew from a first Sunday attendance of three to more than 250 in a half dozen years.

The Latin congregation at Central City Church is a separate and essentially autonomous congregation, and there is very little fellowship between it and the Anglo congregation. This is because there is very little base for identification between the groups. The language barrier is obvious, but even those who are bilingual identify and fellowship with their own group. Anglo identity resides in the ethos of its white middle-class culture, and the concerns of these members are the ideals, values, and happenings of that culture. For the Latins, on the other hand, identity is anchored in the traditions and folkways of their homeland. Their concern is to maintain a stable sense of identity in the face of culture-shock and disorientation.

The Latin congregation functions for the local Latin community in much the same way as the original congregation functioned for the European ethnic community three-quarters of a century earlier. The Latins come to church not only to worship God, but also because the church has become a meaningful center for their lives. In their involvement they are meeting religious, social, and personal identity needs. They are finding a security from which they can meaningfully affirm and become involved in the new urban culture of which they are a part.

These very human concerns of personal identity and group membership are crucial realities that the church must recognize, for religious experience and identity are centrally intertwined. It is the church that helps a person to comprehend life in terms of ultimate reality, but to do this it must meet the person where he is—or more to the point, where he sees himself to be. It is the church that provides channels by which an individual can come into a relationship with that ultimate reality. The church must recognize that people have difficulty in fellowshipping with persons of widely differing social and cultural identities. Even in the church, in which a person's allegiance is seen to be to one Lord and where he is called to identify with one kingdom, social and cultural identity is, with few individual exceptions, still the fundamental basis for fellowship and brotherhood.

Personal Need and Religious Fellowship

The second lesson of the experience of Central City Church is that most people join a congregation primarily to have their own personal needs met, and if those needs are not met they are not likely to commit themselves to serving others. This lesson is vividly illustrated by the Central City Church's effort to develop three outreach ministries in addition to the formation of the Latin congregation.

Other than providing transportation, emergency food, and used clothing and furniture, members of Central City Church had little personal involvement in the Latin ministry. But the new message of the pastoral staff—that the call of Christ is to discipleship and servanthood, not merely to church attendance— began to affect some of the members of the church. They looked further into the local community to see what other needs might be met. During the next few years they developed ministries to young people, the aged, and to the non-English-speaking immigrants.

Thus, in a matter of a few short years a church that had ignored its community for three decades had now turned to that community and was actively engaged with it on four separate fronts. A youth ministry was developed, and a part-time director engaged to lead it. In addition, a number of the members formed a ministry group to back up the youth ministry by meeting the needs of the families of these young people. The church joined an ecumenical cluster of churches in the central city to fashion an outreach to the thousands of lonely aged in the downtown area. Some of the members volunteered their services for visitation, counseling, and nutrition programs. Finally, a number of the members in the church formed a literacy center to teach English as a second language to the members of the Latin congregation and to the residents of the community. There was great fervor and excitement over the new ministries. The church seemed to have a new purpose and was developing a new image as a central city mission church. New ministries were in the planning stage, and an effort was made to recruit volunteers from other churches in the suburbs to help in extending God's redemptive power to the people of the central city.

In the midst of all this fervor, however, two significant developments were in process. First, a number of persons were leaving the church because of its growing "social activism." In the initial stages there was definite controversy and discontent over the new ventures, and many families left the church. Even after things had stabilized, there were still some, less vocal in their dissent, who just left unobtrusively.

But what became more obvious as time went on was that some were leaving not because they objected to the church's outreach to the community as such, but because they felt that the church no longer offered anything for them — that their own personal needs were not being met. Indeed, there developed a growing resentment among many of the more prominent members, who felt that the central city concerns were being given precedence, and that their needs were being neglected.

It became quite evident that the majority of the members could not personally identify with the new program. Indeed, a statistical survey revealed that fewer than twenty percent of the members were active in community ministries, although another twenty percent could be counted on as vocal supporters of these ministries. In other words, a majority of the members saw this community outreach as a diversion from the main purpose of the church — which they perceived as *meeting their own needs.*

Clearly, the pastoral staff and some of the more active members at Central City Church were trying to mold the congregation into something that a congregation by its very nature is not and can never be — *a prophetic missionary community.*

A local congregation is a group of people who gather for worship, fellowship, meaning, and security. The members of a congregation are there because of their own identity and meaning needs—and they hire a pastoral staff to create a context in which those needs can be met. They are not there to be trained to go into the highway and byways of life as suffering servants. Neither are they there to challenge the status quo, for, by and large, they affirm the status quo and are comfortable in it. To be sure, they can tolerate—maybe even participate in — selected services to the community. The local church has always engaged in some home missions endeavors. But these efforts are seen as subsidiary to the primary program of meeting the religious needs of its members.

Dean M. Kelley makes a similar observation:

> It is commonplace today for some of the most concerned and committed young leaders in the churches to address their constituents as "agents of change," calling them to storm the bastions of the status quo and to bring in the new kingdom of righteousness and peace. It has been disillusioning for them to find the rank-and-file membership, by and large, rather recalcitrant to that summons. The members have shown themselves to be more concerned with stability and security than with change. . . . Furthermore, they look to their religious organizations to undergird and enhance that stability and security rather than to foment unpredictable innovations.[5]

Here again, the very human concerns of personal need and group membership are crucial realities that must be recognized by the church. The church as a social institution is a vehicle and channel for meeting people's need— specifically their religious need. In spite of the announced arrival of the secular man, the continuing contemporary passion for meaning and cosmic orientation seems to suggest that man is as basically religious as he has ever been, and most persons seek such meaning through their culture's religious institutions.

People go to church because they have a personal religious need that they want fulfilled, and they expect the worship, teaching, and fellowship of the church to provide the means for that fulfilment. To be sure, this does not preclude missionary prophetic involvement. Indeed, for some it requires such involvement. But the majority — whose involvements and activities are channeled in a variety of ways, from vocation and family to avocation and community — come to church to have their lives anchored in ultimate meaning. They want to make some kind of sense out of the whole thing. They come to church having been sensually bombarded, cognitively overloaded, and decisionally harried — suffering from what Toffler calls "environmental overstimulation."[6] The last thing they want to hear is a call to "storm the bastions of the status quo." They want to know how to make life a meaningful experience.

The Local Church in the City

It is apparent that the two lessons discussed above come from actual experience, not theological inference. This has been deliberate. I am convinced that much recent literature about the nature and mission of the church is guilty of theological reductionism — and attempts to define the church solely in terms of biblical images and doctrinal formulations. The consequence has been the creation of an unrealistic vision of the church. With such images as "the people of God," "the new humanity," and the like, many have made extreme claims for the church, fostered unrealistic hopes, and made impossible demands. Others have launched into radical reform programs to mold and manipulate local congregations in accordance with these ideals.

What is needed to balance this theological idealism is a social and psychological realism. Theology sees the church as a prophetic missionary community, but experience has taught us that only a few respond to the prophetic missionary call. Theology sees the church as a brotherhood breaching all socio-cultural barriers, but experience has taught us that only a few are able so to transcend their provincial identity. Does this mean the church should forsake its idealism and sacralize experienced reality? No, but neither should it ignore experienced reality. It must hold these two poles in dynamic tension.

What this means for the role of the local church in the city is this: first, the church should concentrate its efforts on meeting the religious needs of its congregation and community. To be sure, it can engage in certain services to the community. But it will never be a social change agency. It may even spawn and support individuals in certain prophetic or missionary endeavors. But it will never be a prophetic or missionary community. (There is one possible exception to this, and that is what historically has been called the dissenter group.)

Second, the local congregation, because it concentrates its efforts on religious or meaning needs, will in all likelihood find its ministry limited to one social and cultural identity group. These groups are usually divided along racial, ethnic, and/or economic lines, but there are exceptions to this. What will usually characterize a congregation is a common perceptual field or world-view—a common set of ideals and values. And it is here where the local congregation can make a great and significant contribution to the secular city. By affirming its members in their identity, and grounding that identity in ultimate meaning, the church can help to create healthy and stable individuals. Such individuals can then be taught and led to forsake and transcend those neurotic kinds of attachments to provincial identities which lead to that whole "in-group," "out-group" syndrome of prejudice, discrimination, oppression and conflict.

The local church can thus help the city achieve a dynamic unity in which pluralism and diversity are mutually affirmed and respected. As we have said, to affirm the common culture has been one of the key roles of the church in the past. To affirm the newly emerging common culture, with its recognition and affirmation of pluralism, will be a key role of the church in the secular city.

Notes to Chapter 13

1 Harvey Cox, *The Secular City* (New York: Macmillan, 1966), p. 1.

2 Alvin Toffler, *Future Shock* (New York: Bantam Books, paperback, 1971), p. 2.

3 Will Herberg, *Protestant, Catholic, Jew* (Garden City, N.Y.: Doubleday Anchor, rev. ed., 1955), p. 2.

4 Gibson Winter, *The Suburban Captivity of the Churches* (New York: Macmillan, 1962), p. 55.

5 Dean M. Kelley, *Why Conservative Churches Are Growing* (New York: Harper, 1972), p. 7.

6 Toffler, *op. cit.,* pp. 343-367.

14: MULTI-CULTURAL MINISTRY

by Frank Leeds III

It is a fact of contemporary American society that major ethnic shifts in population are going on throughout our country. But no matter what direction these shifts go, no matter how often they take place, the result is the same: people of like ethnic background huddle together.

When the church — or anyone else, for that matter — begins to interpret this, two explanations come to the fore: (1) people are the same, and "uprooting" must be attributed to the sin of racism; or (2) people are different, and all of the "uprooting" is justifiable. Both explanations seem naive to me. My thesis is this: people are different, but "uprooting" may not be necessary.

FRANK LEEDS III is pastor of the Baptist Church of the Redeemer in the Flatbush section of Brooklyn, New York. He holds academic degrees from The King's College, Briarcliff Manor, New York, and from Conservative Baptist Theological Seminary in Denver. He has also pursued additional graduate study at Oakland University in Michigan, the City University of New York, and New York Theological Seminary. His experience includes the pastorate of the Beverly Hills Baptist Church of Birmingham, Michigan, and some time counseling at the Suicide Prevention Clinic in Denver.

As the minister of a multi-ethnic and multi-cultural church in New York City, I cherish and pray for unity. But I doubt that "unity" is the supreme virtue, as some in the Eastern world would seem to be saying. Not only does unity stimulate a feeling of peace, of security, of harmony; it also has a strange ability to ask those people whom it makes to feel good to pay its price. Several years ago I attended a meeting in which urban and suburban needs were the topic. It was my hope that such a meeting would focus on some specific and increasing urban needs. A well-meaning physician testified that there is no distinction between an urban and a suburban hernia, "for, after all, we are all people." The meeting fizzled. People left with the illusion of "unity," while significant differences were ignored. I love unity. I hate to see people mesmerized by it.

In our pursuit of unity, I believe there is a critical fact that must be faced: *people are different*. We have different physical appearances, different conceptions of reality, and different values, mores, and cultures to guide our lives. Much of our personal identity is based on that which makes us different. Consequently, to minister to real people is to minister to people who are different.

In the next few pages, I would like us to look at some of the components that make us different. As well, a review of our national history would be in order, for the United States is in the forefront of bringing different cultures together. Finally, a brief look at how one church meets the challenge of unity and diversity in an urban situation.

Anthropology reveals the following principles, which are imperative for understanding people's differences: (1) culture is a crucial factor in determining our personality; (2) culture is crucial in dictating our needs; (3) cultures are different; and (4) due to cultural difference, people have different needs. These statements are confirmed by a Christian symposium on the nature of man:

> A particular drive, such as hunger for food, cannot easily be isolated as though it existed by itself on an island. Any drive must finally be interpreted in relationship to the whole field of physical, social, ethical, intellectual, and religious motives.[1]

The principalities and powers of one's culture are powerful enough to affect biological drives. But, one may argue, is not human nature the same for us all? Human nature is human nature, isn't it? The anthropologist responds:

> Human nature is not rigid and unyielding, not an unadaptable plant which insists on flowering or becoming stunted after its own fashion, responding only quantitatively to the social environment, but that it is extraordinarily adaptable, that *cultural rhythms are stronger and more compelling than the physiological rhythms* which they overlay and distort, that the failure to satisfy an artificial, culturally stimulated need — for outdistancing one's neighbours in our society, for instance, or for wearing the requisite

number of dog's teeth among the Manus — may produce more unhappiness and frustration in the human breast than the most rigorous cultural curtailment of the physiological demands of sex or hunger.[2]

In light of this testimony to the cultural component of life, the most pressing question before the urban church is whether divergent cultures can be brought together *and* still meet those cultural needs which beat stronger than the physical needs?

Bringing divergent cultures together is no problem: the United States of America has been doing that officially for almost two hundred years. Meeting cultural needs, however, has seldom been a big priority. According to Milton Gordon, these two centuries of American history have seen three distinct ideologies for bringing people together.[3]

Borrowing from Steward Cole, Gordon calls the first ideology Anglo-Conformity. It is based on the assumption of the superiority of the English culture. Settlers in New England had to adopt the English culture. Immigrants were expected to renounce the behavior and values of their ancestral culture in favor of those of the Anglo-Saxon core group. In national life, they were welcome so long as they did not attempt to alter prevailing patterns. They were welcome if they learned their place and kept in it. Similarly, in church life this means giving up a traditional pattern of behavior, renouncing a heritage, in favor of the prevailing pattern. This seems to be the ideology behind many suburban churches even today.

The nation quickly learned that English culture was inadequate to meet the cultural needs of all who were to be her children. Likewise, the urban church learned that in order to meet the needs of city-dwellers it must culturally expand itself. But how?

Many felt the solution was to merge everyone together to form just one, "America" culture. Thus we have America's second ideology: the melting pot.

> Here you stand, good folk, think I, when I see them at Ellis Island, here you stand in your fifty groups, with your fifty languages and histories, and your fifty blood hatreds and rivalries. But you won't be long like that, brothers, for these are the fires of God you've come to — these are the fires of God. A fig for your feuds and vendettas! Germans and Frenchmen, Irishmen and Englishmen, Jews and Russians — into the crucible with you all! God is making the American. . . .[4]

The melting pot ideology sounded excellent at the time, and even today many urban pastors are trying to melt people together. They hope that by bringing diverse cultures together, they can begin an assimilative process that will culminate in a composite of ethnic elements. Examples given for the success of this ideology are similar to this one by Will Herberg.

> The American's image of himself is still the Anglo-American ideal it was at the beginning of our independent existence. The "national type" as ideal has always been, and remains, pretty well fixed. It is the *Mayflower*, John

Smith, Davy Crockett, George Washington, and Abraham Lincoln that
define the American's self-image, and this is true whether the American in
question is a descendent of the Pilgrims or the grandson of an immigrant
from Southeastern Europe — Our cultural assimilation has taken place not
in a "melting pot," but rather in a "transmitting pot" in which all
ingredients have been transformed and assimilated to an idealized
"Anglo-Saxon model."[5]

The importance for the church of what Herberg has to say is its relation to the
models we display. Of course, our model is Christ. Without realizing it,
however, many churchmen hold the Christ of their culture before people.
Consequently, the assumption soon becomes that "the All American Boy" and
"the Christian" are pretty much the same thing. And the melting pot ideology
turns out to be nothing more than Anglo-Conformity under a different guise.

What other way is there? A third alternative, which promises to do
justice both to the unity and the diversity of human existence, is popularly
referred to as "cultural pluralism." As early as 1915 Horace Kallan began
arguing that we should return to the Declaration of Independence's support of
the "right to be different." Kallan's favorite illustration of the meaning of
cultural pluralism was orchestration:

> As in an orchestra, the different instruments, each with its own
> characteristic timbre and theme, contribute distinct and recognizable parts
> to the composition, so in the life and culture of a nation, the different
> regional, ethical, occupational, religious and other communities compound
> their different activities to make up the national spirit.[6]

To the Christian, Kallan's appeal is reminiscent of Paul's appeal to the analogy
between the human body and the body of believers (I Cor. 12). Perhaps an
exposition of Paul, the leading New Testament advocate of a multi-cultural
ministry, would be a key to showing how a church can embrace the diversity of
cultures and be true to all of them. Is not the grace of our Lord big enough to
allow everyone the "right to be different"?

Pluralistic Ministry

If people are different, and if the best way to bring divergent cultures together
is through cultural pluralism, how, then, does one work this theory out in the
practice of Christian ministry?

The Baptist Church of the Redeemer, New York City, like other
churches in an urban environment, is in a community that runs the gamut of
diversity on skin color, religious affiliation, financial assets, and educational
enlightenment. Seeing the blindness of "Anglo-Conformity" and the naiveté of
the "Melting Pot," we have chosen pluralism as our style of ministry.

This pluralism, allowing and encouraging the right to be different, is seen
and practiced in several ways. On a Sunday, for example, we hold several kinds
of services — worship services in English, Spanish, Chinese, and French, and

also separate children's services (for they, too, have their own culture). For the most part, these are segregated fellowships, meeting in separate locations within the building, each reflecting its own language and culture. All of us have the right to be different. When we do worship jointly, all four languages and the cultural aspects of each group combine to form a pluralistic style of service.

By way of contrast to prevailing political and ecclesiastical ideologies, we are doing as much to encourage the English speakers to learn Spanish, French, and Mandarin Chinese as to encourage the non-English speakers to learn English. Again, the rationale is the same — unity *with,* not *at the expense of,* cultural differences.

Cultural pluralism is also applied to our multi-ethnic English-speaking fellowship. Music is a prime example. What type of music will help people who are culturally different worship? All are Baptist now, but some are ex-Lutherans, Roman Catholics, Presbyterians, Anglicans, Methodists, Pentecostalists, Jews, and so on. Applying cultural pluralism, we try to stimulate a context of freedom, allowing cultural tastes to come to the surface. Thus we use any type of music. Our music repertory is expanding to include some very old Jewish liturgical selections, Gregorian chants, Bach and the German classics, spirituals, folk, gospel, and some rock. The choir has combined with one of our members' opera group and performed in Latin, and (with a little transliteration help from the local synagogue) has managed to sing in Hebrew. This has helped accent the origin of biblical themes in the Old Testament and has allowed us to hear how these themes are given expression in another culture.

A more difficult area to apply cultural pluralism is the content and delivery style of the sermon. The traditional sermon is generally education by way of proclamation, but modern educational philosophy calls for education by way of dialogue. Regardless of the respective values of these different methodologies this will affect the church. If schoolteachers in the congregation have learned the value of movable chairs and desks, of visual aids, of discussion, of allowing one's humanness to come through in one's teaching, they may react negatively to sitting in fixed pews, from where they may ask no questions, and having the minister hide behind a pulpit. At the same time, others associate the "dignity" of the gospel with the traditional presentation of it.

To meet these diverse cultural needs, we vary the manner of delivery. For the traditional, sermons are delivered from the pulpit. A transition is made during our monthly communion service, when the sermon is delivered at pew level from behind the communion table. For those whose craving is not to know the office of pastor but to know the man who is pastor, occasional sermons take the form of a family pastoral chat from a barstool at the center aisle.

In addition to these ideas, I should close by mentioning the three biggest concerns of the church. First is for true orchestration, as opposed to four fellowships who "do their own thing" with no awareness of the other three fellowships. The danger that confronts all ethnic-oriented fellowships — German, Swedish, Anglo, Dutch, "whites," "blacks," Puerto Rican, or Chinese — is vision stunted by ethnicity.

Our second concern is well expressed by T. S. Eliot.

> Men who meet only for definite serious purposes, and on official occasions, do not wholly meet. They may have some common concern very much at heart; they may, in the course of repeated contacts, come to share a vocabulary and an idiom which appear to communicate every shade of meaning necessary for their common purpose; but they will continue to retire from these encounters each to his private social world as well as to his solitary world.[7]

We seek to know each other better by sponsoring ethnic potluck dinners, films about foreign countries, and a more effective use of our foreign missionaries. Still, the warning of T. S. Eliot is haunting. A film about a country can never be a substitute for the native of that country who sits next to you during the film.

Our final concern is our own finiteness. People who are involved in ministering to others are not exempt from the hardiness of their own ethnicity. Not only must we be content to function without all the answers but we must be content to function knowing full well that we are victims and benefactors of our own culture. Our own human nature may be plastic, but not infinitely so. There are times when, because of our own cultural enslavement, we will be unbending to others, telling ourselves that our own culture is obviously superior to others. Perhaps that is why all ministries depend on infinite grace and wisdom! Spinoza's words challenge us: "I have made a ceaseless effort not to ridicule, not to bewail, nor to scorn human actions, but to understand them."[8]

Notes to Chapter 14

1 Meehl, Klann, Schmeiding, Breimeier, Schroeder, *What Then Is Man?* (St. Louis: Concordia, 1958).

2 Margaret Mead, quoted in Bert Kaplan (ed.), *Studying Personality Cross-Culturally* (New York: Harper, 1961), p. 16.

3 Milton Gordon, *Assimilation in American Life* (New York: Oxford, 1964), chapters 4-6.

4 Quoted by Gordon, *ibid.*, pp. 120f., from Israel Zongiwell, *The Melting Pot* (New York: Macmillan, 1909), p. 37.

5 Quoted by Gordon, *ibid.*, p. 128, from Will Herberg, *Protestant-Catholic-Jew* (New York: Doubleday, 1955), pp. 33f.

6 Quoted by Gordon, *ibid.*, p. 147, from Horace M. Kallan, *Culture and Democracy in the United States* (New York: Boni and Liveright, 1924), p. 122.

7 T. S. Eliot, *Christianity and Culture* (New York: Harcourt, Brace and World), p. 160.

8 Quoted by Gordon Allport, *Pattern and Growth in Personality*, p. viii.

15: URBAN CHURCH IN URBAN COMMUNITY: A MEETING POINT

by Arthur Luther Whitaker

Urban mission is so central a task of God's people as they bear witness to Jesus Christ in a changing and complex world that one would suppose the evangelical community to have a program prepared to meet the needs of the city-dweller for reconciliation of man with God and reconciliation of man with man.

But as is all too obvious, white Anglo-Saxon Protestants, except for some broader denominational support programs, have little to show in urban ministry. About all they can point to are the massive and obsolete church buildings they have sold black congregations in central cities across the nation

ARTHUR LUTHER WHITAKER is minister of public ministries for the American Baptist Churches of Massachusetts, a position he has held since 1970. He is a graduate of Gordon College; has a B.D. from Harvard University; and holds the S.T.M. and D. Min. degrees from Andover-Newton Theological School. While a pastor in Rochester, New York, he was on the faculty of the University of Rochester; he has also been a visiting professor at Gordon College, and a lecturer at Colgate-Rochester Divinity School, the University of Minnesota, and Bethel College and Seminary, among others. He has served as a consultant to the federal anti-poverty program and to the US Commission on Civil Rights.

as they exited. For the most part the inner city is a place suburban whites pass through on their way to and from work.

While President Kennedy's New Frontier and President Johnson's Great Society improved conditions in urban America (particularly through the 1964 Civil Rights Act, the 1965 Voters Rights Act, OEO, Headstart and Model Cities Programs), these measures were largely the product of social, economic, educational, and political institutions. What few religious models there were of relevance to the city were black-inspired—Dr. Martin Luther King's techniques of nonviolence, begun in Montgomery in 1955 and used throughout the country under the guidance of the Southern Christian Leadership Conference (SCLC); Dr. Leon Sullivan's Opportunities Industrialization Centers (OIC) in Philadelphia; and, earlier, Dr. James Robinson, long-time black pastor of The Church of the Master in Harlem, whose "Crossroads Africa" program became the model for the nation's Peace Corps.

Many American Christians see the city as a place to escape from. This has prevented the kind of communication, understanding, and participation essential for the urban church to be a relevant meeting point for the secular urban community.

Renewal or Removal?

As Gibson Winter has noted, white Protestantism concerned itself with searching for renewal from within its structure at the onset of the 1960s.[1] Few local white congregations were willing to consider the challenge to minister to the newcomers to large metropolitan centers. By 1960 America's ten largest cities—New York, Chicago, Los Angeles, Philadelphia, Detroit, Baltimore, Houston, Cleveland, Washington, and St. Louis—had substantial black populations. Although blacks had been coming to the metropolis since the underground railroad days, the migration intensified after World War I.

As the pastor of a black church in Rochester, New York, located in the heart of one of the city's two black ghettos, I witnessed the gradual movement of white churches to suburbia or residential areas on the fringe of the city. This pattern of removal continues to this day.

The inward look of white Protestants and the heavy concentration of blacks in American cities caught all social institutions, including the church, ill-prepared to cope with the sociology of the disadvantaged or the behavior of minority groups. These factors, as well as the problem of racism, bear a closer examination.

Racism and Renewal

White Christians must come to grips with the hard fact that as they sought renewal, minorities in general and blacks in particular were not welcomed. Winter has reminded us that Protestantism was on the move outward from central city areas to the suburbs during most of the period from 1870 to 1950.

Somehow the white churches in exodus had forgotten that the good news was not for white members only but for all mankind who believed in a personal God, and in Jesus Christ as Lord of lords. Nonwhite Christians who sought membership in lily-white Christian churches were turned away in one fashion or another. Often it was a subtle kind of rejection, as in the suggestion that there was a nice "colored" church whose pastor was "a wonderful Christian" only five or ten blocks away—or across town, for that matter.

Society in general and the church have inherited racism from the historical past. For the most part those within the church as well as those outside have perpetuated and sustained racism either consciously or unconsciously. Consequently, the starting point in understanding the nature and characteristics of the urban community is to accept the fact of inherent racism within American society. Any attempt to minister to minorities in the name of Christ within the urban complex will cause the penetrating judgment of W. E. B. Dubois to resurface again and again: *The problem of the 20th century is the problem of the colorline.*[2]

White Christians failed to see a harvest emerging within the metropolis as minority groups continued to migrate north. Since it was a different kind of people—different by color, ethnic, and cultural background—moving into neighborhoods, liberal and evangelical Christians alike were quick to surrender their witness and mission. During my ten-year Rochester pastorate, one white minister after another told me that he had no choice. His church *had to move* where its members had relocated. There were only a few exceptions.

A decade later most evangelical churches are still pondering the "prospects of their renewal" but failing to "serve the whole life of the metropolis,"[3] as Gibson Winter had advocated in 1961. Sunday morning at eleven o'clock continues to be the most segregated hour in America.

As the church ponders renewal, it will have to accept the fact that the cities of the seventies are in worse shape than they were in the sixties.[4] Furthermore, there is a new black mood evident within the metropolis. The "Afro" look, black awareness, self-determination and control for black communities, schools, and businesses—these are the "in" thing today.

For the most part, black metropolitan churches are well attended on Sunday morning across the nation. The Christian's God is still worshiped in black communities, but black theology and black nationalism are becoming stronger and more vibrant. Many young blacks who have had some conflict with the police, as they are jailed for minor offenses due primarily to their inability to raise bail, have joined the Black Muslim faith of the Nation Islam. A number of attractive black persons have joined boxer Muhammed Ali in embracing the Black Muslim faith—including such entertainment stars as Aretha Franklin, James Brown, Flip Wilson, and Leontyne Price.

When such outstanding black brothers and sisters reject the Christian's

God, evangelicals must admit failure in the staying power of the gospel among the black community. In short, white Christianity has been rejected.

Sociology of the Disadvantaged

Blacks have come out of a slave culture deeply rooted in paternalism. The strains of this paternalism continue to exist today. Due to the high visibility of their color, blacks, unlike other ethnic groups, find it extremely difficult to be assimilated into or accepted by the mainstream of American society.

Against the backdrop of slave culture, where a plantation mentality developed, a subculture of the disadvantaged black was born. Many were unable to throw off their plantation mentality as they migrated to large metropolitan centers, where poor housing and overcrowding produced an extension of the old plantation mentality into a new form—ghetto mentality and substandard living, the victim of white slumlords and shop owners who lived outside the ghetto.[5]

The result of this ghetto entrapment has been frustration, hopelessness, and deep despair. Subordinate relationships destroyed a sense of selfhood and dignity prior to the black revolution and the new emphasis on black pride. Subordination also imposed a subculture that persists in spite of black awareness; those who have been segregated out and discriminated against and entrapped in the ghetto have a different value system. The ghetto mentality produces in the disadvantaged a loss of the sense of neighborliness, groupness, values, and wholesome social attitudes. Sociologically, this is the lot of all disadvantaged groups, but it is most true of blacks.

Understanding the Behavior of Minority Groups

It is important to understand that the existence of a minority group in a society implies the existence of a corresponding dominant group enjoying higher status and greater privileges. Minority status carries with it exclusion from full participation in the life of the society. The minority is treated and regards itself as a people apart.[6]

Since blacks constitute the largest among minorities in America, it is significant that behavioral patterns emerging among blacks are the end product of the contradiction between the American creed of democratic values and the actual treatment they receive at the hands of the dominant group in society. Anger, alienation, hostility, hopelessness, despair, and violence are key words in the description of the urban minority group experience.

If the urban church is to meet the urban community with a vibrant ministry of the good news, then, it will have to understand these factors and minister to whole persons with patient, accepting love, recognizing the origins of these frustrations and seeking effective ways to change the background and the experience.[7] Our urban communities are teeming with every social pathology known to mankind, largely due to the "benign neglect" of government and churches.

The Church's Ministry to the City

Urban blight is typically the worst in the area adjacent to the downtown business section. This zone has undergone constant change since the late 1940s. Blight in inner-city areas takes on a variety of forms, involving crime, ecological and aesthetic deterioration, social injustice, transience, and poverty.

If Christians are sincere about having a mission to the whole man, perhaps they would do well to reread *The Surburban Captivity of the Churches.* An evangelistic life-style, such as that called for by Key '73, must be equally weighted between a personal gospel and social ministry concept. To *proclaim* the Word of God and not to be committed to its implementation within the individual life and society is to belie the gospel of Jesus. The church cannot be renewed solely from within.

In the words of one of Boston's beloved ministers, the Rev. Dr. Frederick M. Meek, the "downtown church is called to be a Christian conscience." He expressed optimism that the tide is changing, that downtown churches can become, once again, alive and important.[8] If that is ever to happen, it is extremely important for the church to accept its leadership role in the urban community and to take seriously the New Testament mandate: "God was in Christ reconciling the world to himself . . . and entrusting to us the message of reconciliation" (II Cor. 5:19, NEB).

Let us consider some of the implications of reconciliation in relation to the church's ministry to the urban community. I am convinced that reconciliation is one of the marks of a Christian who is empowered by God and committed to be both catalyst and enabler in our society.

1. Coping with New Family Patterns. If the church is to cope successfully with new family patterns, it must understand the single-parent family in particular. Usually the female has the dual parental role in such families due to abandonment or desertion by the real father. The difficulties of the female parent who is single for whatever reason — desertion, divorce, widowhood, or separation — are enormous. While the single male parent has his problems as well, society does not seem to *take* advantage of him as much as it does of the single female parent.

Organizations like Parents Without Partners have offered immeasurable assistance to male and female single parents. The urban church is in a unique position to offer counseling, individual or group, to "parents without partners" through regular counseling services under the leadership of the pastor or other staff members trained in clinical pastoral education. If the church in an urban community is unable to provide full counseling services, it should offer a referral service. Even if full counseling services are available at the church, periodic referral to other skilled and competent professionals within the community can help extend one's own skills and professionalism.

2. *Coping with the Time Factor.* The church in the inner city will soon learn that for some black Americans and some Latin Americans the notion of time is different from that of white middle-class Americans who no longer live in the inner city. Time weighs heavily on all minority groups and the poverty-stricken people caught in slum pockets across the land and excluded from full participation in society. Consequently, some individuals in these minority groups may be late for appointments. The weight of time itself and poor public transportation exacerbate the situation of getting to the church or meeting other appointments on time. The time factor within the culture of black America is less exacting when it comes to beginning and ending any particular meeting or program, including worship services. During my boyhood and teens in metropolitan Boston, I heard repeated reference to "C.P.T." or "Colored People's Time."

Latin Americans, too, do not share middle-class concepts of time. A Latin American will agree to meet someone at a particular hour; but if he happens to meet a friend or someone else who needs assistance along the way to the appointment, an hour's delay will not be a problem for him.

The church must learn how to cope with the different notion of time in other cultural groups as it plans its program to meet human needs.

3. *Coping with Transience.* The transience of great numbers of people in any large city is one of the most difficult problems for the urban church to solve. It is extremely difficult to build a stable ministry around people who are constantly moving. Attempts must be made to establish a core membership, a group of committed persons who by virtue of financial stability and Christian conviction are willing to serve as catalysts and enablers in task-force ministries within the community-at-large. Accomplishing this will be less difficult if the church's program is tailored to the way of life of the various minority groups to which it ministers, highlights some of their problems in the community, and, more importantly, emphasizes the contributions they have made to America and society.

Above all, action, not words, is important for our times. Standard curricula need revision. No single model of ministry will do the job. There are common problems experienced by all human groups, but different approaches, strategies, and programs must be devised to meet different people at their "growing edge."

I must say in all candor that I worry a great deal about the inability of most Americans to understand the dynamics of social change and their unwillingness to accept change and create models to solve the problems inherent within society itself. The 1970s must be a decade of developing mastery of human relations. We must learn a sense of timing and coordination in human relations. We must put out fires rather than allowing them to happen or even starting them. Both short-term and long-range programs and projects must be designed and coordinated by social institutions (including the church), agencies, and community-based organizations. In our pluralistic, multi-racial society, no group can do it alone.

What will it profit the United States if we gain the moon but lose our soul from within? The very soul of America is at stake as urban church and urban community strive to know each other, to work together with the gospel to reconcile man with God and man to man.

Phony Christianity and gimmicks will not do in our time. If we believe that "God was in Christ reconciling the world to himself," we must ask, "Watchman, what of the night *and the day* in urban America during the 1970s?"

Notes to Chapter 15

1 Gibson Winter, *The Suburban Captivity of the Churches* (New York: Doubleday, 1961), p. 39.

2 W. E. B. DuBois, *The Souls of Black Folk* (Greenwich: Fawcett, 1961).

3 Winter, *op. cit.*, pp. 129f.

4 See Robert K. Yin (ed.), *The City in the Seventies* (Itasca, Ill.: F. E. Peacock Publishers, 1972).

5 Arthur L. Whitaker, "The Sociology of the Disadvantaged: the Negro," professional paper prepared for the Project Head Start Training Program, Rochester Institute of Technology, 1965.

6 Louis Wirth, "The Problems of Minority Groups," in Ralph Linton (ed.), *The Science of Man in World Crisis* (New York: Columbia U.P., 1945), p. 347.

7 Gibson Winter, *op. cit.*, pp.129ff.

8 Quoted in the *Boston Herald Traveler*, May 14, 1973, p. 3.

16: URBAN EVANGELISM: CHRIST AS CREDIBLE

by Edward V. Hill

But you shall receive power when the Holy Spirit has come upon you; and you shall be my witnesses in Jerusalem and in all Judea and Samaria, and to the end of the earth (Acts 1:8).

Urban evangelism is commissioned by this call to witness for Christ, beginning at home and then spreading throughout the earth. One should approach the urban community as he does all other communities, realizing that people without Christ are lost. Unfortunately, during the twentieth century American Christians have tended to ignore or avoid this commission to urban evangelism.

EDWARD V. HILL is pastor of the Mount Zion Missionary Baptist Church of Los Angeles, California. He is a graduate of Prairie View College, Texas, and served a pastorate in Houston before moving to Los Angeles in 1961. A life member of the NAACP, he is in frequent demand as a lecturer and consultant. He has served numerous offices on boards, committees, and commissions; and is now president of the United Benevolent Society, an economic development corporation in California; president of two housing projects; vice president of the planning and zoning commission; and chairman of the board of directors of the Los Angeles chapter of the SCLC; among other involvements. He is also director of the World Christian Training Center, an evangelistic outreach in Watts.

Perhaps some have been afraid. Urban centers are generally characterized by the bold presence of crime and sin. Dope is available in the ghettos; prostitution and gambling are common. The inner-city dweller lives against the backdrop of constant conflict and turmoil between groups who vie for power.

Perhaps others are overwhelmed by the extent of the challenge. The city is often a place of overcrowding, of high rents for substandard housing, of exorbitant prices charged to those who can least afford it. The city-dweller lives in constant temptation to do wrong, be subversive, or participate in activities that ultimately lead to crime.

Still others may assume that there is no real need for evangelism because of the religious heritage of many city-dwellers, especially those in the black community. There may be hundreds of religious groups in a large city. But although many have come out of the background of religious community, few have found the living Christ and many have chosen to become associated with other "isms." The urban community is home to many who are regarded — by themselves and by society — as failures. Thus there are always followers for anyone who wants to do anything within the urban community. Among the sufferings, agony and disappointments of the city, militant leaders find a large following and cults that promise a way out of oppression have thrived. Broadway Avenue of Los Angeles has approximately seventy storefront churches, partly because anyone with a particular gift or who is mysterious can, just by renting a building, attract a following.

Finally, there are evangelicals who assume that the urban community will not accept evangelism. Yet when Christ is presented as he is, in boldness, people open their hearts to him. Among those over thirty, Christ has been an answer to life in a community that was almost unlivable at times. In recent years younger people have become very skeptical of Christ. Perhaps, even in the city, this has been partly due to the economic advancement of their parents.

When I was a child, I, like my mother, had to learn how to depend on the Lord because there was no other solution. Modern-day urban parents, in spite of the struggle, have been better able to provide enough for their children, so that many of the children have not had to look further than their parents. And the parents have failed to teach their children about Christ.

Avenues of Evangelism

It is readily apparent that evangelism in the complexity of the urban situation must have a diversified approach. Christ cannot just "be preached." For many he must be demonstrated in acts of kindness. Nor can everyone be reached through the normal activities of the organized church. God reaches each person individually; therefore, we cannot afford to commit ourselves to a single technique. Like Paul, we must be willing to "become all things to all men, that we might by all means save some" (I Cor. 9:19).

1. Mass evangelism. Urban people often are eager to hear and see those of great reputation. Many can thus be reached through mass evangelism. Currently, mass evangelism as known in the white community is relatively unknown among blacks. Attendance at city-wide black revivals has not been large, in part because those persons with the expertise, the funds, and the attractive image have never come into the urban centers. The Billy Graham Association, for instance, with all its resources and potential, has never had an exclusively ghetto crusade. Others who have ventured forth have affected many but do not seem to have the depth of appeal needed yet.

2. *Personal evangelism.* Many city-dwellers will go to such mass rallies or seek God through churches, but in recent years a growing segment of the urban community (perhaps 25%) will come to neither. Instead they give listening ears to those who are hyper-critical of organized religion, such as the Jehovah's Witnesses and Muslims. Thus a great need in the urban community is for believers who are willing to become active personal witnesses. Historically, the average churchgoer has made witnessing the exclusive responsibility of the preacher. Instead of presenting Christ to the persons in his neighborhood or at his job, he will invite people to hear the preacher in the pulpit. There are signs that this is changing, but the change is not as rapid as the growth of hostility toward the organized church.

Personal evangelism and innovative community outreach must be used to the full to reach those usually missed by the organized church. Except for some storefront ministries, most evangelical churches are not significantly ministering to the poor. Street people, welfare recipients, and young people are often ashamed to become part of the middle-class church structures.

We must also begin developing evangelistic strategies to reach the hostile. Persons caught up in radical points of view will not be reached by normal channels. Special people with special talents will have to come to grips with this community; they will have to find ways to communicate the Christ who "has chosen the poor in the world to be rich in faith and heirs of the kingdom" (James 2:5).

3. *Chaplaincy.* Urban institutions like convalescent homes, jails, and juvenile homes can be reached for Christ by chaplains. Persons here may never attend an organized church or be touched by a personal soul-winner or be able to attend a mass evangelistic rally. Thus, a method specifically designed to reach the institutionally confined is much needed. Increased attention should be given to the possibilities of institutional chaplaincy.

Coordination

It will take experimentation, coordination, and use of all of these methods adequately to evangelize the urban community. Other methods, dependent on coordinated use of resources through urban-suburban lifelines, must also be explored. Much larger staffs, many more volunteers, and the cooperative assistance of the total evangelical community are mandatory if we are to reach the millions in central cities for Christ.

Does evangelism in the ghetto have to be limited to a particular ethnic group? Can blacks reach only blacks? Latins Latins? And so forth? I believe that the gospel of Christ transcends racial and cultural backgrounds. Many groups have demonstrated before our eyes that people *can* be led across color lines and background differences. A case in point is the Jehovah's Witnesses. There is a large black church in Los Angeles whose pastor and organist are white, but the question of reaching people across color lines never arises because the minister in charge proceeds as if there is no difference and the people believe it makes no difference. All people can be reached, it seems, if the person sharing Christ does not have a racial hangup himself. I believe that methods used by God for outreach in nonurban areas can often be successfully adapted to various ethnic backgrounds and to the city. People are people. Just as those within races vary in their similarity to each other, so there are those across racial/ethnic lines who can be reached very much in the same way.

The Complete Gospel: Four Bases

Like a game of baseball, the approach of the urban evangelical should have four bases. First base is reconciliation with God through Jesus Christ. When a man has become reconciled with God, or is born again, should he remain at first base or come back to the dugout and wait until Jesus comes? The latter has been advocated by many conservative white evangelicals. Preaching that will not — and should not — be accepted in the urban community. Although we must develop a sound "first base" ministry, the game of life cannot be won by simply making it to first and returning to the dugout. One who has truly experienced new life in Jesus Christ must proceed — under the wise coaching of a biblical pastor — to second base.

Second base is living a Christian life of reconciling men to men. Men who have been reconciled to God should have the courage needed to become reconciled to one another. Ministry in the urban community must be a ministry that seeks to unite men in common goals and common causes that are Christ-oriented. Out of the salvation experience at first base we must make a brotherhood experience at second.

One does not reach second base, however, by going over the pitcher's mound. Some of my Christian friends of liberal persuasion seem to advocate this: once you have hit the ball, the only thing important is to become reconciled with one another. I believe that the essence of reconciliation between persons is reconciliation with God.

But the gospel for the urban man goes on to third base, which is where Christians commit themselves to building a better community as a result of being reconciled with God and one another. The city desperately needs this kind of Christian witness.

All will agree that Jesus was a powerful "first base" preacher. Without hesitation he said, "Verily, verily, I say unto you, you must be born again" (John 3:3). But he went on to ask, more than once, about loving one another — which we have called "second base" in our ministry. What some Christians fail to see is that Jesus was also a powerful "third base" preacher. He said that those who have been born again should let it be known — by loving one another, feeding the hungry, clothing the naked, housing the outcasts, and visiting the sick and imprisoned. We are to be doing that in our cities.

The gospel that the urban community needs is one that will advocate, without apologizing, a true conversion experience. It will insist that as a result of being truly converted we will have a new outlook toward our brothers, and that a community of brotherhood should build a community that meets the physical and social needs of its members. Even this, however, is not all. This gospel is tempting, but it keeps us at third base.

No matter how much our communities improve, no matter how we build, no matter how we try to improve conditions in our world, the gospel that is preached in the city must warn men that they will not be able to stay at third base. It must be a gospel which keeps us "looking for that blessed hope, the appearing of the glory of our great God and Saviour Jesus Christ" (Titus 2:13). When we reach the point where we realize that we cannot meet all needs, this perspective gives us hope.

Vision and Strategy: World Christian Training Center

I will now describe an urban evangelistic program that might prove beneficial to others engaged in evangelism. The World Christian Training Center seeks to train, within every block of south central Los Angeles, soul-winners who will pray and plan strategies to win their whole block for Jesus. In addition, it seeks to create a trained nucleus of soul-winners in every church house in this area, so that each church will be filled with people who personally know Jesus Christ and actively share him with others.

There are five hundred church houses in this area of Los Angeles, yet the area has not been saturated with the gospel. In political campaign headquarters, workers assemble to get information about their candidate, materials supporting him, and the enthusiasm needed to talk to others. In churches, apparently, we assemble to congratulate and praise one another, pray for one another, and then quietly slip back into the community as God's secret army.

This situation must be changed, but not just through sermons or admonitions. The World Christian Training Center is building strategies, providing materials and methods, and training people to take their communities for Jesus Christ. Its plan is to recruit at least three people in every congregation to attend WCTC. This is done through sending volunteers into churches to give testimonies and seek out trainees, and by sponsoring lay institutes in the churches.

WCTC trainees are thoroughly taught about who Jesus Christ is, how to accept him, how to lead others to accept him, how to reach a block for Christ, how to turn a church into a soul-winning church, and how to reach families for Christ. There is also practical experience in personal evangelism.

A trainee who finishes the course is expected to put into practice what he has learned. He returns to his church to share these concepts with members there, and is commissioned as a block worker for WCTC. As a block worker he reports weekly on what he has done in the community to bring others to Christ — persons to whom he has talked, churches contacted, and homes visited. If a person receives Christ his name, address, telephone number, and date of decision are given to the WCTC. The worker is expected to follow up with any persons accepting Christ, and to help them mature in the faith.

When the WCTC secretary receives the name of a new believer she locates the worker living closest to that person. As soon as possible that block worker makes contact and invites him into a neighborhood fellowship. The convert is also mailed a Bible and further materials from the Center. Also the secretary contacts the nucleus of trained soul-winners within the church of the new believer's choice. This group and persons from the WCTC then follow through with the new convert, who may also be trained to become a soul-winner by enrolling in the Center program.

The gospel will work in the urban community if preached in its fulness. The fulness of the gospel is that it offers to us a way of life. It is a way that does not ignore the necessities, problems or pressures of life. In the midst of urban complexity, Christ has come that all "might have life, and have it abundantly" (John 10:10).

PART SIX:
GETTING IT TOGETHER —
PROGRAMS FOR EFFECTIVE URBAN INVOLVEMENT

INTRODUCTION

Effective evangelical urban ministry requires careful thought, dialogue, and planning. None of these takes the place of prayer and the action of God's Spirit, of course. They simply aim at providing strategies[1] and structures through which to communicate the good news to the city-dweller by the most effective use of available resources. The chapters in this section offer some suggestions and illustrations for successful urban ministry.

Planning a Program
On the basis of his considerable experience in secular and church-related program development, Dick Hart provides some guidelines for developing urban ministry programs. To those evangelical groups used to less well-defined ways of doing things, this will sound strange, perhaps threatening. Too many churches simply do not know what their purpose is or how to go about achieving it. Hart's proposed strategy is an extremely practical one. The opening step — need identification — eliminates the endless speculation about what *might be* done and requires direct contact with the community to find out what *needs* to be done. For many churches the mere contact with the

community will provide new impetus and vision for urban ministry. Self-assessment will help keep the goals realistic.

Hart's second step is establishing an action plan to assign responsibility and map the course of action in meeting the need. Those involved in urban ministry will find so many needs that they may be paralyzed into inaction. The third step of priority establishment is thus important in breaking down the overwhelming into the possible and manageable. It is at this point that urban evangelicals must look carefully at the notion of complementary ministry.

Hart's fourth step, the marshalling of resources, becomes important in discussing such alliances. The articles by Craig Ellison, L. Edward Davis, and Michael Haynes are pertinent to this issue as well. There is no need for duplication of effort by the church if secular agencies are meeting a particular kind of need well. Close examination, however, usually turns up pockets of unmet need within these programs. Resources then can be gained from the secular agencies in order to complement their own programs. Finally, Hart points out the need for continuing commitment and application of good management principles in overseeing the effort.

What Kind of Program?

Thom Hopler discusses the varieties of whole-person ministry in which overseas missions have traditionally engaged. The contributions of foreign missions to home urban missions provide a unique perspective and some useful methods. Unique subcultures within the city must be recognized, and the relationship between churches in other countries and those in the city may suggest a strategy for building Christian urban witness (for example, those sharing the Spanish language and Latin American culture). Those who minister in the city must learn how to communicate. They must learn the language, build trust between persons, accept cultural integrity.

Using the model developed in Newark by Africa Inland Mission's Urban Mission USA, Hopler suggests some innovative ways for traditionally overseas missionary societies to build exciting overseas/home-urban missionary links. The wide-ranging missionary efforts overseas show that the kind of whole-person witness needed in the city has always characterized the best of missions. Medical assistance, literature, radio, food, and school development, combined with appropriate spiritual witness, have attracted many to the Christ of compassion and justice. Lessons in cross-cultural adjustment and identification, as well as examples of persistence, faith, and vision, flow steadily from the history of foreign missions. Urban and suburban churches alike must apply these lessons to the city.

Program for Reconciliation

Graham Barnes faces the problem of finding ways to develop positive understanding between blacks and whites so that regular communication and systematic cooperation in urban ministry is possible. Using experience gained from his involvement with the Fellowship of Racial and Economic Equality, Barnes gives examples of some typical hang-ups and shows how, through a combination of group process and one-to-one counseling, both blacks and whites can overcome racial barriers. Until the process was brought onto the concrete level of personal feelings expressed in a problem-solving situation, little change occurred.[2]

The simple sharing of common biblical beliefs does not automatically mean that healthy interpersonal relationships will exist. A dynamic program of guided sharing, Barnes suggests, will help Christians make Philippians 2:2-4 a reality: "Complete my joy by being of the same mind, having the same love, being in full accord, and of one mind. Do nothing from selfishness or conceit, but in humility count others better than yourselves. Let each of you look not only to his own interests, but also to the interests of others."

Lifelines

Complementing a program of reconciliation like that suggested by Barnes, the suburban-urban lifelines presented by L. Edward Davis seem to be a genuine possibility. Davis, pastor of an inner-city church, portrays the suburbs and city as interdependent. Proper evangelical community includes both in several mutually beneficial ways. The Body of Christ needs to be renewed so that it knows what its mission is and comprehends the incarnational nature of its message.

Davis calls for a new strategy of urban ministry. In a highly stimulating discussion he points out six objectives and suggests specific possibilities for implementation. There are rich opportunities here for building lifelines with the suburban church, between urban churches, and even with foreign evangelicals who share the culture and language backgrounds of various city-dwellers.

Co-belligerents

Numerous cooperative endeavors can be undertaken between evangelicals and secular groups. Instead of trying to duplicate better-run and better-funded secular programs, evangelicals might better seek an active part in shaping and running such programs.

Michael Haynes speaks on the basis of his own experience in describing how such Christian-secular cooperation can be a direct help in communicating the gospel. Such cooperation can, for example, help to bring about legislative changes necessary to correct injustice. It can help churches obtain funds to build housing either for its own elderly or poor, as well as for evangelistic outreach. Noncompromising witness for Christ can be amplified rather than diminished by evangelicals who become co-belligerents against evil and injustice with those in secular society who fight for compassion and justice.

Alliances

Another type of cooperation that would greatly strengthen evangelical witness in urban centers is the formation of multiple urban alliances. Craig Ellison discusses such alliances. These would involve local churches as well as the working arms of the church, and would provide a forum for dialogue and problem-solving, as well as a catalyst for specific noncongregational ministries. At another level, this exchange process could be broadened to include several cities in a defined geographical area. Special conferences could be held periodically to provide ideas and inspiration. Finally, at the national level some form of association or center for evangelical urban affairs could be established. Consultants from one city where a particular problem had been imaginatively confronted could be provided for those in another city. Precautions, of course, must be taken to prevent such alliances from becoming inept ends unto themselves.

Working Model

Roger Dewey, co-director of ECUMB, closes this section with a description of a working model for evangelical urban involvement that combines many of the suggestions made in this section. He traces the difficult development of this comprehensive agency and should inspire many to a broadened concept of urban ministry and with the realization that such extensive ministry is possible. ECUMB is probably the most advanced, evangelical urban model functioning in the United States today.

Notes to Part Six: Introduction

1 See George A. Torney (ed.), *Toward Creative Urban Strategy*, Waco, Texas: Word Books, 1970, for an earlier examination of innovative and practical strategies for urban involvement.

2 *Inside* magazine (November 1973) has developed an intriguing game called "Slumopoly" which might be used to develop initial awareness of racial hang-ups and increase sensitivity to inner-city problems, using this concept of emotional role-playing. And *Psychology Today* has produced the "Blacks & Whites" game, which operates on the same principle. Such role-playing experiences obviously need to be supplemented by real-life involvement and experiences such as Barnes describes if fundamental attitude and behavior changes are to occur.

17: STEPS IN URBAN PROGRAM DEVELOPMENT

by Dick E. Hart

Isaiah challenged the godly man "to draw out his soul to the weary, and satisfy the afflicted soul." Paul encouraged the early Galatians to bear one another's burdens. Again in the New Testament, we are told to rejoice with those who rejoice and weep with those who weep. In the stresses of the urban environment of the post-industrial society, the Christian has thrust on him the need to supply much succor to a disturbed society, ranging from the level of the metropolis down to individual neighbors.

Facing the broad problems of our cities requires resources beyond those of a single evangelical congregation. The collectivization of effort is required among evangelical churches and groups of churches. This development is seen

DICK E. HART is executive engineer with the Detroit Edison Company. He is a graduate of Purdue University, and has published a number of articles on engineering and energy subjects. A member of the American Society of Mechanical Engineers, the Economic Club of Detroit, and the Engineering Society of Detroit, he is also on the board of deacons at the Strathmoor Judson Baptist Church in Detroit and a board member of the Central City Conference of Evangelicals, and was a member of the select New Detroit Committee established to assist redevelopment of inner-city Detroit in the late 1960s.

in its embryonic stage in the Book of Acts. Paul's collection of money from churches in Greece and Turkey for the needful saints was in effect collectivization of social concern within the church of Christ. In modern times we have a model for collective action in the medical, agricultural, literature, communication, and educational programs undertaken by mission societies and associations. The problems of the large cities of our country should command no less interest and empathy.

The biblical basis for collective action in today's urban environment is discussed at length elsewhere in this book. The physical needs of the disadvantaged were catalogued by the prophets some 2600 years ago. Christ catapulted social responsibility to the very gates of heaven when he explicitly stated that concern would be assessed and severely judged or gloriously rewarded at the end of time. The scathing words of James, the brother of our Savior, nurtured in the center of Galilee's hotbed of radicalism, leave one with no doubt as to the central role social responsibility must play in the life of the Christian. "If faith is not followed by works, it is a dead faith." James warns us to beware of a pervasive materialism and the resulting economic injustices to the powerless.

Although the physical needs of the disadvantaged and the economic needs of marginal groups demand the attention of the Christian, by far the greatest crises in the experience of many city-dwellers are their spiritual, emotional, and psychological struggles. There are staggering numbers at the lower social strata who are not now able to cope with change in their urban surroundings. Synchronized with the biblical imperative, then, is the contemporary demonstration of the need for effective social programs to complement the gospel mandate.

For those who live in our urban centers, social and economic needs seem to inundate the lower strata of our society. The prevalence of need presses some to despair and others to hasty and misguided efforts at alleviation. This is true even of socially sophisticated professional and business people. Many efforts at housing, vocational education, and ghetto businesses are launched with glowing expectation only to flounder and fail within a few short years. Thus when one imagines evangelicals, with pure hearts, deciding to embark on ponderous poverty programs or huge housing projects, one shudders; for they are regularly people with heart-burden, but no expertise in urban affairs and not in vital relationship to the communities they wish to serve. Unless willing to seek sound social counsel, they are doomed from the start.

Basic Steps

The same failure at the outset often typifies efforts at meaningful evangelism and church planting in communities undergoing a dramatic change in racial or ethnic make-up. There seem to be five logical, related steps for implementing successful social programs, evangelistic outreach, and church planting.

1. Need Identification
2. Action Plan Preparation
3. Priority Establishment
4. Marshalling of Resources
5. Execution of Plan

Need identification requires grass-roots contact with the community about us. There can be no falling back on super-spiritual aloofness. While the problems are being investigated, an effective feedback system and sensitive listening mechanisms must be developed. This will require either the creation of a community action group or the infiltration of an existing action group. The end result must be simple and accurate definition of the nature and scope of the need.

Having identified the need, the concerned evangelical will begin preparing a readily understood action plan. This plan will propose systems and programs which will satisfy the needs. Community familiarity with the plan is an absolute must. Furthermore, the plan must be repeated, revised, restructured, time and again, prior to its final development. It must include a schedule for implementation of its various components. No action plan can hope to succeed if it does not define responsibility and recognize authority as a prerequisite to successful execution.

The third step in effective programming is the establishment of priorities. There is always a time-order in the appropriate and efficient satisfaction of need. Some facets of an action plan will have to be implemented immediately; others may be delayed; still others may be found, after careful study, not to be necessary at all, and thus may be delayed indefinitely. There is always a limited pool of resources in men, materials, and money, thus requiring a painful counting of the cost.

When the action plan has been developed and priorities established, resources must be marshalled prior to action initiation. Economic scarcity always demonstrates that there are not enough men, materials, and capital to achieve the goal effortlessly. Men with talent and skill are always in short supply, and in social action programs supported by secular agencies or evangelical groups much of the expertise must be supplied voluntarily. Materials will be required, and, unlike in normal business enterprises, social projects must rely a good deal on donations. Depending on the program, dogged effort will be required to obtain low-interest loan credits or outright grants to the project.

Finally comes the execution of the plan. This calls for disciplined administrative skills. Budgets, inspection, control, and adjustments necessary due to unforeseen conditions must all be purposefully and relentlessly applied if the project is to be successfully carried out.

Youth Summer Program

The implementation of such a program is applicable whether it is a program dealing with people or with facilities. A one-time recreation and evangelism summer project in the central city will serve to illustrate the effectiveness that can result from orderly implementation of a person-centered program.

The identification of need came about rather informally in the early spring when a significant influx of minority children into the Sunday School was observed. By visiting the homes of these children, members learned of a need for summer activities for children in families that could not afford the traditional, middle-income summer vacation. The number of children would be considerable—two each from eighty to a hundred families. The minimal need, it was determined, was a half-day program five days a week, with a variable recreational and Bible teaching emphasis. As results later proved, a genuine grass roots contact was achieved, and the feedback system enabled effective program changes all summer.

By the middle of May an action plan was well under way, effectively defining the needs of the community youth. Numerous alternatives presented themselves, and it developed that the program would have to be built on variety, encompassing athletics, meaningful handicraft, day-camps, cultural center visits, and Bible teaching with evangelism adapted to children with impoverished spiritual backgrounds. It was determined that the program should last for ten weeks.

On the basis of careful evaluation of the action plan, responsibility for the program seemed best assumed by a college student director, who was given complete responsibility for program arrangement within the plan and for recruitment of volunteer staff. These efforts were completed two weeks after the day schools closed for the summer.

The early success of the program required that priority events be set which required minimum qualifications on the part of the staff and little preparation of materials. Recreational programs were readily established, as were activities involving prepared audio-visual aids. More difficult craft preparation and meaningful field trips were planned for later in the summer. Finally, a two-week camping experience was scheduled to complement all that had preceded in craft, Bible teaching, and body development.

Marshalling the resources of manpower, materials, and money was a significant challenge, since by mid-spring plans had yet to be formulated. The director was obtained from a Christian college with no more than the promise of a minimal salary. A detailed budget for materials and equipment, representing great expectations, was developed in faith. Specifications for assisting personnel were developed and recruitment completed just prior to the initiation of the program. Donation lists for equipment and funds were drawn up carefully. This orderly procurement of resources provided a solid base for the earnest prayer effort undertaken concurrently. As a result, there was always a timely resource supply.

The delight of the youth recreation and evangelism program was in its execution. The response of young minds and hearts to wholesome activity and probing evangelism always more than compensates for the effort extended. Still, implementing the program required disciplined management and leadership; and there was a continuing need to apply program changes, shifting in staff, and transferring of funds from one part of the project to another. Flowing from change was an improved program. Earlier action planning, priority establishment and resource assembly all proved highly beneficial to final execution. The result was that a number of young people made decisions that eternally identified them with the Lord Jesus Christ.

Demonstration Project

To illustrate these same five steps in a successful "brick and mortar" program implementation, a look at a low-income housing project will be instructive. In this case, identification of need required a careful analysis of the inner-city census tract involved, a study of the City Planning Commission's existing housing condition evaluation, a door-to-door gathering of data on family size, and a probable ten-year housing spectrum based on numbers of bedrooms. Following this objective and somewhat impersonal analysis, it was necessary to organize a community group to determine desired life-styles of the present occupants. All of this effort, which took six months, led to the decision to establish a nonprofit organization with a local congregation as the sponsor.

The establishment of the nonprofit corporation, assisted by legal volunteers, created the group through whom an action plan could be developed. The development of the plan began with the retention of a competent land planning and architectural firm. A careful house-to-house interviewing of over five hundred families in the community determined the details of family size, living styles, aspirations for better housing, and those features that would be desired in a new community with modern housing. A functional land-use plan was then developed, which fostered the operation of a viable community, reducing those influences of traffic, congestion, and noise that destroy human settlements. This plan was discussed and revised repeatedly at the suggestion of the active community members. Finally, with community approval, the land plan was carefully reviewed with the City Planning Commission to assure that it conformed to the overall city plan and building code.

Extensive individual interviews and community discussions sought to discover the life-styles of the future occupants, who were now living in deteriorated houses in the neighborhood. Some of the important features that came out of the discussion were clear and unobstructed views to play areas, pedestrianways to schools, adequate front stoops, and common backyard play areas. Basements were insisted on for storage and indoor play for the family. The structure and arrangement of the dwelling units had to take into consideration the need for great durability and minimum maintenance. This required detailed discussions and, often, compromises.

When a design satisfactory to the occupants had been found, Housing Commission approval was needed. Where advisable, waivers of building code regulations were sought to allow for the use of new materials and structural forms whose service life would be comparable to conventional material, but whose cost would be lower. A very painstaking forecast was made of the number of bedrooms needed in the several hundred dwelling units for the first ten years. Specialists were called in to help find the best means for financing the construction of the project.

The selection of the construction firm was an exercise in which the community group participated. They were permitted to see the economic analysis of the bids, to examine the construction schedules, to question the firms about their minority hiring practices, and to talk to representatives of the construction trade unions. Representatives of the community groups visited nearby construction projects. The final selection of a firm was made with the aid of a panel of professional architects, engineers, and land planners.

Similar precautions were taken in selecting the firm to manage the housing installation. Within two years, the firm was to train a project manager and maintenance crew to be selected by the group from its own membership. Those responsible for management were required to provide the new occupants with training in proper cleaning, maintenance, and use of the facilities, since many of the occupants would come from deteriorated dwellings, requiring them to learn a whole new life-style in order to preserve the new structures and accommodate the rights and needs of others within the community. Strict rules were adopted and enforced by the community.

Finally, rents were established for dwelling units of various size, tenants were selected, and rental subsidies secured from city and county agencies for eligible occupants.

The span of time from need identification to the occupation of the more than two hundred dwelling units was more than three years. Perhaps this seems unnecessarily long and quite inefficient. But if a disadvantaged community is to be permitted to participate in planning and decisions that bear directly on the residences it will occupy, such time is always well invested. The current level of occupancy of units and maintenance costs attest to the care for and involvement of the community. However, of equal importance was the careful effort given each step in the successful implementation of this program.

18: LEARNING FROM FOREIGN MISSIONS

by Thomas Hopler

What can foreign missions offer to people in the city? One of the strongest voices of protest against foreign missionary methods comes from urban centers. The heartfelt cry is: "Why are so many personnel and millions of dollars invested overseas while little concern is expressed for the cities of our own country?" The purpose of this essay is not to address that question, but, recognizing the faults of foreign missions as practiced today, to sift out the positive contributions of overseas experience and learn from the methods that apply to the city.

Urban churches have seen the impotent gospel of those who hope that a few mission meetings, paper tracts, and sermons in the park will change people and make the city good. They know the sterile gospel of the do-gooders

THOMAS HOPLER is coordinator of urban mission for the Africa Inland Mission, and has begun a pilot work on this project in Newark, New Jersey. He is a graduate of Barrington College, Rhode Island, and holds the master's degree from New York State Teacher's College. For nearly ten years he and his wife served as missionaries in Kenya, before becoming intrigued with the Africa Inland Mission's new interest in the inner city. In September 1971 they moved to Newark to head the program in which they are now involved.

who felt that a bit of whitewash, some new buildings, and better schools will change the city and allow "good people" to be good. If the church is to be effective in communicating its message to the world, we must look for instruction from those who have seen the need for a more complete expression of the gospel and have experienced situations paralleling those in the urban church. Some of those parallels may be found in foreign mission work.

In drawing these parallels we shall part company with those who feel the methods of foreign missions are sacrosanct, but we shall also remind those who see foreign missions as no more than a facet of Western colonial expansion that the commission comes from Christ as head of the church.

Concepts

To avoid confusion we shall begin by elaborating on some concepts that will be important throughout our presentation.

Foreign Mission is cross-cultural communication of the gospel from a culture in which the church, as the living and dynamic body of Christ, is known and visible, to a culture in which the church is unknown or irrelevant. This communication can be considered effective when people in the host culture understand the gospel and, empowered by the Spirit of God, are able to communicate the gospel to people within their own culture.

Individual Witness is telling of one's personal experience with Christ. It is useful for edification in one's church, perhaps also for stimulating someone in one's own culture to accept Christ. It is very rarely of use for evangelism in the initial contact of a foreign culture.

Missionary. A person with unique qualification and gifts that can be recognized by his fellow Christians, who is sent by the church to establish the gospel in a new culture. Not every individual who wants to help someone overseas or in the city is a missionary. The present trend in some quarters to classify every Christian as a "missionary" is not a very helpful use of words.

Mission Field. A culture to which the gospel has not yet been made relevant. Until recently cultures have been seen as synonymous with geographical boundaries; hence the geographic expansion of missions. The layman refers to Kenya, for example, as a mission field. The missionary knows that Kenya comprises 57 tribal groups, each with a distinct language and culture, so that it must be reached separately. The city, like Kenya, is multicultural. It must be seen as a mosaic, both as a whole and in its separate pieces. The church in the city is not monolithic: there are black urban churches, traditional denominational churches, independent integrated churches, Puerto Rican churches, Latin American churches, and so on. There are also pieces of the mosaic that are unchurched — certain large project areas, some ethnic groups, the night-time community.

Ethnocentrism is an anthropological term meaning the tendency for any people to put its culture or reference group in a central position of priority and worth.

The contributions of foreign missions to the urban scene fall into two categories. The major contribution is the dynamic of a new perspective from a unique position in time and space. The second contribution is in offering some useful methods that have been tested on the field.

Dynamics

Missions have been the cutting edge of church expansion for two centuries. Today there is progress on a myriad of fronts around the world. We shall look at three general ways in which the dynamics of foreign missions can activate a more meaningful response to the urban challenge.

The first is the idea of a universal church. Incredible growth has occurred during the last two decades in the churches of Africa, Latin America, and Asia. Increasingly in mission circles a universal or world church is being recognized. Diverse manifestations of the Spirit are being expressed independently but still forming a definite "whole." This is a much more promising development than the organizational unity without spiritual unity often associated with the ecumenical movement. Latin America is redefining evangelism; Africa is redefining our concepts of God; Asia is redefining piety. Mission societies and national churches around the world are engaged in an open-ended dialogue that could ultimately be as significant to the Body of Christ as the Council of Jerusalem (Acts 15).[1]

It is inconceivable in this context to think of the church in the city as a mere copy of white suburban churches. Those churches who follow their members to suburbia indicate thereby their inability to meet the needs of the city. An awareness of the universal church enables one to see that Spanish-speaking churches in sections of the city with heavy Latin American concentrations will not only relate better to those whose native language is Spanish, but will no doubt benefit more from the insights of thousands of different churches around the world than could a church patterned after white suburban models.

Mission societies have the obligation to share the results of church/ mission dialogue with urban churches. For instance, the rise of nationalism in Africa has caused the national church there to see itself and foreign missions in a new light. Confrontations that have been painful for mission societies have resulted, but lessons have been learned in these exchanges which could be very important for urban black churches. It is encouraging to see several mission societies, especially from Latin America, bringing national pastors into service in American cities. An even more deliberate attempt must be made to incorporate the leadership of "third world" (Latin America, Africa, Asia) churches in America's urban missions.

Paul the Apostle was called by the Holy Spirit to the Gentiles. Because he forced the issue at Jerusalem (Acts 15) the church broke out of its Jewish confines. Centuries later the Jesuits became a prodding force for change in the Roman Catholic Church. Early European missionaries went out against the wishes of the church, often in the face of open harassment. Here we see the second dynamic of foreign missions: because of its opportunity to see God at work in new soil, the missionary involvement has often been the prophetic voice of renewal to the home church.

Perhaps the greatest failure, then, of the movement in the last half-century is that it has not spoken with force on issues about which overseas experience has qualified it to comment. Many of the attitudes that prevent American churches from penetrating the city were identified by foreign mission experience decades ago, but were never communicated to urban ministries. To take one example: if missionaries accept polygamy as a non-Christian norm, why not accept the transient habit of the urban black male as a norm? A more important lesson is that isolated individuals in society are always easier to win for Christ, but churches are built from community participants. Very few urban ministries are aimed specifically at the average citizens of the city.

Voices from the national churches of Asia, Latin America, and Africa, as well as from American youth and the black community, are saying that Christianity is unacceptable in its Western garb. Any one of these voices can be brushed aside. Together — and this is the third dynamic of foreign missions — these minorities represent a majority to which we have no choice but to listen.

Within the Western world, Francis Schaeffer has begun to expose the weaknesses of the church in a post-Christian culture, and from outside the West David Barrett, giving reasons why more than five thousand new churches have broken from mainline Western church groups, says, "Here lay the crux of the whole matter: in the phrase 'to share and sympathize'. In regard to this one small facet only — love as close contact with others involving listening, sharing, sympathizing and sensitive understanding in depth as between equals — missions in many tribes had failed."[2] When the urban black says, "We do not have a black problem, it's a white problem," he is voicing the same criticism. Western man too often finds himself incapable of loving. He produces or consumes but he cannot relate as a human being.

Under attack from national churches—and, more recently, from youthful candidates — mission societies are the first to sense how immense the changes are which must take place before these attitudes are corrected. A few societies have had the courage to make significant structural changes. In return they are finding the day of missions is not over. *The urban mission must realize that the cries of America's minorities for identity, understanding, acceptance, and genuine love are the cries of what is in fact the majority around the globe.* In the face of that we must seek new mission structures that do not interfere with direction from the Holy Spirit.

Methods

Those overseas missionary methods which will be useful in the city are the ones which are neither ethnocentric nor geographic in their orientation. We must stop using such terms as Christian/non-Christian culture; sending/receiving country; developed/undeveloped country. *If we define foreign mission as cross-cultural communication of the gospel, our cities are foreign mission fields.*

We shall look at the application of foreign missionary methods to the urban mission under four headings: communication, individual witness, corporate witness, and foreign mission. Every city has sections to which each of these stages is appropriate.

1. Communication. Before the gospel can be presented, lines of communication must be developed. This may be an arduous process, as illustrated by the well-known example of the Auca tribe in Ecuador. Years of language study, research, airplane flights, gifts ended in the death of five men. With perseverance others pursued the task and finally broke through incredible barriers to establish communication. At present the lines of communication between urban and suburban communities are, if they exist at all, garbled. Let us compare present church methods of evangelism with the strategies foreign missionaries have learned.

The first line of communication has to do with language. Disrespect toward Southern black dialect, or urban youth language, or Spanish is ethnocentric and reflects rejection of the person. The heart of the problem is probably the content of words. Overseas, many spend hours selecting the right word for a translation of a biblical passage. It seldom seems to occur to us that in America there are English words which have an entirely different meaning in an urban context from their suburban meaning. If the same word produces a different mental image in the hearer from that in the mind of the speaker, it does not communicate. A long list of key words — including "church," "help," "Jesus Christ," and "love" do not communicate in the city what suburbanites think they do. Time must be spent learning the language *before* we attempt to communicate.

Secondly, before communication can begin, the question, "Why are you here?" must be answered. Every missionary spends some of his first term building mutual acceptance with the people to whom he came to minister. For the earliest missionaries in many tribes, this process took several years. Similarly, we must understand and accept the city, then we must be accepted by the community to whom we will minister, *before* we can communicate the gospel. The gospel cannot be rejected before it is communicated: as Jesus says, "If I had not done among them the works which no one else did, they would not have sin; but now they have *seen* and hated both me and my Father" (John 15:24). The gospel is sometimes rejected because of the method of communication, not the message.

The gospel is an intensely personal message. Unless we have common personal ground, we find it inconsistent to discuss the gospel. Pre-evangelism is commonly accepted in foreign mission. Building trust relationships that do not communicate the gospel is a necessary step to evangelism in a non-Christian culture. Christ intensified the message he proclaimed with each level of trust he developed. It was not until his final week that he told the whole story, and even then he said there was more. If we are ever to communicate the gospel to the *whole* man, there are acts of mercy to be accomplished before we can win the right to share our faith.

The third step in communication is recognition of different values. The uniqueness of the gospel is that in it God comes to us where we are. If satisfaction in my culture involves owning two cars and a color television set, whereas I have only one car and a black-and-white TV, I may feel a need. Christ can deal with that need. If satisfaction in your culture is having ten children and an acre of ground, and you have no children, you may feel a need. But if Christ is to deal with that need, you must know what Christ has to say about having no children, not about how to get along without a color television. In other words, if we do not understand the value system of the city, we cannot communicate to the people in it.

God felt it essential to live as a human from infancy in order to communicate with humans. How can we presume that he will perform the supernatural to save us the pain of living in the ghetto? The marriage patterns, sex mores, and entertainment habits of the city-dweller are no more sinful than the gossip, love of affluence, and lack of concern of the suburbanite. A bar on every street corner is no different from a liquor cabinet in every home. We may grow accustomed to "our kind of sin," but God does not. When we develop lines of communication, then, we must remember our sins as well as "theirs."

2. Individual Witness. The second stage of foreign mission begins when a few nationals have comprehended the gospel, accepted it, and find their lives being changed. They can then give witness of how Christ is important within the normal life of their culture. The typical emphasis on evangelism to the abnormal—to the drug addicts, drunkards, and gang lords—emphasizes the rejection of urban society by most American suburban Christians. For every drug addict there is a schoolteacher, shopkeeper, taxi driver, lawyer, or housewife who also needs Jesus Christ. Win a schoolteacher and you establish a witness before a few hundred children and several hundred parents. Win a shopkeeper and you establish an on-going witness to the community. This is what churches are made from. One of the greatest needs in urban mission is the systematic documentation and publication of Christ's influence in the normal lives of urban people.

These first converts are tender transplants in a hostile soil. They need nourishment, protection, and growth. After a brief period of witness in Damascus, the Apostle Paul went to Arabia for three years and then to his home town of Tarsus. We may assume that as a result of the growing influence of Paul's witness in Tarsus, Barnabas joined him (Acts 11:25).

New witnesses in the subcultures of our cities seem often to face two unsatisfactory options. Either they can refuse all contact with the Body of Christ and live in isolation, or they can be inundated with an organized Christianity so powerful that it soon stifles their individual identity. This is self-defeating. We must find out how to encourage growth in urban Christians without interfering with the work of the Holy Spirit. Discipleship, not institutionalization, is called for. God could have programmed his angels as missionaries, or written the gospel in the sky, or implanted Christian faith directly on the minds of men, but he has chosen to communicate it through us. It is by our dealing with people that God deals with us. If we send money, graded curricula, well-printed tracts, without being empathetically involved as people, we are abdicating our responsibility in mission. This depersonalized gospel and standardized results can crush the tender new witness, with the result that the indigenous church is not established and the city remains its pagan self. Urban Christians living in the urban culture must be encouraged to discover how Christ is important in their lives.

3. Corporate Witness. Bringing together indigenous witnesses to form a corporate witness to the community — the visible church — is the next stage in a foreign missionary strategy. The dynamic witness of this body to the community will depend on how strong are the roots of its individual witness. Churches that are imposed on a foreign society can fail completely. Rigid structures that ignore the flexibility demanded by the life-style of city-dwellers will not work, and are perhaps the clearest example of how essential it is for the church to grow out of its own community.

During this stage of missions outside help can be very useful, provided that discipleship, not institutionalism, is the goal. Corporate witness will take into account what God is doing in a particular cultural setting, not try to transfer institutions proven effective elsewhere. Missionaries are, of course, accountable to the people back home who pay their salaries. Consequently the temptation is great to impose on the foreign contexts discipline that produces behavior pleasing to the people of the sending church or society. Denominational boards are particularly eager to maintain similarities between sending and developing churches. But genuine church discipline is the structuring of living experiences on biblical principles, not the teaching of "Christian living" by Christians from another cultural setting. What are some of the issues urban missions should investigate?

Local church forms have arisen out of crowded conditions—especially in Southeast Asia—that could be adapted to American cities: rooftop churches in Hong Kong; small out-churches or chapels under the leadership of a large, central church; fellowships of house churches that meet monthly for communion in a rented hall.

Mission societies have proved that social needs which prevent the church from becoming a complete community must be met. If people cannot read, schooling is necessary; if people are dying, hospitals must be built. In some countries mission societies have borne the needs of an entire country until government was able to take over. But the needs of the community must be discovered in a process of building corporate witness, not in sterile dialogue with government or para-government organization. For example, suppose organization A says the only solution to the educational problem is to bus 30% of all city children to suburbia. The church should not be forced into taking a yes or no position on this. Perhaps the better response would be to think about developing Christian schools as an alternative means of education for children in the city.

The church should also sense the crippling effect that welfare has on a person's self-image. How can a person believe that God sent his Son to die for him if his entire life is controlled by the regulations essential to get that check? Similarly, the proliferation of drugs, of corruption in government, the callousness of industry prevent the church from being the church. The church must expose opposition and find a way through it if it is to be the light on a hill to all people. When this brings it into conflict with authority, it must nonetheless stand for truth.

New discoveries from the field of church growth are important to the church's approach to the city. Anti-denominationalism and membership loss in ethnic churches have led to a trend toward church consolidation rather than church planting. This thought pattern must be reversed. Mobile urban society requires the multiplication of dynamic, fruit-bearing congregations.

Theological education by extension is a Latin American development that is very promising for the growth of urban missions. We must recognize that theological institutions tend to meet the needs of a single constituency. American theological institutions are entirely unrelated to the black, Spanish, Chinese, and other ethnic groups of our cities. Adequate leadership training for city churches must be developed. The multiplication of store-front churches in urban areas, not dependent on heavy outside resources, indicates that flexibility in form and on-the-spot leadership training are important contributing factors to church growth.

A final lesson about corporate witness that foreign missions have taught is this: we must unify at least for the sake of evangelism. Church groups with broad diversity have worked in considerable harmony overseas. The fractured witness in American cities is dismaying, to say the least, to anyone who has been involved in foreign missions. This is not the fault of those who are there, but of those who are not. There is a serious need for organizations with a nationwide constituency to become involved as unifying forces in urban mission.

4. *Foreign Mission* is not an *option* for mature churches, but an essential part of church growth, a necessary phase before the initial mission process is

complete. A church that does not develop its own cross-culture communication process will compromise with the society around it and will thus lose its message. If it remains at all it will only be as another empty religious system. There are vestiges of such churches today in India, Africa, Russia, Europe, and America.

A foreign mission vision is not easily caught. The Book of Acts leaves no doubt that the Holy Spirit had to break down a good deal of resistance before the Jews were willing to include the Gentiles in their number. Similarly, the black church in America has been isolated from mainstream Christianity by the attitude of racial superiority on the part of the white church. This isolation has had predictable results in its missionary vision. Most urban churches have a strong local concern but have been prevented from developing a world-view of evangelism and mission. The breach between foreign missions and the urban church must be healed before the urban church can be a living and dynamic force in the world. Foreign mission societies are responsible to examine what steps are necessary to open lines of communication to all biblically oriented city churches. Urban churches must examine what they have to do for a vision of world evangelism.

Under severe attack as "colonialist" and "imperialist" in recent years, foreign missionaries tend to be defensive about a global vision. The fact remains, however, that the lines of communication for world evangelism and church planting are largely in the hands of foreign mission societies. At present the flow on these lines of communication is largely from the Western, technologically oriented churches to foreign communities and their churches.

Suppose national churches were encouraged to reverse the direction on these lines of communication. In addition to suburban white churches sending missionaries to foreign countries and to urban centers, we could have foreign countries who receive missionaries also sending missionaries to urban America. Urban America would then be receiving missionaries from suburbia and from foreign countries, and the next step would follow quickly: urban churches, having met nationals and gained confidence in the mission society, would send missionaries to the foreign country. The final step is obvious *and essential:* nationals from the foreign country would team up with members of urban churches to become missionaries to suburban America. If this last step comes as a surprise, perhaps it is because we have not understood the process of missions as the crossing of cultural boundaries through the supernatural guidance of the Holy Spirit. If Christ is the Lord of his church, made up of people from around the world, and his concern is that all people come to him, the Holy Spirit will surely call on any of his servants to fulfil this task anywhere.

The present mission agency, transformed to something international in make-up, would coordinate the flow of personnel and finance in any direction between suburban America, urban centers, and foreign countries. The source of supply would be churches. Every church would be missionary minded.

Christ can override the impersonal forces that consume human lives and spew their living remains into ghettos. Churches have too long attacked each piece of the mosaic without understanding the relationship of that piece to the whole. Foreign mission societies have too long been concerned with a world-view and not aware of how important their experience is to the local church back home. The urban mission must be the combined forces of the church concerned with urban centers around the world. First, we must attack the concept of the city as a powerful whole. Let us then move into each ethnic group, power clique, class of people, and communicate Christ until he is understood, and his church stands as a peaceful haven to all who would enter.

Notes to Chapter 18

1 "It was a curious fact that while in the United States five (and later eight) older denominations strove valiantly to merge through the Consultation on Church Union (COCU), probably a new denomination a day was springing up with vigorous life in the Non-Western World." Ralph D. Winter, *The Twenty-five Unbelievable Years 1945-1969* (South Pasadena, Cal.: William Carey Library, 1970), p. 31.

2 David B. Barrett, *Schism and Renewal in Africa* (Nairobi: Oxford U.P., 1968), p. 155.

19: BLACK-WHITE UNDERSTANDING: COMMUNICATION AND PARTICIPATION

by Graham Barnes

Jason (a pseudonym, as with all personal names in this chapter) sat at one end of the semicircle of an interracial group, his legs crossed away from the group. The position of his body formed a barricade to the other members of the group. He said he wanted to do something about the uncomfortable feelings he experienced around blacks. These feelings were getting him into constant trouble in his work at a predominately black institution.

"I want to learn to be close to members of the *opposite* race—of another race," he paused. Sitting next to him was Larry, a black, whom he had blocked

GRAHAM BARNES is president of the Southeast Institute and director of the Fellowship for Racial and Economic Equality (FREE), headquarters in Chapel Hill, North Carolina. He has studied at Roanoke Bible College, Abilene Christian College, Harvard University, and Boston University. He is also a teaching member and a member of the board of trustees of the International Transactional Analysis Association. Previously he served as vice president of the board of directors of Shalom Apartments, an inner-city experiment in multiracial living in Lynchburg, Virginia. Generous support needed to conduct the research and develop the practical tools presented in this chapter was provided by the Irwin-Sweeney-Miller Foundation from 1969 to 1971.

off completely. Larry asked, "What is keeping you from being close to blacks in this room?"

"Perhaps my own insecurity, not being sure of myself," Jason replied.

"What do you mean by insecurity?" I asked.

"Not being sure of my own competency, my adequacy . . . and as I begin to get hold of that, maybe then, this is where. . . ." His voice trailed off.

"How are you going to go about getting hold of your competency, your adequacy?"

After rambling for a moment Jason mentioned his failures in personal and professional relationships with blacks. His most recent failure was in his work under the direction of a black woman.

Members of the group offered Jason their impressions of his behavior in the room. Someone called attention to his body language: Jason asked to have the videotape of the session played back. Another member of the group mentioned Jason's slip of the tongue in the phrase "opposite" race and suggested that he might be substituting racial for sexual differences.[1]

Jason learned two important things about himself in the session: that he had bought into a strong "white" cultural and parental message not to be close to or trust blacks; and how he was setting himself up for failure.[2] He was reinforcing his decisions not to be close to blacks and to fail by trying, from a superior "rescuer" position, to help blacks, whom he saw as victims.[3] Usually, blacks reject his help, so he feels "frustrated" and "hostile."

Through his intensive work in the group Jason decided to reinforce his commitment to racial justice and to discover his ability to respond to injustices as a problem solver. Jason became aware of his racial "script," the basic decisions he had made about people of other races early in life.[4] He decided to stop living as an unwilling slave to childhood decisions based on inadequate or distorted information from parents, other adults, or society as a whole. These early decisions had become the basis for an unreflective way of living, characterized by unwitting game-playing and collecting bad feelings.

After his decisions to stop setting himself up for failure and to be close to and trust blacks and others, Jason found a new positive response from those in the group, especially blacks. One of these was Larry. Before Jason had worked through his impasse, Larry had told him, "I have some problems trusting you. You're interested in me as a part of the black race, not as a person." Now Larry responded to him with trust and warmth, and Jason's work gave him permission to examine his own feelings. Larry confessed to members of the group that he felt uncomfortable around whites who occupied positions of authority. He did not feel close to or want to trust these people.

Someone asked what would be the worst thing that could happen to him if he continued to distrust white people in positions of authority. "I would be tricked, used, and exploited," he replied.

"Is it a fact that you *can* be used or tricked or exploited?"

"Oh, I could be if I were unaware. But there is no way that I'm going to walk into a place with my eyes blinded."

The leader asked Larry what would happen to him if he were tricked. "I would feel put down," he declared.

This exchange helped Larry become aware of how he had been setting himself up to be put down by whites. Larry related a traumatic scene from childhood. He had gone into a gas station and asked to use the rest room. A surly white attendant had rudely refused permission and scolded him. Larry decided then and there never again to risk trusting a white person in authority. He also became aware of how he had been setting himself up to be kicked by some whites as a way to collect bad feelings that would reinforce that decision at the gas station.

What Jason and Larry accomplished illustrates a process I have discovered to enable blacks and whites, and others, to become aware of themselves, of the games they play, and then to become "centered."[5] To experience awareness and become centered is to begin to understand others, to open lines of communication, and to find ways to cooperate that elicit participation.

The Fellowship for Racial and Economic Equality (FREE) was started to help whites, especially evangelicals, take seriously the mandate of their theology, as well as the American creed, to eliminate racism. Those who worked in FREE share the basic framework of meaning, the same basic values and ethics, the same general rules for how Christians ought to behave and what they should do in response to the racial crisis in the United States.

It was at the level of implementation that we experienced difficulty. Many sensitive evangelical leaders have taken their theology seriously and they attempt to give attention to structuring their lives in harmony with the teachings of Christ, at least as commonly understood within the American ethos. Given this fact, documented by social scientists,[6] we were not startled that for most evangelicals the elimination of personal and institutional racism was close to the bottom of the list of priorities. The radical evangelical ethic has not been used to criticize institutions and society and to bring about racial, economic, and political justice.

Our appeal to the framework of meaning (theology) and the framework of values and ethics made no perceptible difference in the behavior of most of our early evangelical clients and their institutions. We called attention to what others already knew: that evangelical rhetoric abounds with righteous indignation and confessions of guilt, and climaxes in an exercise called repentance, which brings forth nothing.

Nonevangelicals provide some instructive parallels. Several years ago Ralph Potter examined the positions taken by the churches on nuclear weapons. He concluded that the problem was not that the churches had not spoken but that they had not spoken well. Similarly, in the area of racial justice, the problem, especially with evangelicals, has not been the quality of their utterances but the paucity of their actions.[7]

In short, after listening to carefully formulated theological statements we still witness the same behavior and virtually no change in oppressive institutions. We find the same behavior patterns among evangelicals as among nonevangelicals. We have not detected any noticeable difference between religious and secular institutions, except that some secular institutions are more committed to racial and social justice.

So we felt it was necessary to help people define the racial and social context or situation as they *experienced* it, rather than as they though they ought to see it.[8] We stopped telling people what they *ought* to do — they already knew that. We discovered that problems are invented either to be solved or to be frustrated about. People in our groups learned how to define racial problems that concerned them and to look for "how-to-get-on-with-it" tools. Our response was to find and share techniques that could be used to solve these problems.

As we developed our capacity to listen to people define the situation,[9] we saw some leaders leave our sessions with new and practical solutions to racial problems, only to return to their organizations and sabotage the very cause they had championed. Since we had decided not to be satisfied with less than effective institutional and personal change, we added other criteria. We would not consider our work with a leader successful unless he or she returned to his or her organization with increased awareness of a capacity to solve problems more effectively than before working with us.

With this in mind we decided to give attention to the unpleasant behavior and feelings each person wanted and needed to change. We saw that we could not isolate racial feelings and behavior from other troubling experiences. We have learned to concentrate not on how people *should* behave, but on how they *are* behaving; not on how they ought to think or feel but on what they are experiencing in the here and now; not on what they say they want to do or will do, but on what they are actually doing in the group.

In this context people wanted to deal with repressed hostility towards parents, high frustration, feelings of inadequacy, interpersonal alienation, sexual confusion including repressed sexuality, projection of undesirable feelings (this included whites using blacks as a "living ink blot"[10]), and distrust of others, especially people of other races.[11] To meet this need we integrated psychotherapy theory and techniques with social and racial concerns. We have discovered that as people overcome their unpleasant feelings they become more aware of their power to solve social and racial as well as personal problems.

Sidney is an example of how prejudice and racism can be related to other troubling experiences. Sidney came to FREE as part of a white church's mission to prepare its leaders to communicate with blacks. During the first session he made the following statement about himself:

Everybody tells me that I can't make it, but that makes me want to try that much harder, especially with my brother. He puts me down and my dad put me up to put me down by comparing him with me: "Dave always does a better job *than you will.*" That makes me try that much harder. Ha! Ha! Ha! *I always resented my brother.* He was older than I was. Dad always looked up to him because he did things to please Dad. I never could do anything that would meet his standards. I think that made me try that much harder to show that I could *be.* Maybe that's the wrong way to do.

Sidney says several things about himself here that become important when he describes his racial feelings and behavior: (1) He has decided that he will not make it. He tries hard but he does not think he will ever live up to his father's unrealistic expectations or do as well as his brother. (2) He feels put down by his brother. His father set him up to put him down or kick him. (3) He tries hard to stay alive. (4) He collects feelings of resentment. (5) He got a message from his father and brother not to be close to them.

When Sidney said these things about himself he was not fully aware of the extent to which he was living with unfinished business with his father and brother dating back to when he was a child. Later, when Sidney decided to work with his feelings about blacks he said:

I have a racial problem and it's concerning my job. . . . I have played with blacks from my youth up. For the last six months I have resented them more than before.

We have a nigger . . . ahh black man, George, over at the Shop who holds the same position I do. And he's a married man too. He is flirting with one of the white women over there. This gets my goat. This tears me up. It makes me resent him. I just sometimes would like to walk up and grab him in the nape of the neck and punch him in the mouth—just take my fist and drive it right through his face.

Then we have another one over there, Randy. He is impolite and he is all time running into me, bumping into me. And I try my best to get out of his way, to excuse myself from his presence and things of that nature. But he is always there bumping into me. In the last six months or so it's really been getting my goat.

Now there is one colored gentlemen over there that I work with. I think just as much of him as my own flesh and blood. I believe I would fight you over him right now if you said a cross word about him, or anything. But these other two they get my goat and I just resent them.

Sidney was then asked how he would like to change that.

I'd like to have a better understanding with them, you know. I would like to be able to—maybe to—find out what makes them do the things they do so that I can understand them and maybe be more forgiving and not hold a grudge or anything. Of course, I don't go around with a chip on my shoulder. I'd like to be able *to overcome this problem and work through it. I want to understand myself better and get over the resentment.*

In these last two sentences Sidney articulates what he wants to change about himself. He has moved from wanting to *change* George and Randy, which he did not have the power to do, to wanting to *understand* them, a more realistic goal. When he says he wants to understand himself and give up his resentment, he is in contact with a part of himself that he does have power over and can change.

At this point I asked Sidney to pretend that one of the three blacks he had described had come into the room. He chose George. I placed an empty chair in front of him and asked him to put George in the chair and tell him what he was feeling. After explaining some of his opinions and beliefs, Sidney said, "George, I have tried to witness to you but you always put me down and make fun of me. All the time. . . . You guys have me labeled as a fanatic. . . . I don't go up to you and say, 'If you don't change your way you are going to hell,' or something like that. I try to drop a hint when the occasion arises. I try to put Jesus in there when I can."

After considerable dialogue between Sidney as himself and Sidney playing the role of George, Sidney told George: "You don't know what you are missing. It is wonderful. I mean your whole life would be changed if you had a little bit of Christ in you — *if you quit resenting* him and let him come in."

What happens in Sidney's relationships with blacks? First, Sidney sets himself up for failure in these relationships. Second, he sets himself up to be put down. Randy bumps into him all the time and George puts him down. He has found two blacks on the job who treat him as his father and brother did when he was younger. Third, this pattern of behavior reinforces Sidney's feeling that he has to struggle to stay alive. He tries hard to get people to give him permission to live. Instead of getting people to like him, he antagonizes them to bump into him and to put him down, which reinforces his death wish. Fourth, Sidney has decided not to be close to or trust blacks. Again, blacks take the place of father and brother. Fifth, he continues to collect resentments. This is of course especially dangerous, because eventually Sidney's resentment may boil over into violence.

Later in the workshop I asked Sidney to re-create a scene from his childhood with persons of his choice in the group posing as family members. This exercise helped Sidney become aware of his decision long ago not to live up to the unrealistically high standards of his father. He remembered that he decided as a child that a safe way to get recognition or attention from either parent was to send secret or ulterior messages to them so they would put him down. Then he felt hurt and later turned the hurt into resentment. Sidney recalled that his mother had never told him she loved him and that he felt as a child that if he would die then she would love him. He cried, "All I want is for my mother to say she loves me." I asked him to give up waiting for her love and to decide not to kill himself accidentally or purposely. The air was electric with emotion as he gave up believing in the magic of childhood and decided to live and to take care of himself.

He also imagined his father, and later his brother, in empty chairs and told them how much he resented their demands and expectations. He confessed to them that he had kept these gnawing feelings in his guts for years. At this point Sidney became aware that he had repressed the hostility toward his parents and his brother and had taken it out on blacks; that he had projected his feelings of resentment and undesirable sexual impulses onto blacks.[12] He had selected whites to portray all the members of his family except his brother when he had created the early family scene.

Sidney worked through these early feelings. He forgave his parents and his brother. In so doing he learned the joy and usefulness of living in the here and now. Later when Sidney returned to a group meeting he reported, "At work I haven't felt that old resentment for my fellow employees."

Conclusion

How can whites, blacks and others develop understanding and open lines of communication? I have seen no simple solutions. I only want to share what I am finding useful both personally and in my work with others.

I am beginning to feel about others—whites, blacks, Indians, Chicanos— that they are all right. I am of inestimable worth and they are too. I am learning to separate acceptance of them from agreement or disagreement with them on political, social, racial, theological, and other issues. After resolving some very uncomfortable personal issues I am beginning to face up to what I feel, even when it is not the "right" thing. In so doing, I can take responsibility, and by taking responsibility I can decide what to do with my feelings. It is not always easy to feel compassion and concern for those whose behavior I find reprehensible, but I feel more comfortable in this position than when relying on the dogmatic assertions of those (including myself) who advocate violence and punishment to control behavior.[13]

My behavior is filled with fewer indirect or secret messages. I am concerned with the consequences of my actions. I am learning to trust my intuition. By relying on my own integrity I do not need rules to control my behavior or prohibitions to tell me what I should not do. I do not need to manipulate others, nor am I easily manipulated, especially by those who use high-sounding rhetoric to produce guilt in unsuspecting victims.

My effectiveness in working with others can be measured by the extent to which I refuse to put myself in an oppressor, rescuer, or victim position. By becoming more aware of myself and others, by owning my power, using my creativity, developing my capacity to participate in decision-making, I am overcoming my racial isolation and joining with others to tackle the racism deeply embedded within the structures of our culture.

The cultural prohibition against trusting or being close to people of other races is one that people adopt as children and transmit as parents and leaders. Generally it cannot be overcome by appeal to theology, values, or ethics. It lies, often dormant, in the depths of the person to influence or determine, perhaps in subtle ways, feelings and behavior.

Jason and Larry are examples of how people can identify and overcome these archaic injunctions. The case of Sidney illustrates how prejudice and racism related to other troubling experiences can be resolved. These people met for specific purposes: first to become more whole and effective, and then to define and solve institutional problems.[14] A group is wasting its time when it meets to "discuss racism." Books abound with all the information people need to educate themselves out of their ignorance of blacks, native Americans, Chicanos, whites, and others. Merely talking about the evils of racism perpetuates despair, stifles creativity, encourages bad feelings, and keeps us all stuck.

When we form groups with a specific purpose—to break racism down into its economic, political, social, religious, and personal components—we can use our personal power and creativity to devise strategy, and our collective power to change structures and influence public policy.

Notes to Chapter 19

1 Some studies indicate that race may serve as a functional substitute for difference in sex. Gordon W. Allport, *The Nature of Prejudice* (Garden City: Doubleday, 1954, 1958), abridged edition, pp. 349-50, who cites J. L. Moreno's research in this area.

2 Joel Kovel, *White Racism: A Psychohistory* (New York: Vintage Books, 1970), delineates three "ideal" types of racism in the United States: dominative (characterized by bigotry and the threat and/or use of force), aversive (characterized by avoidance and distance), and metaracism (characterized by feelings, attitudes and actions that are unconsciously racist). What Kovel calls aversive racism—a set of feelings and behaviors that permeate our society—appears to me to be what I see clinically in the form of an injunction: "Don't trust blacks" or "Don't be close to blacks." When this is merged with what Kovel calls metaracism—programs to help blacks devised by whites with good intentions and feelings of superiority—the consequences may be disillusionment and despair.

3 James Comer, *Beyond Black and White* (New York: Quadrangle Books, 1972), mentions three kinds of whites blacks don't need: the rescuer, the masochist and the ally. People in these positions form a drama triangle of oppressor-victim-rescuer (cf. Stephen B. Karpman, "Fairy Tales and Script Drama Analysis," *Transactional Analysis Bulletin,* 7:26, April 1968, pp. 39-43). Whites who see blacks as victims needing to be rescued are advised to see that rescuers are still in a superior position. Help offered from this position, even if not rejected by the "victim," may not be very constructive. Cf. Eric Berne, *Games People Play* (New York: Grove, 1964), pp. 143-47. The rescuing or paternalistic aspect also finds expression in religious sentiments. Paul A. Riemann argues that Genesis 4 is not meant to substantiate our idea of "brother keeping." "Am I My Brother's Keeper?", *Interpretation,* XXIV: 4 (October 1970), pp. 482-92.

4 The key factor is to take responsibility for feelings, thoughts and actions. Cf. Seymour L. Halleck, *The Politics of Therapy* (New York: Science House, Inc., 1971), p. 216, for a discussion of responsibility as accountability. Redecision, the resolution of an impasse or of early conflicts, is not the same as good intentions which end up in the verbal garbage pail. It serves as a prerequisite for change, involves the commitment of the whole person, and requires owning conflicts and bad feelings and giving up childish fantasies of helplessness. See Robert Goulding, "New Directions in Transactional Analysis: Creating an Environment for Redecision and Change," in *Progress in Group and Family Therapy,* Clifford J. Sager and Helen Singer Kaplan, eds. (New York: Brunner/Mazel, 1972), pp. 105-34; and Robert L. Goulding, Mary E. Goulding, and Paul McCormick, "Marathon Therapy with a Marijuana 'Loser', in *Human Development: Selected Readings,* third ed., Morris L. Haimowitz and Natalie Reader Haimowitz, eds. (New York: Crowell, 1973), pp. 412-26.

5 George D. Kelsey, *Racism and the Christian Understanding of Man* (New York: Scribners, 1965), pp. 11, notes that a racist lacks centeredness. An uncentered person would rather trust his fantasies and prejudices than rely on his ability to process data, to test reality and to use intuition. A racist society is alienated and fragmented, preferring violence to communication and acceptance of diversity. Cf. Arnold R. Beisser, "The Paradoxical Theory of Change," in *Gestalt Therapy Now,* Joen Fagan and Irma Lee Shepherd, eds. (New York: Harper, 1970), p. 80. Also, Gordon W. Allport, *The Nature of Prejudice,* chapter 24, "Projection"; and Frederick S. Perls, *Gestalt Therapy Verbatim* (Lafayette, Cal: Real People Press, 1969), p. 37.

6 See David O. Moberg, *The Church as a Social Institution: Sociology of American Religion* (Englewood Cliffs: Prentice Hall, 1962), chapters 3 and 17; Thomas F. Pettigrew and Ernest Q. Campbell, *Christians in Racial Crisis* (Washington: Public Affairs Press, 1959); Joseph H. Fichter, "American Religion and the Negro," *Daedalus,* 94:4 (Fall 1965), pp. 1085-1106; Louis Schneider, ed., *Religion, Culture and Society* (New York: John Wiley and Sons, 1964); and *Psychology Today* 3:11 (April 1970), articles by Rokeach, Stark *et al.,* and Brannon. However, Allport, *op. cit.,* chapter 28, calls attention to positive religious factors and experiences that offer alternatives, especially on the personal level. Also see Allport, "Prejudice: Is It Societal or Personal?", in *The Person in Psychology* (Boston: Beacon, 1968), pp. 187-207.

7 Ralph Potter, "Silence or Babel," *Social Action,* XXXII:5-6 (Jan.-Feb. 1966), pp. 34-45.

8 Cf. William I. Thomas, "The Four Wishes and the Definitions of the Situation," in *Theories of Society,* Talcott Parsons *et al.,* eds. (New York: Free Press, 1961, 1965), pp. 741-44. Thomas notes that most groups seek to define the situation for their members and then devise corresponding rules of conduct.

9 See the work of Carl Rogers on listening as noted by George Prince, *The Practice of Creativity* (New York: Collier, 1972), pp. 42-45. Prince also discusses a useful exercise in listening called "spectrum policy," pp. 46-52. Also, Franklin H. Ernst, Jr., "The Activity of Listening," in Haimowitz and Haimowitz, *op. cit.,* pp. 373-81. Discounting is another mechanism that gets in the way of listening. Discounting is thinking that one's own ideas, thoughts, or feelings are more significant than what the other person is saying, doing, or experiencing. See Aaron Wolfe Schiff and Jacqui Lee Schiff, "Passivity," in *Transactional Analysis Journal,* I:I (January 1971), pp. 71-78.

10 Cf. Gordon W. Allport, "Prejudice and the Individual," in *The Person in Psychology,* p. 214.

11 Cf. Bernard Berelson and Gary A. Steiner, *Human Behavior: An Inventory of Scientific Findings* (New York: Harcourt, Brace and World, 1964), pp. 493-525, chapter on "Ethnic Relations," especially p. 517 where they cite the work of Suchman *et al.* (1958) that correlates these items with the prejudice-prone personality. I do not see prejudice as part of our nature. It is both "taught" and "caught," and in both instances learned and bought. This means it can be unlearned and dropped. Every generation may have to deal with new prejudices as well as some of the old because of both the irrational basis of prejudice and the disguises in which it is passed down from generation to generation. In addition to the personal side of prejudice, we need to see its social, political, historical and economic aspects. See Bruno Bettelheim and Morris Janowitz, *Social Change and Prejudice, Including Dynamics of Prejudice* (New York: Free Press, 1964), chapter 3, "The Psychology of Prejudice," pp. 49-77, especially pp. 50-53, for a critique of the disregard of these factors in psychoanalytic studies. These factors are interrelated. "Every personal problem is a social problem, and every social problem is a personal problem"; James Luther Adams, "Social Ethics and Pastoral Care," in *Pastoral Care and the Liberal Churches,* James Luther Adams and Seward Hiltner, eds. (Nashville: Abingdon, 1970), p. 199. Prejudice and neurosis may be social symptoms of the sickness of a society. Marshall Edelson, *The Practice of Sociotherapy: A Case Study* (New Haven: Yale U.P., 1970), calls attention to the tendency of psychological interpretations to ignore the social situation and its impact upon the individual. See chapter 11, "The Sociotherapist's Use of Social Theory," especially pp. 312-314.

12 Sheldon B. Kopp, "The Refusal to Mourn," *Voices* (Spring 1969), pp. 30-35, emphasizes that as we mourn the unfinished past, bury our dead, and give up trying to redeem our disappointments and our losses, we open ourselves to feelings of love and warmth in the here and now. An important step in obtaining awareness, spontaneity, intimacy and compassion is by getting what Berne, *op. cit.,* pp. 182f., calls a *friendly divorce* from all parental influences – past and present – including one's own mother and father.

13 Cf. S. L. Halleck, M.D., "Even Punishment of Powerful Offenders is Wasteful," *The Chapel Hill Newspaper,* Sunday, June 17, 1973, p. 9D.

14 This process requires the assistance of highly skilled, trained group leaders who offer support, understanding, acceptance and permission to change. Cf. Morton A. Lieberman, Irvin D. Yalom, and Matthew B. Miles, *Encounter Groups: First Facts* (New York: Basic Books, 1973).

20: SUBURBAN-URBAN LIFELINES

by L. Edward Davis

By "suburban-urban lifelines" we mean those relationships between bodies of Christ (or Christian churches) that enable them to coordinate their efforts and cooperate in doing the will of God and accomplishing the work of Christ in urban society. The hyphenated form "suburban-urban" in our title is meant to suggest coalition. More often today it seems to suggest "suburban versus urban," a fragmentation that tends to polarize the body. Accepting the secular norm of quantity rather than quality,[1] the church has divided itself between urban and suburban. It has become an institutionalized church out of its desperate need for self-preservation, a racist church, and thus an impotent church.

How can we redefine "suburban-urban" to indicate a vital relationship of working together. The Master Plan and Program of Urban Development of the

L. EDWARD DAVIS is pastor of the Central Alliance Church in Detroit, an inner-city parish near Wayne State University. He is a graduate of Nyack College and holds the M. Div. degree from New Brunswick Theological Seminary. He is co-chairman of the Detroit urban coalition, the Central City Conference of Evangelicals, and has served his denomination, the Christian and Missionary Alliance, in developing a master plan for urban ministries.

Christian and Missionary Alliance recognizes that "the urban structure is essentially three-layered, i.e., the inner city, city residential, suburban residential fringe." Rather than a compartmentalized vision of the church's task, therefore, a new strategy, based on this integrated concept of the essential unity of the urban world, made diverse in a three-layered structure, must be articulated in order to build the kingdom of God within urban society.

But before we can even talk about future cooperation and coordination the present absence of lifelines between the city and the suburbs must be remedied.

Remedial Prerequisites

What does it mean to be the Body of Christ in light of Scripture? What is the nature of the church in an urban society? That is the first question confronting us if we wish to awaken ourselves, repent, and return, lest the Lord come to us and remove our lampstand from its place (Rev. 2:5). The Body of Christ must be defined in terms of its biblical identity as the present, incarnate body over which Christ is head and through which Christ ministers in the world (Eph. 1:22-23; 4:4-6, 11-12, 15-16). This is the church universal. The local church is one member of that body, which functions in a particular location for the same purpose as the church universal — to edify the body and disciple all persons.

The local church should be a microcosm of the world within which it ministers. In an urban center, there is usually a multi-cultural cross-section of peoples, which may include Appalachian whites, ghetto blacks, middle-class university students, international students, persons who are employed by the city, and so on. Such a cultural diversity demands of the local church a cross-cultural fellowship that reflects the unifying effect of the Body of Christ, which transcends the diversity and plurality of human society. Some research would suggest that church growth comes best through homogeneous groupings because of the practical limitations of a cross-cultural church. But Howard Hageman asks whether it is not "something near blasphemy to say we cannot preach Christ except to members of our own class and race and culture."[2] The diversity of a cross-cultural church is its blessing as well as its bane, and it seems to me that we need to work carefully for a combination of homogeneity and heterogeneity.

Our second question is this: how do we define "mission"? "Mission" is the function of the church.[3] The church's mission is to disciple, by going, baptizing, and teaching (Matt. 28:19-20), to Jerusalem first, then to Judea, and finally to the remotest parts of the earth (Acts 1:8). Ralph Covell suggests that the urban crisis of today is the measure of the church's commitment to this mission: it may be, he says, "God's provision to the church to test our integrity, to force us to be honest, and to keep us from congratulating ourselves for a ministry abroad that we are loathe to practice at home."[4]

I once ministered in a city where the slogan of a large evangelical congregation was "One of America's Great Missionary Churches." But then the black tide began to flow towards that church. Every kind of effort was exerted to keep the church white, but the suburban members soon began to rebel against traveling to that part of the city. The outcome was inevitable. "One of America's Great Missionary Churches" sold out and relocated in the safety of a suburb—from which point, incidentally, it still proclaims the same slogan. Acting out of some conscience, the congregation tried several times to do evangelistic work in the area from which it moved. Not surprisingly, its efforts met with little success.

An almost inevitable accompaniment of the evangelical's flight from and loss of concern for the city is the erosion of his conscience. Christ's parable of the Good Samaritan reminds us that those who ought to be the most sensitive to need are often the least sensitive. A desensitized social conscience makes it difficult to exercise real compassion. The suburban church thus has much to gain by investment in the mission of the total urban world, for it may earn back its integrity and therefore its vitality. True lifeline communication— mission extended with healing power out from the urban center to the suburbs, and with supporting resources from the suburban churches to the inner city—must be established.

Third, what is the message? How do we convey it? The key word is "incarnation." Christ himself, the message the Father proclaimed to mankind, is a message-receiver, a message-sender, and a message. As message-receiver, he claimed to receive his truth from God the Father (John 7:16-17); as message-sender, he proclaimed God's truth to mankind; as the message, he revealed himself to be God by his works, attitudes, and behavior (John 5:19ff.).

As Christ's body, we must study more closely the way he taught and acted, so that we can also be message-receivers from the revealed, written Word, made understandable and practical by the Spirit; message-senders, who disciple and teach; and finally ourselves a message, by our actions, behavior, attitudes, motivations, intentions, and deeds. When our message fails to reach people, it is not because the message is false or impotent, but because the Word has become words rather than flesh.

Finally, what is our restored vision? It is simply Christ's vision: "I will build my church" (Matt. 16:18), and no cosmic reality can prevent the accomplishment of that vision. We are, as his servants, the instruments for the building of his church. The vision is *the doing* of what the Body of Christ has been called *to be*.

One Christian with vision was A. B. Simpson, who wrote of a two-part vision—a local church in the city for those left churchless by poverty and social disadvantage, with an outreach to the "sick and suffering";[5] and an effort to disciple those without the gospel across the face of the earth. Over the course of a century, the worldwide phase of this vision has been militantly fulfilled. The vision for local urban churches has been obscured.[6]

Renewal and reconstruction begin only when the church hears the Spirit's voice and awakens to its tragedy. It is not easy or comfortable, but it has to be said—we have failed. "What will it take before we realize that God means business when He tells us to go to Nineveh in His name? For us modern Jonahs, our Nineveh is the inner city."[7]

Mobilization — A New Strategy

Many urban ministries erupt and flow out of a genuine but undefined and uncategorized response to the need of "getting at it." Problem-solving has preceded problem-analyzing. The wisdom of hindsight must not be depreciated, but it comes at a high cost. Goal-setting may seem tedious to the activity-inclined person, but energies invested in it are not wasted. Urban workers have to learn to face failure, but many failures are quite unnecessary, resulting from the lack of clear goals and crisp priorities.

Research and evaluation is, indeed, a practical starting point, but it must be an ongoing process as well. There must be regular examination, in the light of new research, of what one is doing. "Mission work always implies a willingness to begin anew, and in the process to take into account that God has not yet exhausted his new possibilities and most probably still has some surprises in store."[8]

How may the church transcend its suburban-urban impasse and tackle the vast mission field of urban society? Talk is cheap, but it is not what the world or God's kingdom needs. The work is hard and singularly unrewarding. We must be open to risk and willing to experiment. In what follows we shall sketch some practical suggestions for mounting an overall strategy for building God's kingdom in urban America. We shall delineate six objectives, with specific goals and implementation suggestions for each.

I. Church Planting

Objective:

Systematic planting of churches in urban areas left without adequate testimony by the migration of churches to the suburban residential fringe.

Goal:

To establish a base within the urban area in order to

(1) disciple all peoples;

(2) minister to the elderly, the socially disadvantaged, the culturally deprived;

(3) bring peace—spiritual, social, and racial—to the inner city.

Implementation Suggestions:

(1) recruit persons gifted in urban techniques for leadership training and for development of specialized ministries like urban evangelism;

(2) distribute copies of the Bible and Christian literature that are written in contemporary language;

(3) organize "high interest" ministries through clubs and classes for children and young people;

(4) explore in depth the relationship between economic, cultural, and social conditions, and church planting, growth, and congregational life;

(5) follow the principle that the mother church must give of itself in stewardship to establish new fellowships and provide essential support resources of people, prayer, substance;

(6) apply the replacement principle, which suggests that if a congregation or ministry relocates, a replacement witness relevant to present needs must be secured;

(7) follow McGavran's eight principles for church planting.[9]

II. Renewed Structure

Objective:

Development of an adequate parish structure and program to build and nurture the Body of Christ across cultural lines and to develop indigenous leadership.

Goals:

(1) to develop understanding of black and other minority groups' needs and dynamics;

(2) to shore up floundering parishes;

(3) to provide a base for nonparish ministries;

(4) to provide multi-congregational and para-denominational facilities where these will effect necessary economies;

(5) to encourage self-discovery of purpose with consistent goals.

Implementation Suggestions:

(1) take advantage of church consultant services, which can bring their expertise to bear on attempts at renewal of life, ministry, and structure;

(2) support community centers, such as parish houses, centers for social services, and other nonparish ministries;

(3) arrange strategies such as pulpit exchanges to enrich the experience and viewpoint of both urban and suburban churches;

(4) educate according to a Christian education curriculum that is urban-oriented and sensitive to minority problems and needs.

III. A Total Ministry

Objective:

Articulation of a biblical concept of ministry to the whole man and discovery of various channels of implementation for this.

Goals:

(1) to research comprehensively the biblical attitudes to the total man, in light of Christ's concern for the whole person and the social mandate expressed, for example, in Isaiah 58:6-7;

(2) to research the needs of the total man;

(3) to meet such needs as hunger, poverty, and poor education, thus facilitating an encounter with the needs of the soul;

(4) to help evangelicals whose fear and misunderstanding of the inner city cripple their good intentions to understand and identify the realities of urban life.

Implementation Suggestions:

(1) pool the services of Christian professionals in a comprehensive program of crisis centers, family counseling centers, medical clinics, and the like, but avoid overlap with existing secular agencies and personnel;

(2) make available vocational training and placement service through Christian business owners and management experts whose talents and opportunities may be shared with the needy;

(3) present a Christian school system as a viable alternative to train and educate the Christian family in the context of theistic values;

(4) begin a reading program, particularly of urban and black literature, with updated reading resources made available periodically.

IV. Long-Range Planning

Objective:

Development of long-range planning that makes the best possible use of all the Christian resources in the metropolitan area.

Goals:

(1) to provide for ongoing research and evaluation;

(2) to build a working foundation on which national and regional coalitions can develop;

(3) to develop a new concept of cooperation;

(4) to provide channels for matching needs and resources.

Implementation Suggestions:

(1) establish dialogue groups between existing churches, especially between suburban and urban congregations, cross-cultural and para-denominational whenever practical;

(2) work to organize a coalition of current evangelical urban ministries;

(3) establish a centralized resource file with card entries on gifted personnel throughout the urban area;

(4) begin a "united fund" for giving and sharing financial resources needed for Christian social services, job placement programs, and the like;

(5) organize action programs for those eager laymen, especially in the suburbs, who are now saying, "What can I do?";

(6) publish a news and prayer letter to communicate needs and resources, and to build a prayer ministry.

V. Use of Present Resources
Objective:

Mobilization of churches and believers within the metropolitan area to penetrate cities as a part of the mission for urban outreach.

Goals:

(1) to saturate the urban community with the good news by consolidating the vast evangelical resources;

(2) to cause the name of Christ and his mission to be made known widely in major metropolises;

(3) to help churches realize their missionary potential;

(4) to tap hidden resources capable of being trained for urban mission;

(5) to help each believer discover his own gifts for edifying the body.

Implementation Suggestions:

(1) convene urban missions conferences;

(2) establish a missionary-in-residence program, manned by a person with expertise in foreign, urban, cross-cultural work. This could involve redeployment of foreign missionaries for short-term urban work; internship in urban work for missionary candidates; or one-year residence of furlough missionaries in urban settings, ministering as home missionaries associated with existing churches;

(3) challenge writers and editors to produce new literature suitable for the cause.

VI. Leadership Development
Objective:

Recruitment and training of indigenous urban leadership.

Goals:

(1) to find young people willing to invest their lives in mission to urban society;

(2) to acquaint young people and adults with the needs and problems of urban residents;

(3) to train people in the principles of discipleship and discipling;

(4) to provide the skills and materials for urban outreach.

Implementation Suggestions:

(1) start a lay institute of theology and church renewal, employing proven learning and communication skills;

(2) make financial aid available for minority students who wish to enrol in existing Christian institutions of education and professional preparation;

(3) establish an urban internship to offer on-site exposure for potential urban ministers;

(4) open live-in residences within the city to afford young people the opportunity to secure training in discipleship and in urban ministries;

(5) develop Bible study materials for urban distribution, home study, and follow-up work, focusing on outreach evangelism with the goal of conversion.

To close this section, let me add some precautions. Both the mobilization of a new strategy and its implementation are contingent on appreciating certain characteristics of urban society. Some points of special concern are these:

(1) *Racism,* which projects a superior attitude toward the less fortunate, whether by an individual or by an entire congregation, whether in word or in deed;

(2) *Paternalism* — the pity and condescension that many whites adopt when they speak to, rather than share with, blacks, or do something for minority groups rather than work with them;

(3) *Spiritual commuting,* which fosters only a superficial identification with a community by persons outside.

(4) *Reactionary conservatism,* which frustrates constructive change. A. B. Simpson said: "Everything is going on as it has gone on for many, many years, and there is no place for fresh seed to fall."[10] That a theology of change is necessary is seen in Christ's own words and actions. Christ's word to the recalcitrant, resistant Pharisees was, "Your traditions make null and void the Word of God" (Mark 7:13).[11]

Our lampstand will be removed if we do not awaken, repent, and return; our lamps will go out if, like the five foolish virgins, we are not prepared for the coming of the Bridegroom. We become prepared by first fulfilling Christ's command to disciple all people, going into urban society, baptizing new disciples, and teaching them Christ's commandments. We must take time now to redefine our biblical purpose and mission and message, to realign our priorities in terms of urban society, and to implement our objectives by cooperatively tapping our vast, sleeping resources. Thus will we infuse life into the Body of Christ and develop lifelines for the mutual benefit of all members of that Body, both urban and suburban.

Notes to Chapter 20

1 In Gibson Winter's words, "Suburbia has introduced its concept of success into the very center of church life. Advancement, monetary and numerical extension of power–these are the criteria by which suburbia measures all things"; "The Church in Suburban Captivity," *The Christian Century,* Sept. 28, 1955, p. 1113; quoted in *The Congregation in Mission* by George W. Webber, p. 43.

2 Howard Hageman, "Christ in the Inner City: What's Holding Him Back?", *Eternity,* Dec. 1969, p. 23.

3 Excellent discussion, especially for group study, of this theme of "Church and Mission," is provided in *Who in the World?,* ed. Christians, Schipper, Smedes (Grand Rapids: Eerdmans, 1972), originally prepared for Key '73.

4 Ralph Covell, "Urban Crisis: Test of Our Missionary Concern," *World Vision Magazine,* Oct. 1969, p. 12.

5 Cf. Simpson, *Natural Emblems of Spiritual Life,* p. 101.

6 And continues to be so! The author's denomination commissioned the drafting of an Urban Master Plan in its general assembly of May 1971, tabled the study committee proposal work until May 1973, and then, adopting only a portion of the total program, ironically refused to authorize any expenditure to implement such.

7 Hageman, *op. cit.,* p. 13.

8 J. C. Hoekendijk, *The Church Inside Out,* p. 23.

9 Donald McGavran, *Understanding Church Growth,* pp. 285-95. McGavran obviously leans towards indigenous churches, with a small crumb thrown toward the cross-cultural church, but insists on a theological foundation for an egalitarian society. Why not egalitarianism within the fellowship itself, as a microcosm of what the society can be?

10 Simpson, *op. cit.,* p. 86.

11 Cf. Robert Roxburgh, "Addenda: A Resource of Ideas for Change in the Church," in *Pattern for Change: A Handbook for Church Renewal,* pp. 61ff.

21: CHRISTIAN-SECULAR COOPERATION

by Michael E. Haynes

Urban renewal has left the cities of America in serious straits, suffering from decadent housing, violence, rising taxes, decreased municipal services, floundering educational systems, massive flights to suburbia, new political trends, and impotent church institutions. As the evangelical community faces the city, it faces a great opportunity to engage in bold strategies and methodologies for mission that are new to it. By pursuing these, evangelicals can offer more meaningful and comprehensive pastoral care, alleviate some of the complex needs of the non-Christian masses, and ultimately provide for themselves the right to be heard as they give verbal expression to the gospel of Jesus Christ.

Apostolic teaching clearly indicates that the Christian community is engaged in warfare against a powerful enemy. We must adopt a strategy that

---

MICHAEL E. HAYNES is senior minister of the Twelfth Baptist Church, in Boston, Massachusetts. He received his formal education from Berkshire Christian College, Gordon College and Seminary, and the Boston University School of Social Work. For five years he served in the Massachusetts House of Representatives, and he has also served as a member of the Commonwealth of Massachusetts Parole Board. He has served on some thirty social welfare, governmental, education, and religious boards.

will allow us to move into and permeate the whole of society, bringing hope and healing and pointing mankind to the claims of Christianity. Consider the full implication in the mandate of Jesus that the Christian community is to be "the salt of the earth." Consider the total meaning of his prayer that the disciples not be taken out of the world but be kept from evil (John 17:15). We are to be involved in the world, while not being tainted by it.

There are times when the Christian mandate to infiltrate society is best accomplished by working with secular institutions, influencing them to usefulness for God's purposes. Paul states that he became "all things to all men, that [he] might by all means save some" (I Cor. 9:22). Christians today must act with the same flexibility.

Let us consider a few examples of undertakings that can raise the quality of life, say to the masses that the Christian community cares about how a person lives here and now, and in so doing provide openings for the ultimate and direct witness of the gospel.

Model Cities

Although the federal administration has stated that drastic cuts and changes will be implemented in many such programs, Model Cities has provided a means for churches to get involved. If government funding is curtailed, the possibilities of encouraging big business to continue successful phases of this program should be explored.

In the Roxbury section of Boston, a Presbyterian church of meager financial resource with a white pastor, a remnant of white members, and predominant low-middle-income black membership, got a new lease on home missionary life through an outreach program subsidized by Model Cities called "Teen Town." As in a similar project in my own church, this program provided Christian leadership that was involved with the masses, full- and part-time jobs for community people, collegians, and seminarians, help for boys and girls with school-related problems, and a whole gamut of tutorial services, drama opportunities, recreation, counseling, and community organization features.

Twelfth Baptist Church, which I serve as senior minister, is involved in a somewhat more comprehensive Model Cities project. Our Board of Missions long felt a need to address itself to the needs of the many senior citizens living in old age homes, nursing homes, rooming houses, and private homes in the area. Too many senior citizens in poor urban ghettos are afraid to walk the streets, and thus spend day after day bored and lonely, often neglecting both their physical and spiritual health. Our meager financial resources and limited staff, however, kept our dreams of service to them from becoming a reality.

Through Model Cities we have been able to address ourselves to some of the needs of these elderly people. In so doing, we have been able to reveal to them a body of Christians who are concerned about the totality of their existence. Although the program — too detailed to describe here — is still in the early stages, we are so convinced of the need of efforts of this type that we are seeking private funding that will allow us to continue after the initial Model Cities' subsidy is no longer available.

Carefully and prayerfully we have cooperated with Model Cities to develop this three-phased program for senior citizens. The first phase provides senior citizens of the neighborhood with a two-day-a-week program at the church with crafts, sewing, crocheting, music, and social fellowship. A light lunch is provided and transportation is provided to and from the church for those who need it. Often the groups are taken on short trips and tours. The second phase provides staff and volunteer visitation to nearby old age homes for those unable to venture out. Phase three is directed to helping senior citizens who live in their own homes or apartments by providing them with meaningful social contact and helping with errands and housework where appropriate.

The complete outreach program Twelfth Baptist Church has developed along with Model Cities has two other components: a weekday program for children and youth, which includes drug education, music lessons, tutorial help, drama, personal counseling, and recreation; and a young adult basketball team that involves committed Christians, marginal Christians, and unchurched parolees. The latter group provides male role models who in turn teach younger children basketball and basketball officiating.

The program is not restricted by race or religion. The secular sector provides the funds and other professional services, and the church provides the program and the leadership — which, significantly, is Christian.

There are numerous similar programs in which the evangelical community could become effectively involved and thus enhance its "witness quotient."

"In Prison and Ye Visited Me"

Attica 1971 painfully focused the attention of the world on conditions in our prisons. The sensitive Christian believer will not stop with lamenting the tragic events there. Touched with compassion for those in prison, he will look for opportunities to show forth love and understanding within the walls of jails, houses of corrections, and state and federal penitentiaries.

Sociologists indicate that, with few exceptions, prison populations consist of the poor and ethnic minorities. The epidemic of drug addiction in America has created an entirely new type of offender and consequently a new type of inmate. At the same time, new techniques and attitudes in corrections have created a new approach for dealing with those incarcerated. There is new sentiment for *community-based* correction facilities for both juvenile and adult offenders.

Here is a largely untapped potential for cooperation with secular agencies! A small group of believers in the Boston community is discussing the possibility of the establishment of a halfway house for juvenile offenders by the Christian community. At this writing, both federal and state monies are available to contract services for offenders on both the juvenile and adult level. A private organization committed to providing "starter money" to aid discharged prisoners has offered our church an opportunity to be the vehicle to administer some of these funds. In Massachusetts the parole board has released a number of drug-addicted inmates to Teen Challenge, a program sponsored by a national evangelistically oriented group. This program raises its own funds.

Secular institutions show considerable interest in cooperating with the church in developing programs to help combat drug abuse. Local medical authorities, law enforcement agencies, and social welfare organizations have been most cooperative with Twelfth Baptist Church in sponsoring workshops, clinics, and seminars for all age groups on the subject of drugs.

It should go without saying that sound research and planning must precede the development of any projects in these delicate areas. A good starting point for determining what can and should be done is to visit the local or regional United Fund headquarters. Such umbrella organizations for human services usually have their fingertips on what is happening. In most states and countries the department head for corrections usually has a staff member to develop new programs and work with community groups. Seek out an early meeting with this person. He can be an invaluable resource. In Boston the following organizations and persons provide helpful information and advice for church groups who wish to develop programs for prisoners: the United Prison Association, the Massachusetts Council on Crime and Delinquency, and government-employed chaplains assigned to specific prisons and jails. There are counterparts to these in other states and on the national level.

Politics and Government

Recently evangelicals have become constructively involved in the affairs of state. The masses need to hear our voice on such issues as war, abortion, legalized gambling, and a whole array of subjects that enter the halls of legislation.

Black and white evangelicals alike supported and campaigned for me in three overwhelmingly victorious campaigns to the Massachusetts House of Representatives. One suburban evangelical church made it possible for me to engage the services of an outstanding Christian layman for my legislative staff so that I could better serve the needs of my constituency. Thus, I became a better representative for the cause of righteousness and justice in government.

A Place To Lay One's Head

Housing remains a critical problem in urban America. Large low-income families, single people with moderate incomes, and the elderly find it difficult to secure a decent and safe place in which to live.

St. Mark's United Church of Christ in Roxbury, Massachusetts, became the first church group in the nation to sponsor low- and middle-income housing under federal urban renewal provisions. In this same community, Charles Street African Methodist Episcopal Church, Grant AME Church, Union United Methodist Church, People's Baptist, and a Unitarian group have all availed themselves of secular aid in order to help raise the quality of living by sponsoring new housing. Emmanuel Temple Church and Bethel Pentecostal Church have provided the Boston ghetto community with extensive units of rehabilitated housing for low-income families. Twelfth Baptist, Concord Baptist, Ebenezer Baptist, Eliot United Church of Christ, and several other church groups have plans on the drawing boards which, if approved by the federal administration, will make more housing available for the poor.

A recent article in *Ebony* indicated that the Christian church, especially the black church, has been a prime mover in development of federally aided housing for low- and middle-income families in urban areas throughout the whole country in the last decade. Cooperative ventures such as these give the Christian community a voice within the ghetto. A Christian can more effectively verbalize the gospel when he has already stated by positive action to poor urban masses, "I care about you as a whole person."

All Work and No Play?

A significant percentage of the black leadership in the Roxbury community acquired a college education by a scholarship won because of athletic talent. Skilled youth leaders and social workers have been able to use a young person's interest in sports as a motivational tool to inspire a youth who might otherwise not have achieved a higher level of life.

Recreation is a most effective tool for molding lives and attitudes, and church leaders who deal with young people would do well to keep this in mind. Recreation is another area in which the church can become cooperatively involved with the secular society. Several members of Twelfth Baptist Church serve on the board of the local Boys' Club — a remarkable modern facility. Two members of the church are full-time members of the staff. In addition to taking advantage of their educational programs, we also use their recreational facilities for church activities from time to time. This cooperation can go the other direction as well: a nearby Baptist church (subsequently closed and demolished) made its large gymnasium available to secular youth clubs in the community who could not afford to rent other facilities.

Individual Ventures

Some of the finest examples of cooperative ventures between the Christian community and secular society are seen in the accomplishments of dedicated individual Christians.

My own life was strongly influenced and guided by Dr. V. Simpson Turner (now the minister of Mt. Carmel Baptist Church in New York City), while he was a student at Gordon College, which was then located on the edge of the Roxbury district of Boston. As a committed believer studying for the ministry, he worked for a local secular social service agency. Skilful in his group work techniques and impressive in his athletic leadership, he used the quiet forum of the secular agency to prove that he cared about a person's life. If his was only a word of testimony, a Bible verse, or a tract handed me, I probably never would have been convinced of the worth of the Christian message. But he saw me as a whole person and reached out accordingly. Through his position in a secular agency he manifested the love of God through his continuing concern and help.

Christian-secular cooperation is the Christian teacher in a public school, the Christian worker in the Department of Public Welfare, the Christian prison guard or state representative or Congressman, the Christian registered nurse — each employing all of the resources made available, by reason of secular employment, to be an instrument in the hand of God.

Christian-secular cooperation can be the concerned automobile dealer making a van available for transportation in a drug halfway house program; or a foundation making a grant available to an interracial outreach program in Chicago; or a state commissioner of banking giving advice to a church group that wants to set up a credit union in a changing urban community; or the Black Panthers administering sickle cell tests in and with an involved church, both sharing the concern that young black children do not die before they really get a chance to live — even in this life.

James reminds us that "every good endowment and every perfect gift is from above, coming down from the Father of lights" (1:17). The evangelical Christian community would do well to use every honorable resource available, even seemingly secular gifts loaned of God to mankind, to the end that eternal light may penetrate the depths of urban density, deterioration, and dilemma, flooding the souls of the lost people there and leading them to the truth of the gospel.

22: TOWARD EVANGELICAL URBAN ALLIANCES

by Craig W. Ellison

The history of Protestant Christianity has been a repeated chronicle of splinter denominations and groups that have discovered particular biblical or theological emphases which have led them to dissociate themselves from the mainstream. To speak to Protestants of cooperation outside their own group, then, is to suggest going against a firmly established trend. Among evangelicals such a proposal may be even less favorably received for fear that this might play into the hands of the antichrist in the formation of the one world church.

Suspicion of cooperative efforts has no doubt helped shield the theological integrity and biblical basis of many groups who have rejected coalitions with those who do not believe in the essentials of biblical faith. But it has also weakened their outreach and deprived them of fellowship with other Christians. Instead, we find competition between evangelical churches as fierce as that between competing merchants, needless duplication of resources and waste of effort, failure to learn from each other, and arrogance. With so much to be done in the city by so few, such attitudes are devastating.[1]

To talk of urban alliances is in no sense to suggest that we abolish the local church. As a body it may have a unique ministry as well as providing spiritual support to its members. But it is doubtful that any one church will have sufficient resources for the many and complex needs around it. Individuals from several evangelical churches working together may be able to face a specific need for which those from one church could not marshall enough manpower or interest.

I use the plural "alliances" in the title, because several forms of alliance are necessary for effective urban ministry. In addition to alliances for specific community-oriented projects, prayer, and fellowship within small areas of a city, an informal grouping of evangelicals within an entire city may be helpful. Groups such as the Central City Conference of Evangelicals (Detroit) and the Evangelical Committee for Urban Ministries (ECUMB) in Boston identify and gather resources for larger projects, provide a forum to exchange problems and ideas, and encourage cooperative efforts in subregions of the city. These groups tend to work as an arm of the churches in the city, whereas subregional alliances involve local congregations as such. The larger groups can serve as catalysts for city-wide evangelism and action projects aimed at meeting human needs, as well as channels of communication through newsletters and radio programming. Such communication will make urban evangelicals aware of each other and of pertinent information, and might also be useful in making suburban churches aware.

An alliance between urban evangelicals on the regional level would also be useful. Persons actively involved in urban ministry from several cities in a defined geographical area might periodically meet together for instruction, exchange of information, and encouragement. The attention of the general evangelical and secular communities can be turned to this vital facet of Christian ministry, and resource persons can be more easily obtained than in a one-city alliance. The exchange of ideas and information about functioning urban ministries may renew the hopes of those discouraged and provide new ideas already tested in another city.

Finally, some form of alliance would seem of great importance at the national level. I am not certain what is the most appropriate form for such an alliance to take, but if it is to do more than provide an annual conference for those who can afford to travel — and thus exclude many of those most involved in urban ministry — careful thought will have to be given to this question. Let us look at one possible model.

An Evangelical Center for Urban Ministries, with paid staff members responsible for maintaining regular contact with cooperating groups in various cities, could be formed. Its advisory council or executive board would include representatives from each geographical region in the United States (each region would include five to nine major cities).

The relationship of the Center to these regional and city alliances could include many facets: providing financial resources, encouraging the education of Christian college and seminary students sensitive to urban concerns, publishing materials by evangelicals involved in central cities, publicizing and carrying the legitimacy of the urban mission to the general evangelical community, facilitating minority-majority understanding and cooperation, establishing a placement service matching services needed with persons available, developing short-term urban mission involvements.

The Center would thus seek to lift some of the fund-raising, development, and administration burdens of spreading and legitimizing urban ministry. It would become closely involved in supporting action on the local scene, but its ties with the local groups would remain loose. It would not supplant or dictate local efforts, though it should have the freedom to suggest and evaluate where asked.

Careful thinking about how to finance the center will be necessary. Several possibilities are foundations, churches, association fees, individual donors, and real estate development. The source of the money used will be no less important than decisions about how it is most wisely to be spent.

To insure that the grassroots workers receive full benefit from the Center, the Director should plan to be mobile. Rather than assembling everyone annually in a single geographical location, the Center might limit itself to regional conferences at which selected personnel would be present as resource persons. The emphasis would be on the day-to-day ministry and building contacts within cities and regions.

Some Cautions

Red flags may already be raised in the minds of some readers. Whether or not the proposed model for urban alliances is the best possible one, there are six concerns that should be aired at this point.

1. Organizational Oppression. Careful structuring will be required to avoid the creation of organizations that exist for their own sake. No one seriously involved in urban ministry needs another organization that will just take him away from his work. Hence our stress on loose, working relationships between the national center and the regional and central city alliances. The kind of voluntary associations called for in entire cities and areas within them would seem to hold a great deal of promise for lightening everyone's load. Wise strategy and common efforts can conserve energy while increasing output.

2. The Local Church. The value of the local church is not to be played down. Effective urban ministry simply will not occur unless local churches are at least centrally involved in strengthening their members to carry out ministry and undertaking some efforts unique to their particular setting and membership composition. Not every effort has to be cooperative. On the other hand, the local church should look carefully at the possibilities for cooperative endeavor before beginning institutional projects, and should encourage its members to do the same.

3. White Intrusion. A critical concern of many black Christians today is that such alliances, as well as the general call to urban ministry among evangelicals, can only result in an unwanted influx of paternalistic whites. Continuing dialogue must take place on a national level with such groups as the National Black Evangelical Association (N.B.E.A.), as well as on local levels, to make sure that this does not happen. Those most affected by the city are those who live there. They must be in direction of evangelical urban efforts. I do not believe that this means there is no place for the white in today's American cities. I do believe that every step of involvement for the white in urban ministry must be carried out in sober dialogue with his black (and other minority) brothers. Black Christians also have a responsibility to help create an atmosphere where such learning and exchange can take place.

4. *Representative Leadership.* It is essential that the leadership at every level of urban alliance must be integrated not only racially, socially, and economically, but also with regard to laity and clergy. Effective alliances will be speaking to various kinds of needs, and will thus require input from businessmen, educators, community representatives, politicians, medical and mental health personnel, and general Christian laymen of every professional and laboring background.

5. *Tolerance.* A great deal of understanding will be needed if such alliances are to be representative. Some sectors of the alliance may place the initial emphasis on strategy development; others on immediate action. The truth is that probably both are needed. The danger is that either side will stop listening to the other before things get off the ground. Naturally it is most comfortable to do things our own way. Effective ministry in the city, however, will require stretching, listening to others, and loving each other. If Christians cannot show Christ's love to each other as brothers, it is hard to see how they will ever demonstrate it to unbelievers. That is easy to say; but given the diverse participation necessary for effective urban alliance, it will not happen easily. Perhaps special encounter sessions will be necessary at the outset to lay bare underlying feelings and varying perspectives in a constructive way.

6. *An Adequate Concept of Ministry.* A recurring theme of this volume has been that if urban mission at any level is to be thoroughly effective and evangelical in reconciling to Christ those with multiple needs, we must have a concept of total ministry. Proclamation of the word is necessary, but not at the expense of disregarding the individualized work of the Holy Spirit. God made us to be integrated beings, and has bestowed a variety of gifts on believers (Rom. 12:4-11; I Cor. 12). Because of the multiple social, physical, psychological, and spiritual needs of city-dwellers, the form of witness must be flexible and sensitive. As Bill Pannell has said, the urban-involved Christian "must scratch where people itch."

Pessimism and Vision

Some will regard all this as "pie in the sky." Those who have ministered to the city for years, understaffed and virtually ignored by the broader evangelical community, may have difficulty accepting "Johnny-come-lately" proposals for action. With good reason, many blacks will regard any such efforts initiated by white evangelicals with suspicion. On the other hand, many whites will doubt that they can engage blacks. Still others will just be too tired to care about association: they have too much to keep them busy already.

A new sense of vision, inspired by God's Spirit, will be necessary if such alliances are to be formed and sustained productively. There will have to be persons at the various levels who can visualize the potential benefits. Perhaps these persons will emerge from some of the Christian programs of urban education discussed above, persons of varying races and backgrounds with the enthusiasm and the willingness and the skills to undertake the initial steps. Perhaps they will be persons who are tired of being isolated and trying to go it alone. The key is to not quench the Spirit before he has a chance to work. A pessimistic perspective at the beginning will probably be self-fulfilling. Let us rather be cautious but optimistic, open to the vision God gives for more effective cooperation in urban ministry.

Notes to Chapter 22

1 For a comparative discussion of urban coalition refer to C. W. Ellison, "Third World in America," *The Other Side,* May-June 1972, pp. 42-43; and C. W. Ellison, "The Urban Challenge," *Inside,* January 1973, pp. 30-34.

23: A COMPREHENSIVE MODEL FOR EVANGELICAL URBAN INVOLVEMENT

by Roger L. Dewey

Perhaps no one should be so presumptuous as to write an article such as this. The reaction of some will be: "More whites coming into the cities? Who needs them?"

Let me try to clear the air. Scattered throughout the churches are thousands of biblically oriented, suburban Christians who are genuinely concerned for basic social change. If somehow enabled to share their resources and coordinate their efforts they could have major influence. They could restore parts of the church into dramatic models for society, raising a dynamic witness to the reality of Christ's power to transform life-styles and relationships. They could transform parts of society as well. I am writing to them. They do not need convincing that the Bible commands social concern; they are (at least vaguely) aware that their role is not in the black community, that

---

ROGER DEWEY is co-director of the Evangelical Committee for Urban Ministries in Boston (ECUMB). He is a graduate of Cornell University and has worked as an architect. For two years he studied city planning at Harvard. His involvement with ECUMB also includes serving as editor for the bi-monthly journal Inside, *which records the ministry concerns of ECUMB and presents a forum for evangelical opinions on current social crises.*

integration is a goal only on the basis of justice and human development and self-determination. They are aware that racism and structural oppression exist and require a massive effort at change.

Yet there are few answers to their question of "what can I do?" This article will be my attempt — incomplete, oversimplified, perhaps missing the target in some places. The central question is, What kind of structures will enable suburban participation in Christian efforts at genuine positive social change, while utilizing minority initiative and control?

Those who attempt to respond to urban problems usually find themselves constricted by two opposing realities. On one hand, they quickly discover that even the most modest objective requires a nearly superhuman perseverance because of bureaucracy, various external pressures, and the limited resources available. But at the same time, restricting one's focus usually means leaving unchallenged the basic causes of the problems and contenting oneself with remedial efforts. The ever-present danger is that of cementing oneself into a two-dimensional program, as though urban problems were separate and distinct issues.

The Christian trying to be of genuine service in the inner city knows this is not the case. He knows that each person he contacts has many interlocking needs. The mother to whom he provides hot meals, for instance, needs this assistance because she is unemployed. She cannot accept employment because she has no access to day-care facilities for her children. There is no other source of income because she is deserted by her husband. He is unemployed, because his education was deficient. She buys inadequate food partly because she spends too much of her income paying rent to her slum landlord, partly because food prices are highest in the poorest areas, since no insurance is available to protect the present stores and there are no bank loans for developing more efficient supermarkets. She receives too little income from welfare because the state, under pressure from suburbanites who have no communication with the realities of poverty in the city and no realization of how their votes affect real flesh-and-blood human beings, has cut her benefits. And finally, her faith in a loving God who answers prayers and meets needs often seems quite unreal and impossible because of everything else.

In this situation it is unfair to criticize the efforts of urban evangelicals as being "Band-Aid" measures. The Christian who provides the hot meals knows all these complex problems, but he can become swamped simply by the logistics of preparing and distributing the food. He has little time for trying to change the real causes of the problem and, besides, each cause is itself interlocked with all the others and quite beyond his reach. When he does try to reach out beyond the immediate provision of assistance on a one-to-one basis he is criticized for becoming "over-extended" and for going in the direction of some governmental programs with their gross inefficiency and lack of concern for individual people. The pressures to continue operating solely at the level of remedial efforts are enormous. When you begin to understand the city, it seems impossible to do almost anything else.

A friend once commented that evangelical efforts within the cities seem much like the beginning stages of putting together a jigsaw puzzle: there are few pieces on the board, they seem nearly unrelated, and although colorful they give little clue to the nature of the final picture. One should add that no one is more painfully aware of this than the "pieces" themselves. As long as Christian efforts to begin eliminating the causes of urban problems are undertaken by isolated groups here and there, the charges of overextension will be not only valid but inevitable.

We need a far more coordinated and comprehensive approach by Christians to the inner city. We need an alliance of evangelical churches, individuals, organizations and denominational groups capable of pulling together the resources of evangelicals throughout an entire metropolitan area. We must have the same vision as those who developed the foreign missions outreach of the church. Christians must be enabled to present a living Christ who, in power, is truly the answer to the real questions that real people are asking. Those of us who recognize that Christ can change the inner man, providing inner peace, and inner security and inner joy, must recognize and demonstrate that he came to do far more than that.

The scriptural concept of the Body of Christ bears directly on this question of poverty and need. The Body of Christ is *one* body, urban and suburban together, dependent on each other whether we realize it or not, responsible for each other's welfare. It is not at all a collection of "local bodies." The local church is certainly important, but it should never proudly think of itself as a well-rounded, self-sufficient entity. Denominational churches must find some way around the separatism and provincialism their orientation sometimes generates. The biblical image is that of a single living organism composed of a multitude of apparently unrelated parts, totally dependent on the unselfish sharing of all resources and consequently enabled to accomplish a common task. The Body has within it all the necessary resources for the healing and nourishment of its various parts.

No congregation builds a church without looking to the future. The Christian community *is* the church; in building it we should attempt now to assess its future needs and prepare to meet them. Some problems are simply too complex to face without preparation. As individuals we buy insurance policies, as the church we plan ahead. Is not this the lesson of the apostolic church, who prepared for a famine in another land *before* it occurred (Acts 11:27)?

To propose a "Christian Answer" to the complex problem of the inner city would be just a bit presumptuous. Yet without question the very complexity of the problem requires this planning ahead, twenty years or even more. The vision, of course, must be repeatedly updated, helping to guide us, to unite us, and to challenge us to our best efforts. This must not become some grand attempt to predict the future; the vitality of life and our relationship with Christ rest in the fact that our humanity is open-ended and continually a risk. Yet we must look ahead and take that risk. Far-off goals, if realistic, could help various Christian groups, inner-city and suburban, make short-range decisions in a way that would support each other's efforts. This alone would be a significant step.

Our concern for whole persons, our ability to integrate these activities with our view of man as in need of personal salvation, will prevent our efforts from becoming just another frustrating and ineffectual materialistic exercise. What is required is a working together in response to a common vision, the vision of God for this era as well as for the wider metropolitan areas in which most of us live. What is required is genuine person-to-person contact, so that we are sharing our real selves and not simply our money. The relationships between suburban white and inner-city black and poor are vital for the health of both. If understood and nourished, those relationships will produce strength and vitality and love and a testimony, but when ignored or undervalued they encourage prejudice, fear, materialism, and an affront to the Lord whose image we collectively bear.

We say it so easily: "Christ is Lord of our lives." Yet he is to be Lord not only of our personal lives but over everything that touches our lives and over every means by which we affect others. He is Lord of the whole man – social, physical, intellectual, economic, and political. We must discover what that means in the context of our everyday lives. Every vote, every business transaction, every purchase is a moral statement. Christ is Lord of all the elements that go into making our cities. He is Lord even over the dehumanizing system we call welfare. The present deterioration of our cities and the injustices towards our poor are simply evidence of what happens when governments are run autonomously from the moral law of God and when Christians feel that the economic and political areas of their lives do not come under his lordship. The present isolation of most Christians from these problems is simply the natural result of our individually choosing our own personal vision, without reference to any overall vision.

Some Basic Principles

It will not be easy to implement a vision that is large enough to affect some of the causes of the problems, and at the same time intimate in its personal concern. But the first and foremost principle in developing an alliance of evangelicals is that of *local initiation and control.* Urban ministries cannot be developed by commuters. Most Christians now realize that whites cannot work in positions of leadership in the black community. They would still be astonished, no doubt, at the degree of hatred they would encounter in lower-class white neighborhoods.

Little is more frustrating than to spend years of struggle against seemingly impervious conditions only to have one's efforts overshadowed by relatively well-financed outsiders. Even if their achievements meet some very real and basic needs, they will still be resented unless their programs originate within the urban community and are under its direction and control. One need not be born in the city to be effective, but one must certainly live there and be committed to staying there.

Part of a Christian perspective on urban problems is that we do not think of oppression, sin, and conflict as *solely* structural problems of society. There is a need for individual, personal reconciliation to God and to each other, as well as for basic changes in society's organization. But recognizing that we are insufficiently reconciled to each other means accepting the conflict that will arise when we try to work out that reconciliation. Criticism will develop around this issue of initiation and control, but if faced honestly and openly it can be a positive force. We must not seek to develop programs that omit conflict. If we are conscious about the criticism, if we "pay our dues" by taking some abuse along the way, we will learn what to do and we will grow personally.

For the suburban white with a sincere concern for the city but without the compulsion to move there to involve himself in direct assistance, another principle becomes of central importance. *Everything we possess has been given us by God.* We are stewards of it, not owners. Our salaries, time, and specialized abilities are given us by the Lord not primarily for our own use but to be distributed for the nourishment of the entire body. Apparently few of the Christians attempting to assist urban people have been given the gift of raising funds, with the result that nearly every mission is limited in its effectiveness *primarily* by lack of funds. At the same time, many of those to whom God has given that gift, to whom he has "loaned" the funds by providing the resources, time, and energy necessary for education and "success," have the idea that they were meant to keep their income. Each Christian should be much more aware that his "secular" earning power is a gift from God to be used for his purposes. This may demand reordering our personal priorities and recognizing the degree to which we have allowed the secular god of materialism to limit our service to Jehovah.

A third principle involves persons and information going the opposite direction, from the city out to the suburbs. *Urban missions is a two-way street.* While the inner-city Christian — black, white, Spanish, Chinese — needs the input of suburban experience, financial resources, and expertise in organization, the suburban Christian also has much to learn. Through pulpit exchanges, publications, seminars, and especially through personal involvement, he can be exposed to how the Christian in another culture thinks and works and lives for Jesus. He will see it is possible to be freed from slavery to the clock, to exercise patience under extreme duress, to express his emotions openly, to live a faith not muddied by theological debate. He will learn that much of his religious upbringing was simply a result of his white, conservative culture, for it is definitely not shared by his Christian brothers in these different urban cultures. Many will have to repent of un-Christian attitudes toward blacks and towards those on welfare. It is our culture that teaches us to associate stillness with reverence, tidiness with goodness, peace of mind with spirituality, order with God, busyness with godliness, and justice with the laws of the land.

Suburban outreach beyond the personal and the theological is also necessary. It will take a massive educational effort to inform suburban evangelicals of the degree to which their economic decisions and political opinions are responsible for the oppression of the poor, both black and white. Many cannot comprehend that their desires for lower taxes and a comfortable life-style translate directly into further denial of opportunities for the poor. Mere suburban education, of course, will be insufficient; far too many are too comfortable to change. Pastors will need encouragement to preach against the sins of materialism, racism, and political apathy. Yet this, too, will have little effect unless it helps produce a genuine revival. The root problem is sin. Some, fortunately, are beginning to see that our standard of living is not a blessing but a curse, that they are only being asked to give up their shackles and accept the freedom that Christ died to give us.

The final principle is simply that *nothing is excluded as being outside the Christian's realm of concern.* Our God made a man's neighbor his personal responsibility, without an extended discussion of eligibility, race, status, or classification of any kind. The extent of our response to another human being is dictated simply by the extent of his need, not by the degree to which we feel he "merits" our assistance or by the nature of the assistance required. Whether the need is for housing, food, spiritual counseling or education; whether the need is felt by an individual for a job or by a whole community for national justice, the Body must stand together and provide the necessary healing. This is the beginning of true Christian community and ministry.

Getting Started

I shall briefly describe the beginnings of the Evangelical Committee for Urban Ministries in Boston to give a context for understanding the more comprehensive concept of the alliance elaborated in the following section.

ECUMB really had two simultaneous beginnings. The first was when a few suburban pastors consulted Rev. Michael Haynes, a black pastor in Boston, and at his suggestion collected about $3000 for scholarships to send black students to Christian colleges. About the same time a group of white college students began attending Rev. Haynes' church. They also asked his advice and soon had developed a tutoring program. Weekly discussion sessions between black and white students suggested the idea of a publication to inform other white Christians about the experiences and insights being gained. When the two groups discovered each other, I became the first coordinator for their combined efforts.

The first issue of our magazine, *Inside* ("the voice of Christians living inside the city"), had a run of eighty copies. It was nearly a year before there was sufficient income to pay a salary and nearly another year before a secretary could be hired. However, at the end of the first four years, more than $41,000 had been distributed in scholarships, an average of thirty-five tutors had worked each school year, over 150 Christian black students had been flown to Boston from around the country for a conference they had organized, the magazine had begun to achieve its goal of informing and unifying the efforts of urban-sensitive evangelicals around the country, and a group of inner-city residents, predominantly black, had been given a substantial boost towards the development of their dream of a Christian day-care center. The project later collapsed before opening because of a federal cutback in Model Cities funds.

Beginning as a fully volunteer effort insured a very slow initial growth. Our list of accomplishments was unimpressive, perhaps. Yet this gave us all the time to learn and to grow personally. We made many mistakes, some nearly fatal, yet the Lord blessed these efforts — possibly because our journey was so definitely through unchartered territory that we were continually aware of our dependence on him.

By the fifth year, our progress in building suburban support had grown to where it was possible to hire a part-time black co-director, Rev. Theodore Moran. This encouraged suburban Christians as a measure of progress and our income began to grow significantly. Within *six* months our staff had increased to five, including a full-time black co-director, Rev. Eugene Neville. We began developing several new ministries — prison visitation, a learning-disabilities program, a street evangelistic ministry in cooperation with Young Life, and extensive counseling of black Christian students in area colleges. We had finally recognized *Inside's* limitations for attitude change (people just do not read what they strongly disagree with) and had begun using it to develop strategies for those who were already concerned but needed direction. In each case our approach has been to cooperate with other organizations, sending workers to them in preference to developing our own parallel programs. Through such penetration of secular organizations, we hope to have as much influence on them as on those to whom we minister through them. At this time, our suburban outreach was only beginning to establish its goals and strategies. Nearly forty churches and many hundreds of individuals were supporting us financially, yet we had never had the time or manpower to even begin following up all those leads. That was yet to come.

Let me briefly list some of our early mistakes and the lessons we learned from them. Tutors initially came from a wide geographical area. When a third failed to live up to their commitments, we began soliciting tutors only from churches and colleges within a very few miles. The tutoring program nearly folded when its black director moved. Now we concentrate on developing strong local leadership and semi-autonomy within each of the centers where tutoring takes place. Scholarship commitments were established in relation to *anticipated* income, an act of faith, but they continually ate up funds which could have hired a sufficient staff to enable more solid expansion. The community board of education for the day-care center was developed too early. Before we could collect the $14,000 necessary for "start-up" funds, several key persons had lost interest, concluding that "these whites" were not much different from others who had made big promises. Key leaders were not kept sufficiently informed and some hurt feelings resulted. A "People Bank" (to be described later) was poorly promoted to suburban pastors. Presented to them while it was in the early conceptual stage, it gave the image of a casually developed idea that would not be realized.

We also had some strong forces in our favor. In the first place, we were extremely concerned with obtaining grassroots control. Sometimes — as in the case of the scholarship fund — this meant starting a program ourselves in response to a local suggestion and then continually offering someone full control over it until it had become large enough to spark his interest and to warrant the commitment of his time. Second, although much of our difficulty was financial, we did attract a growing number of small contributors who felt personally involved and well informed through our magazine and prayer letters. This kind of support gave us the freedom to experiment and to make mistakes without having our financial rug pulled in by large but nervous contributors. As a result our budgets increased by 50% to 100% each of the first four years. Finally, the magazine gave us the chance always to keep the larger vision before our supporters even while we were necessarily involved with small and tentative first steps. The more usual plan of identifying with one specific, limited objective attracts sponsors whose interest is also limited to that objective and fails to attract those with a larger vision whose support might enable that very expansion. At the outset we did not foresee how essential the publication of *Inside* would become in forcing the kind of analysis necessary. From these and other experiences came the emphasis and the components of the comprehensive model proposed here.

A Comprehensive Model
It requires no great vision to make a rather lengthy list of things that need doing. The more important questions are how, by whom, under what priorities? Ironically, most of the efforts we envision for our urban areas have long been undertaken by evangelical foreign missionaries — the building and staffing of schools and hospitals, the construction and repair of private housing, the training of pastors and community workers and the development of food co-ops and job training centers. Beyond this, the evangelical church is

beginning to understand that a returning foreign student will often be a more effective proponent for Christianity in his home country than will someone from our culture. Therefore, some are now trying to provide nationals with the ability to set up job training programs and other social projects. We have not recognized that the average black American is no doubt as different culturally from the average suburban white as is someone from India. The urban community needs to hear the good news from someone within its own culture. Urban Christians similarly need resources to be effective. The primary question, then, is how to get the necessary resources to the right people.

An informal, in-depth, totally nonpublicized, very personal survey of the city takes a lot of time. But it is essential to know who is where, doing what, and with what resources. Duplication and competition must be avoided. But more than that, whatever is eventually developed must be done in accordance with that first principle of community initiation and control.

Structure

Assuming, then, that there is contact with community leaders who have some vision, the next question that arises is that of structure: "Where do we get a board of directors?" This raises the basic issues of initiation and control, purpose, and relationship to existing groups

ECUMB began in the traditional manner with an advisory board of well-known local Christian leaders, and a slightly less public board of directors. There was no job description for me as interim director, and probably could not have been for this exploration into the unknown. The problems that arose were numerous. The advisors couldn't advise, the directors couldn't direct, and I didn't know what to do but to do whatever I could. Fortunately, through time we have developed a very workable structure, genuinely responsive to a variety of needs.

The Urban Action Level. ECUMB has two co-directors, who split their responsibilities generally along urban/suburban lines. Each has one or two advisory boards concerned with such specific functions as suburban outreach, the magazine, urban ministries. These are working committees. They establish their own agendas and frequency of meetings. When an advisor displays a major commitment, or a desire to understand other facets of our involvement, he becomes a prime candidate for the board of directors.

One of the advisory boards is called the urban Council. It is composed of two black Christian students from each of the area colleges. They help us initiate and develop programs in the black community. They also organize conferences or projects to strengthen their own witness and coordinate the area's black Christian students.

We have only recently begun discussing the situation in the poor white communities of Boston. The racism there is often undisguised. Fear, resentment, and sometimes hatred are nearly tangible. Those people need our love. In ministering to their overwhelming needs, as Christ would have us do, we may eventually be able to build some bridges between probably the two most alienated groups in our society.

The next level of this metropolitan alliance is suggested by ECUMB's relationships with other urban ministries. The most promising of these is our contractual relationship with urban Young Life — a high school oriented evangelistic effort of long-term personal relationships at the street level. Young Life is soon to begin hiring street workers who will be under the supervision of ECUMB and reporting to both organizations. Each of us retains our distinctiveness, yet sufficient cooperation is structurally required so the relationship should survive even when new personalities take over the organizations. We see this as a developing model for cooperation among related organizations. If there are no specific long-term programs undertaken in concert, the best intentions of both parties are often not sufficient to maintain the communication.

Another variation is the nature of our cooperation with the Southern Baptist ministry in Boston. Though an official programmatic merger with a denominational effort is not possible, we share office space and their director attends most of our staff meetings. We have worked together on one project and are beginning to coordinate in several ways.

Whenever possible, we have also coordinated our efforts with non-evangelical churches and secular agencies. Many of them have already gone far beyond us in the areas of our own interest and we have much to learn from them. The local cerebral palsy association is assisting with our learning disabilities program; the YMCA, boys' club, legal assistance society, and young parents programs are all willing to cooperate, each of us referring contacts to the other. We are developing many potential relationships through which Christ can eventually be made known.

The Suburban Action Level. Parallel to the above, several activities and relationships are developing in the suburban branch of ECUMB. At one early point we spent a great deal of time and effort contacting suburban churches. Within the first couple of years I had spoken in nearly a hundred. My intent was to reach as many people as possible. We needed so much help it seemed inconceivable we would discourage *any* volunteers. And yet the contacts were superficial, the actual possibilities for involvement negligible, and the financial return limited. Our ministries were not yet sufficiently developed to excite much interest. Beyond all this, that form of suburban outreach required too much time.

Our direction now is to find a contact person in each of the forty suburban churches supporting ECUMB, someone respected by the church and able to represent the pastor in meetings with us. Once every month we would have an orientation for these contact persons at our office, meeting our staff or students on scholarship. Lectures, seminars and discussions would be devised to enable them to return to their church and say, "I have seen with my own eyes. I understand their motives." We would encourage them to form small groups, meeting regularly to pray for urban ministries, and attempt to provide them with suggestions for leading discussions on racial, economic, theological, and political issues. We are only beginning to discover what is possible in the area of attitude change through these small-group discussions.

Of great assistance in this outreach is our publication, *Inside* (and the somewhat similar *The Other Side* which we also mail to our subscribers). Some issues examine in depth the various problems of social injustice. Others sketch out the broad picture of what is happening in our culture and where we fit in as persons attempting to bring all aspects of our lives under the lordship of Christ. The magazine also fills a fund-raising role; though subscription is $6, the average renewal check is for $25 for support of our urban ministries.

One of the most difficult concepts to get across in the evangelical church is collective responsibility. Even those who enthusiastically support political and economic activity on behalf of the poor do not always see the connection between the existence of poverty and their own economic or political decisions. We have tried in several ways to illustrate this need for justice. One new approach explains how a church's purchasing of goods and services is really a series of ethical decisions; if purchases are from firms with discriminatory practices then the church is indirectly supporting that oppression. We have begun investigating the practical problems of carrying this through.

Politically, the same general point needs to be made. An early objective is to be able to describe for a suburban congregation the effect that their political opinions have on those in the city. We hope to be able to relate specific examples of hardship and assistance to the votes of their own representatives. We support efforts to develop a Christian political consciousness, a unified movement transcending the humanistic labels of "liberal" and "conservative." Yet we reject the oversimplified position that all politicians are basically the same and that short-term "lesser of two evils" political activity is not valid for the Christian. When the issue is survival, impoverishment, or dehumanization we cannot be silent, even though there is no ideal solution.

Making It Work

While this illustrates the potential involvement of ECUMB in many worthwhile efforts, it is far from exhaustive. If you add the number of ministries undertaken by churches, denominations, and other Christian organizations, there still remains much to be done: housing, schools, clinics, job-training, food co-ops, legal services, and so on. But dreaming about what might be done is helpful only to the extent that it points out why it is not being done and what can be changed so it will be.

The same four closely related limitations seem to face all Christian attempts at social change: research, manpower, financial resources, and a communally developed world-view. It seems an approach could be developed to deal with these four problems as a coherent whole. Such an approach should probably be centered in a specific physical location. Interested persons could go there to learn what is happening throughout the metropolitan area and where they could become volunteers or staff; students could coordinate their courses with Christian projects so their field education and research papers would also contribute to the work of Christ; representatives from Christian groups could find help in writing government and foundation proposals; individuals with a specific vision for Christian action—from day-care centers to political campaigns—could be put in touch with the necessary research, financial support, workers and consultants; young Christians could attend seminars on the biblical world view, discovering what it means for Christ to be Lord over all aspects of their lives; volunteers and staff from many organizations could be trained in the skills needed for their programs (such as counseling) and followed up to insure a higher standard of Christian activity; group leaders could find a sense of vision, relating their efforts to those of the entire metropolitan Christian community.

To help people share their abilities with others, the center would include a computerized "People Bank." Christians would deposit themselves, their talents, their technical expertise in a single resource bank, to be drawn on by churches, secular agencies, and individuals. Resources are shared, local leadership is maximized, wasteful duplication and overhead are avoided and Christians are enabled to contribute personally and directly, rather than just financially or through organizations. To be served by the People Bank the recipient persons and organizations would have to coordinate with it. Thus even secular agencies would come into contact with the biblical world-view.

The specific goals of such cooperation will vary from city to city, yet I would suspect that every urban alliance will eventually include both an educational and a health component. In the twenty-year plan this may mean starting schools in different sections of the city. It may mean establishing free health and dental clinics, if not hospitals. It would certainly involve developing for residents a listing of the various social services currently available. Since the urban church is usually the place of first resort for help, it should at least be enabled to provide a complete referral service to other agencies.

Of course, none of these efforts is unique. Several of them have encountered some real obstacles, such as government job-training programs for which no jobs are available to the graduates. To avoid this, short-range goals should be established to contribute directly to the achievement of the twenty-year goals, so that all components will interact and support each other. The jobs developed should be jobs with opportunities for advancement. For instance, companies should probably be formed to design, build and manage the needed schools, clinics and housing. This would make possible on-the-job training in business administration, building construction, architecture, printing, and numerous other fields. Local ownership of these companies and of the housing could be arranged through low-interest (or better, no-interest) loans from the alliance and from Christian businessmen. We would ask local firms, beginning with those headed by Christians, to share the expertise of their companies. Perhaps one of their employees could work full- or half-time with these urban groups for a one-year period without loss of salary. This would be a way to involve a Christian who had indicated willingness to join the People Bank. The aim is to eventually liberate people from their undue dependence on others, enabling them to help themselves and therefore to develop the kind of self-esteem we all should have before our Lord. Essential in all of this is that the long-range view links together all current efforts and the development of those linkages is accepted as the definition of the short-range objectives.

The need for such a unifying vision is obvious. Throughout most cities there is a wealth of Christian talent, expertise, and insight waiting to be tapped. More Christians are looking for a sense of direction, and are willing to respond radically and sacrificially, than we are able to place. We do not need or want one big organization. We do not need or want centralized direction, but we do need the development of a sense of community in the Body of Christ. We need a united purpose, seeing ourselves as co-laborers in Christ's kingdom and therefore shedding the parochialism and possible sense of superiority inherent in a single-church mentality.

Twice in the past few years, ECUMB has sponsored "unity banquets" to try to develop this kind of coordination and cooperation. Neither worked. We have not yet learned to think of ourselves as a united movement rather than separate organizations. The Christian community needs a sense of cohesion and a sense of purpose like the black community has begun developing these past decades. That is the essence of the vision we need.

Community will not develop, however, by simply selecting a common purpose, as important as that is. Individuals need to know their heritage and derive their efforts from it. We Christians interested in social change need to know who we *are*. Our social change must be *in the name of the Lord*. Few Americans are motivated to man the barricades for such innocuous goals as an increase in social security benefits (as necessary as that may be). That is the problem with the materialistic goals of political liberalism. But when Christians feel implicated in sin by our government's improper care of the elderly, it becomes a crusade, taking on a forcefulness, direction, and perserverance unmatched by the fickle tides of public whim.

The word "crusade" requires an understanding of the Christian world-view. There is more to being, for instance, a Christian businessman than not lusting after one's secretary, being honest in business practices, witnessing occasionally, and being loving to those one meets. The biblical standard of love must be applied to every relationship between management and labor; the biblical standard of equality before the Lord must be applied to the organizational pyramid; the biblical measurement of human worth must be related to salary increases above the level of one's true needs; the biblical fact of one's responsibility for his neighbors must confront the existence of wealth in the midst of poverty.

This center would therefore also be a place for study and reflection — a place where people can go and listen to tapes, attend seminars, participate in discussions. By incorporating this intellectual study with the numerous activist elements mentioned earlier, the center could encourage both relevance and depth. By aggressively sharing the resources of the church throughout the metropolitan area it would encourage efficiency, strength and vitality. By thus relating Christ to all aspects of our lives, we would get to know him better. Seeing him at work throughout our society, we could witness more effectively to his power and relevance. It could mean a dramatic change for many Christians and, perhaps, a revival in many churches and in many places of business. We finally would see the beginning of the many-faceted alliance, an effective cooperation which till now has remained the dream and the prayer of many isolated Christians.

SUGGESTED READING

Culture

Eliot, T. S. *Christianity and Culture.* New York: Harcourt, Brace and World, Inc. (A Harvest Book), 1949.

Glazer, N. and Moynihan, D. P. *Beyond the Melting Pot.* Cambridge, Mass.: M.I.T. Press, 1963.

Niebuhr, H. R. *Christ and Culture.* London: Faber and Faber, 1952.

Van Til, H. R. *The Calvinistic Concept of Culture.* Philadelphia: Presbyterian and Reformed Publishing Company, 1959.

History

Cairns, Earle E. *Saints and Society.* Chicago: Moody Press, 1960.

Smith, Timothy L. *Revivalism and Social Reform.* New York: Abingdon Press, 1951.

Race Relations

Allport, Gordon W. *The Nature of Prejudice.* Garden City, N.Y.: Doubleday & Company, Inc., 1958.

Ellison, Ralph. *Invisible Man.* New York: The New American Library (Signet Books), 1952.

Franco, Sergio. *The Other Americans.* Boston: Beacon, 1973.

Haselden, Kyle. *The Racial Problem in Christian Perspective.* New York: Harper and Brothers, 1959.

Jones, Reginald L. (ed.). *Black Psychology*. New York: Harper & Row, 1972.

Pannell, William E. *My Friend the Enemy*. Waco, Tex.: Word Books, 1968.

Salley, Columbus and Behm, Ronald. *Your God Is Too White*. Downers Grove, Ill.: Inter-Varsity Press, 1970.

Silberman, Charles. *Crisis in Black and White*. New York: Random House, 1964.

Stone, Shelley C. and Shertzer, Bruce (eds.). *Minority Groups and Guidance*. Boston: Houghton Mifflin, Guidance Monograph Series VI, 1971.

Wilcox, Roger C. *The Psychological Consequences of Being a Black American: A Collection of Research by Black Psychologists*. New York: John Wiley & Sons, 1971.

Urban Ministry

Cully, Kendig Brubaker and Harper, F. Nile. *Will the Church Lose the City?* New York: World Publishing Company, 1969.

Ellul, Jacques. *The Meaning of the City*. Grand Rapids, Mich.: William B. Eerdmans, 1970.

Furness, Charles Y. *The Christian and Social Action*. Old Tappan, N.J.: Fleming H. Revell, 1972.

Grounds, Vernon C. *Evangelicalism and Social Responsibility*. Scottdale, Pa.: Herald Press, Focal Pamphlet No. 16, 1969.

Kemp, Charles F. *Pastoral Care with the Poor*. New York: Abingdon Press, 1972.

Miller, Kenneth O. *Man and God in the City*. New York: Friendship Press, 1954.

Moberg, David O. *The Great Reversal: Evangelism versus Social Concern*. Philadelphia: J. B. Lippincott Company, 1972.

Mumford, Lewis. *The Culture of the City*. New York: Harcourt, Brace, Jovanovich, 1970.

Ryan, William. *Blaming the Victim*. New York: Vintage Books, 1971.

Torney, George A. *Toward Creative Urban Strategy*. Waco, Tex.: Word Books, 1970.

Winter, Gibson. *The Suburban Captivity of the Churches*. New York: Doubleday, 1961.

Christian Periodicals

Inside, Evangelical Committee for Urban Ministries, 130 Walnut Avenue, Boston, Massachusetts 02119. Bi-monthly, $3 per year.

The Other Side, Fred A. Alexander, P.O. Box 158, Savannah, Ohio. Bi-monthly, $3 per year. Can order through *Inside* and receive both periodicals for $6 per year.

The Post-American, P.O. Box 132, Deerfield, Illinois 60015. Monthly "underground-type" format. $5 per year.

DATE DUE

ILL # 7527595			
APR 29 1985			
J.L.L.# 8550166			
OCT 17 1985			
DEC 18 1985			